*An Island Called California*

AN ECOLOGICAL INTRODUCTION
TO ITS NATURAL COMMUNITIES

# An Island

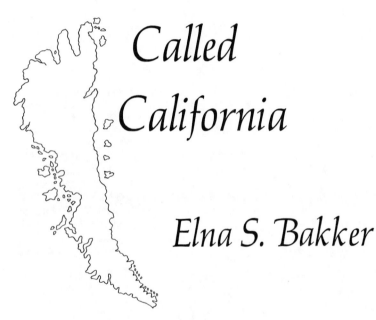

# Called

# California

## Elna S. Bakker

FIGURES BY GERHARD BAKKER, JR.
PHOTOGRAPHS BY PHILIP HYDE

UNIVERSITY OF CALIFORNIA PRESS
BERKELEY, LOS ANGELES, LONDON

University of California Press
Berkeley and Los Angeles, California
University of California Press, Ltd.
London, England
Copyright © 1971, by
The Regents of the University of California
First Paperback Printing, 1972
ISBN: 0-520-02159-2
Library of Congress Catalog Card Number: 70-107657
Printed in the United States of America
Designed by Dave Comstock

3 4 5 6 7 8 9 0

*to Nancy Thomas Neely*
*who started it all*

# Contents

# Illustrations

PLATES

# Preface

Around the year 1510, some eighteen years after Columbus' discovery of the New World, Garci Rodríguez Ordóñez de Montalvo of Spain wrote a highly popular though decidedly fanciful account of a queen who ruled over a rugged country of Amazon-mannered black women. Among other quaint customs was the feeding of surplus males to trained griffins, keeping only enough men, either born to them or captured by raiding vessels, to serve as studs to these enterprising women. Gold was the only metal known, incidentally.

Montalvo is not hesitant about locating his mythical queendom. He instructs: "Know ye that on the right hand of the Indies there is an island called California, very near the Terrestrial Paradise. . . ." Fact and fiction were not altogether inseparable in those days when tales of the New World spread through the homelands of the returned adventurers. Inn and courtyard rang with truth and fantasy mixed, at best, in equal proportion. No wonder then that the early explorers making their arduous ways up the west coast of Mexico drew what seemed to them the obvious conclusion that the land across the Sea of Cortez would continue to be separated from the mainland. If so, this surely was the famous island of griffins and bold rocks, California.

In time, of course, the misconception was corrected. Baja California is a peninsula, and lands to the north are fixed more or less firmly to the North American continent. I say "more or less" since the San Andreas Earthquake Fault is supposedly shifting the portion of California west of this great rift to the north. Be that as it may, there is ecological validity in thinking of California in insular terms. Not only is it isolated by a combination of topographic and climatic features, it differs from the rest of the continent in a number of significant ways which, involving as they do both species and the natural communities where they live, form some of the basic themes of this book.

During the years of writing this manuscript, the author was working as a consultant naturalist for The Oakland Museum, part of a team developing an exhibits program that features an ecological orientation of California's biotic communities. The visitor to the Natural Sciences Division of this new museum complex is invited to think of his visit as a "walk across California," beginning with the Golden Gate, turning south at Mono Lake, and ending in the deserts of southern California.

It seemed logical to pattern this book in the same fashion— to take a slice of central California from west to east, a transect some 65 miles wide whose southern border is latitude 37° 20" (San Jose) and whose northern edge lies along the 38° 14" parallel (Petaluma). (See Map 3, the foldout map at the back of the book.) The boundaries are admittedly arbitrary, but they enclose representative examples of the biological communities typical of the state's heartland. By exploring these communities as thoroughly as is necessary in a book of this scope and by venturing elsewhere within the state when needful to fill out a particular ecological story, it is hoped that the book will present an adequately substantive account of natural California. Following the example of the museum, the journey continues south into the desert portions of the state.

Among the many patient people whose expertise, and generosity with time and helpful suggestions provided invaluable aid are: Gerhard Bakker whose knowledge, encouragement, and artwork have greatly contributed to the completion of the manuscript; Edith Kinucan, research assistant; Dr. Richard Vogl, Botany Department, California State College at Los Angeles; Dr. Hans Jenny, Soils and Plant Science, University of California, Berkeley; Dr. C. Don MacNeill, Natural Sciences Division, The Oakland Museum; Don Greame Kelley, formerly Acting Curator, Natural Sciences Division, The Oakland Museum; Dr. Robert Stebbins, Museum of Vertebrate Zoology, University of California, Berkeley; Dr. A. Starker Leopold, School of Forestry and Conservation, University of California, Berkeley; Dr. H. Thomas Harvey, Department of Biology, California State College at San Jose; and Dr. Jack Major, Botany, University of California, Davis. All of the above reviewed the portions of the manuscript appropriate to their special fields.

*An Island Called California*

Map. 1. California

Surf, Garapata Beach

# 1. The Seashore

Where the far edge of California gives way to the ocean, landscape shifts to seascape, a meeting ground with its own kinds of confrontation of the two great worlds supported by our planet. Beaches fringe a restless surf; headlands thrust obstinantly into churning swells; and islets persist in spite of the sea's aggression. These are outposts of California, stubborn and steadfast.

Stony point, sand or pebble beach, lagoon, and cliff are common features of shorelines everywhere, created by the struggle of the two adversaries, land and sea. Each supports typical aggregations of living things that vary from one habitat to another. Rock outcrops often usurp the beach line. Where they do, pools and shallows shelter distinctive forms of life found only in such environments. Here, at low tide, one can rummage for their treasure, peering into little bowls encrusted with all manner of living things—slippery and smooth or roughened and calloused—or crouching beside channels through which the wavelets pulse in gentle rhythm. Then thoughts can move like curious fingers over this small portion of the world of the sea, now open for a while to inspection.

Even the smallest tide pools are worth investigation for their rich assortment of organisms. In no other kind of place can one see more animals in a single visit. Though terrestrial soils may harbor enormous quantities of living things, it is usually difficult to observe them and their behavior without special equipment. Tide pools, on the other hand, are readily viewable, and their inhabitants for the most part are large enough to be easily seen.

Changes in tide level hinder or aid their exploration. The best times are during the very low tides occurring regularly along the California coast. Then one can venture out to usually inaccessible rocky heaps and reefs, and discover miniature groves of sea palms, perhaps catching a glimpse of an octopus slipping like a spurt of dark fluid behind a sheltering projection. To the curious but untutored observer, a tide pool visit can be a frustrating experience. A first reaction often is, "I want to know what they are!" If so, he is in good company as this quest for understanding has been the starting point for a number of avocational and professional experiences in natural science. But simply identifying the organisms found here does not tell the whole story of tide pool life, and we are now beginning to discover just how complex and interwoven are the threads of the drama.

For many years natural scientists were largely concerned with discovering and naming plants and animals or with learning how their various organs worked. In the early decades of the twentieth century they became interested in the communities in which these plants and animals live together. Before, it was enough to know that a fairly small greenish-purplish crab was *Pachygrapsus crassipes*, the lined shore crab, which lives on rocky shores of western North America, scavenging on bits and pieces of organic debris, scuttling into crevices or under rocks for cover. But the shore crab does not live alone. It occurs with other crabs, and a number of plant and animal species share the same tidal environment. They all have evolved ways to cope with their watery home, making use of it in terms of food and shelter. They are living things on which the struggle for survival has not only imposed adaptations for life in tide pools, but has established patterns of interrelationships. A shore crab is aware of some of these interactions and connections in the web of his existence. This bit of debris is good to eat; that one is not. This approaching thing may be dangerous; that one is harmless. This place is too dry to live in; over there is better. With these perceptions, it places itself in a community and sees its world as one in which it lives with other creatures in a place best suited to its inherited habits.

Shorelines provide some of the most fascinating natural communities in California. Their inhabitants reflect the great wealth of living organisms present in the ocean ecosystem, a term used to describe a more or less self-contained unit of nature that includes both physical environment and the plants and animals found there. Tide pools and beaches are on the edges of this world-within-a-world, and depend on its food resources in a variety of ways.

The coast of central California has several major types of littoral communities, depending on their substrate, or base, and their place with regard to tide levels. It has two low and two high tides each day, but of unequal height. There is a high-high and a low-low, with one high-low and one low-high in a twenty-four-hour period. Twice a month the shore experiences extreme tides. When the sun, earth, and moon are in a straight line with respect to the earth, their combined tug causes spring, or extra large, tides. When the sun and moon are in right-angle position with regard to the earth, their influence is less, as the respective pulls tend to cancel out each other. Neap tides of this period have a small rise and fall.

One of the often observed features of rocky shores is the zonation of their plants and animals. The organisms of the littoral are stratified, for the most part, according to the amount of aerial exposure to which they are subjected during tidal rise and fall, though other factors are also at work. Four zones have been described for the coast of central California. The top or splash zone is the highest. Here live animals which can protect themselves from desiccation by withdrawing into shells, or may require only an occasional wetting, or are more adapted to life in the air rather than in water. Generally, the upper part of this zone receives moisture only from spray and unusually high waves. The lower part is visited by high tides. Next down are the midlittoral or intertidal zones; the higher one is exposed twice a day by both ebb tides, and much of the lower during most low tides. Zone four is usually under water. Only extreme lows will uncover it, or the so-called minus tides. Below this is the subtidal zone.

The water on which most animals of rocky shores depend for oxygen, moisture, and food is present or absent according to zone and time; they must adjust to the tidal rhythm, meeting its demands in some way, or perish. Ironically, surf can be their worst enemy, necessary though it is for the life of the community. Not many living things can take the unleashed power of wave surge and splash. This is not the only danger. They, like other creatures, must have some defense against hungry neighbors. A few individuals of each species must remain alive long enough to mature and reproduce if the species is to survive.

How does life go about minding its affairs in this warring ground of land and sea? One only has to do a little rocky shore exploring to begin to understand. It is not necessary to wait for an extra low tide; midlittoral zones will serve nicely. Central California has many beaches along semiprotected open coasts where easily accessible rock outcrops with pools abound: around the Monterey Peninsula, near Santa Cruz, Año Nuevo Island, Moss Beach, and, north of the Golden Gate, Dillon Beach, Tomales Point, and Shell Beach. In places the sedimentary rocks have been upended, and weaker strata have been worn away leaving crevices, some large as a bathtub and some as small as a tea cup. These are the jewels of the shoreline, their still surfaces broken only by the occasional surge of the wavelets characteristic of low tide in quiet waters.

The higher ledges of the splash zone are populated by animals more oriented to life on land than in the sea. Rock lice, relatives of the common sow or pill bug, slip into cracks well above the tide line. Surf avoiding, they are independent of actual contact with water. Slightly farther down are the first of the real marine organisms, at this level highly specialized to resist desiccation. Acorn barnacles scatter themselves on rock that is occasionally quite dry. They are able to exclude sun and air by retreating behind tightly closed doors. When the welcome floods of high tide wash over them, they quickly open and fling out legs to grab what crumbs they can from the rich larder of the sea. Unlike the scurrying rock lice or stationary barnacles, species of littorines, also called periwinkles, wander about on rocky faces at the lower level of the splash zone. These little snails seem to need only an occasional wetting. Like many other marine animals, they have an operculum, a door with which they can block their shell openings, protecting themselves from air. Slow-moving molluscs called limpets clamp their oval shaped shells firmly to rocks; the tight seal keeps the soft bodied animal inside from dehydrating. One common high-dwelling species, *Acmaea digitalis*, apparently needs more moisture than some of its relatives. It ranges up into the splash zone only when covered by high water or sheltered from the direct rays of the sun. Many limpets tend to be night active, when the danger of desiccation is less.

The rocky midlittoral has many hazards for their residents. Even the dwellers of pools whose water levels do not fluctuate much regardless of tide height must contend with possible changes in temperature, oxygen level, and salinity. Breaker impact is equally important. The mid- and lower-zone creatures on the outer rocks of the open coast withstand an incredible amount of buffeting and have evolved many adaptations to the now weak, now strong cadence of surf. Limpets and barnacles are admirably designed to withstand wave action. Water hits and runs harmlessly off their sloping shells. Branched animals such as stony corals absorb wave shock easily. Purple sea urchins are sometimes found in very wave-swept positions. With tough spines they scrape round cavities in the rock. By settling into these, after wandering out for food, they escape some of the surge stress. Many tiny animals such as certain isopods, cousins of the rock louse group, seek shelter in their spines. Living in the same turbulent waters are California mussels, common starfish, and leaf or gooseneck barnacles, often in such abundance as to exclude other forms. The sturdy starfish, attached to the substrate, or base, by the suction of its tubed feet, can regenerate an arm if one is lost in combat or by wave action. Mussels cling by means of elastic threads to these sea-battered outer rocks, and barnacles use a natural cement for secure fastening. Sea palms, erect seaweeds with frondlike clusters on flexible "stems," meet the full force of the breakers. Their holdfasts grip the rocky foundation, and the stem is strong and pliant enough to bend but not break with each new wave.

Seaweeds are most numerous in lower tidal and subtidal zones. They cannot endure the prolonged dehydration of the undependable splash zone, nor can they descend too far from sunlight. Rockweeds and nail brush appear rather high in tidal stratification. Any pool with permanent water from tidal residue usually has a colorful display of seaweeds. It is these more than anything else that give texture and variation in hue to most pools, notwithstanding the more spectacular animals such as red and blue sea stars, purple and burgundy sea urchins, and a brilliant orange-red coral. Limy seaweeds known as coralline algae grow like stiff pink lace on walls, in crannies, and even on mussels and other shells. The cabbagelike "leaves" of red laver and red fan, the waving ribbons of red sea feather, red point, and lissom red sea fire enrich the brocade of tide pool sides with hues ranging from orange through russet to purplered. True browns are contributed by the laminarians—kelp-size plants of lower tidal zones—feather boa, a number of rockweeds, ruffled sword, and seersucker. Beds of sea lettuce, one of the loveliest of seaweeds, are salad green. Ocean pincushion and green rope live higher on the littoral and are richly emerald. Many seaweeds are olive in hue; and yellow, black, and lavender are not uncommon colors.

Some of the larger seaweeds such as feather boa kelp (the common name is inspired by blades and air sacs projecting from the stipe like the plumes of Edwardian era finery) and *Laminaria*, or oar blade, require footholds in lower intertidal zones or just below. Both of the giant kelps, bull and bladder, are firmly fixed to rocks in even deeper water, below the realm of the littoral. Inflated bladders at the base of the "leaves" float the long ropelike stipes of the latter up through the intertidal regions to the surface. The equally long stipe of bull kelp enlarges near the water surface to become an enormous tapered air chamber from which a cluster of blades, sometimes 12 feet long, spreads out. The brown bulbous tops of the air chambers gently rising and falling with the ocean swell are common sights to those familiar with the California coast. Some species of red algae are found at depths down to 600 feet. Because of their pigmentation, they can absorb and thus use blue and green light, the most deeply penetrating wavelengths of solar radiation in water. Dwellers of zone four and below include the great green anemones, multiple rayed sun stars—largest of their group—giant red sea urchins, and various abalones.

While examining the wonderfully rich life of the intertidal rocks, look for channels that run from pool to pool. Here, wave pulse drifts the shredded sea lettuce back and forth as though a tired woman were waving tatters of green chiffon. Rockweeds stiffen and relax as the current ebbs and flows. Unraveling and ragged kelp blades drift coiled in great tangles. On uneven surfaces between the basins, clumps of partly exposed seaweed curl with the flexible crispness so peculiar to these plants. When the upwelling water, back flow or insurge, quickens the pool edge, opalescent bubbles gather and burst in their own tiny rhythms. Hermit crabs skitter and fuss on toothpick-size feet, retreating into or peering out of their portable homes. Blennies and sculpins slip in and out of fronds of rockweed. Nudibranchs, small, often colorful shell-less molluscs, glide over the rough surface, their naked gills rippling delicately; sea stars and sea urchins creep about on tube feet. Smells hover from decaying seaweed and that briny something which belongs only to the beaches of cool and temperate lands. From overhead, or just where the breakers begin to curl, comes the shrill yet muted keening of a gull or a sea lion's hollow honk. Bird and seaweed, hydroid and crab—practically every major division of living forms is represented in the crowded communities of rocky shores. To gain just a little understanding of how their residents live together is to begin a new adventure.

Beachcombing, unlike tide rock exploring, is a gentle sport, and a very pleasant thing to do—alone, with congenial people, or with a dog. Your four-footed companion should be tractable, however, content to walk quietly by your side if you so command. Of course, there is hardly a better place to run a dog, with waves to chase, shorebirds to harry, and a host of glorious smells. So, if taking home a wet and dirty canine is no problem, his company may enrich these pleasurable intervals of sand and wind and surf, as many people have discovered.

There are ways and ways to beachcomb. If your feet can take it, barefoot is best. There is nothing like shoes full of sand,

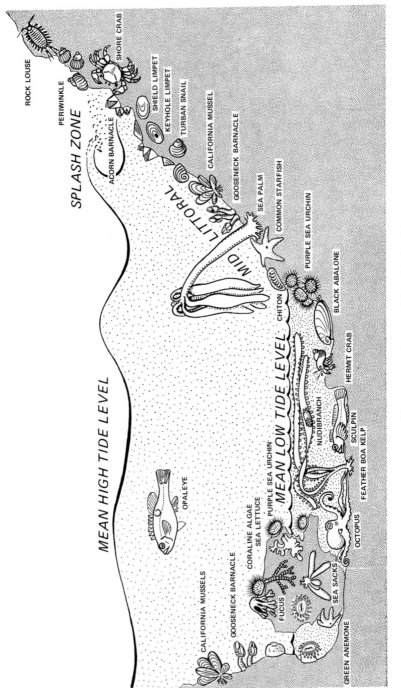

Figure 1. Typical homesites of intertidal and subtidal species

particularly wet, large-grained sand, to make the experience disagreeable. Even sandals are a nuisance as the damp grains encroach between foot and sole. Very high tides compound the problem. You never know when an aggressive wave will chase you back to softer sand, which should be avoided if possible. It is hard to walk through, and it is rather spare of interesting flotsam. Try to keep to the narrow strip of firm wet sand between lower swash zone and high tide mark. Then, barefooted and in swimsuit or dungarees, you will not have to worry about an occasional footwetting.

Beaches vary in place as well as time. Steeper shores have coarser sand. The converse is equally true, and gentler slopes have finer sands. These patterns are closely related to beach position, and a natural sorting out results from the combination of several factors—prevailing swell direction and coastline configuration among them. Many headlands on the central California coast curve to the south, thus protecting inlets and bays to the east. The beaches behind these jutting cliffs reflect this sheltering influence. The most protected are flat, and the sand is fine grained. As the shore opens out to the full force of the northwest swell, the most common wave direction here, the strand slopes sharpen and their grains are larger.

Where bay indentations bite into the coastwise cliffs, they are often sealed off, or almost so, by sandspits across their mouths. The headlands flanking them are subjected to constant battering. Particles torn from the parent rock are picked up by currents that travel parallel to the bay mouth, generated by waves hitting the shores at an angle due to wind and land patterns typical of the coast. Swept by these longshore sea streams, the fragments drop as they encounter the quieter waters of the bay, enlarging shoreline beaches and building sandbanks across its mouth. Gradually the headlands erode back to where the bars have formed, and a comparatively straight coastline is the result.

The long spit beaches with their enclosed lagoons are the beachcomber's boulevards. The flats to leeward are the communal residence of myriad plants and animals preferring muddy bottoms and quiet water. Eel-grass, a true flowering plant, is frequently found in dense patches in these shallower areas and, when uprooted, lies in windrows in place of the piles of seaweed so characteristic of the outer edge.

Where the coves are narrow or the parent rock of larger beaches is a certain nature, the sandy fringe may be reduced to practically nothing, and cobble—collections of surf-rounded pebbles—paves the shoreline. Then the lap and swish of the sea has a sound heard on no sand-bottomed beach. This is the clatter of thousands of pebbles settling into place with each receding wave. Such silibant soughing is quite different from the roar and crash of breakers pounding reefs or headlands.

Aside from the great slow rhythms of coastal uplift and downdrop, erosion and buildup, beach appearances can change from day to day, from season to season. Tides rearrange the shore-edge debris. Storms toss up new tangles of deep water kelp that are often host to creatures, or their remains, less adventurous folk rarely see. The casual visitor down for a picnic or for the day has a whole new world of discovery. He can enter it with but a handful of the bits and pieces from these undulating ribbons of flotsam following the wave line of high tide. Here are the empty cones of barnacles strewn about or still adhering to fragments of rock or to shells secreted by other animals such as mussels and red abalones. Many intertidal forms stay quite clean of encrusting growth, and one can pick up clamshells, starfish, and black abalone looking scrubbed and polished in comparison to molluscs and crustaceans more hospitable to free riders. You can make the acquaintance of some of the more attractive snails by carefully checking over these little mounds of debris. Purple olivellas which live in the fine sands of bay mouths are a collector's joy when perfect and tinted a soft violet. Delicate pectens are the seashells of tradition with fluted fan and squared-off side projections. Several clams have sun-ray markings in pink, violet, and tan. Occasionally there are the dainty slipper limpets or the craterlike hillocks of their ribbed cousins. Horn snails and the banded black-and-white barrel snail occur in lagoons or bay flats and should be looked for there, not on seaward shores. Rock snails and top shells, on the other hand, live in more open waters and their convoluted spirals are often part of the wave-line litter.

Crab remains are common. The cast-off exoskeletal parts, which are periodically discarded as the animal grows, are paper thin or hard as a china plate, depending on the species. Sand dollars are the delight of children who carefully collect them for their perfection of shape and the embroidery of their markings. The "dollar" is the husk covering the soft and vulnerable animal inside, now dead and washed away. Alive it was bristly, much like its cousin the sea urchin whose globelike casing is also part of beach debris. *Donax*, the little shore-dwelling bean clam whose shell often has small round holes drilled by predaceous boring molluscs, occurs as far north as the San Luis Opisbo area. Keep a careful eye out for evidences of boring clams. Scattered in among pebbles you might find rock fragments pitted with round holes quite frequently still cradling the bivalve responsible for the hole. These are dug by chemical means or abrasion. The half-shells, opening and closing in a rotary motion, scrape away the rock particles with the help of sharp ridges on the two valves.

Most of the small rounded pebbles scattered on a sandy beach testify to the grinding action of waves. Rockhounds have learned to tumble handsome rock specimens by observing the power of water, sand, and motion. Jadeite and moonstone, jasper and agate—skin-smooth and grape-round—are the gems of the beach, free for the finding. Crystal clear and looking more mineral than animal, jellyfish and a host of relatives litter the beach from time to time with gelatinous lumps. *Velella*, often called "by-the-wind-sailor," is a small animal whose aggregations drift with the winds and sea currents, hoisting sails of clear plasticlike material. From time to time they are cast up on shore by the thousand, to die and end as flotsam. Much different in color and shape are the egg cases of skates, related to rays and sharks. They look like rectangles of black leather with four hooked projections at each corner. These catch on to kelp fronds, anchoring the case until the embryo within matures enough to emerge from the open end. Wave-ground bits of broken bottles can also be found, as well as knotted twists of driftwood and the snarls and clumps of seaweed—small worlds even now, though ripped from their rocky substrates.

Turn over a pile of kelp and hundreds of beach hoppers and the smaller sand fleas burst like sparks from a beach party bonfire. These little amphipods seek any shelter available on the shore, including driftwood, abandoned picnic litter, and the sand itself into which they burrow. Some are nocturnal, others day active, but all must protect themselves from desiccation though, oddly enough, they will drown in water. They are flattened like their relatives the isopods, or sow bugs. However, amphipods have a humped look as though pinched by two fingers pressing in on each side of the thorax or chest. A sowbug appears to have been flattened by someone pressing a finger down on the top of its back as it scurries along.

But the real treasure of a pile of decaying seaweed is revealed to the casual beachcomber in forms of life seldom seen except by skin divers and tide-pool explorers. One may find baby octopi, kelp crabs, and nudibranchs still alive in the masses of wet seaweed abandoned on the shore by the giant waves of winter storms. Crustaceans seeking the shelter of seaweed and kelp beds such as broken-back and skeleton shrimp stir and wiggle, still alive though their storm-loosened home was heaved up on shore. Sea spiders, small worms, sponges, and tunicates together with stray sea stars, sea lice, and many other intertidal forms spend all their lives in the "roots" and "stems" of the great plants of the kelp forest. Storm wrack is an excellent place to look for these animals, and as soon after high seas as possible.

Here and there in a pile of the larger algae are the torn shreds of smaller and more delicate species: *Plocamium*, mermaid's hair, and delicate sycophant, for example. But a few days of sun and dry air soon reduce these fascinating heaps of sea hay to unattractive snarls, their stems dried to leathery thongs. Any still attached leaves are now toughened and shriveled. The little sea creatures so abruptly torn from their home in the littoral must die unless some high wave gives them reprieve and carries them back for a second chance at life. Odds are they are doomed. Their remains will feed the sand fleas, beach hoppers, and flies that are the last to use the friendly shelter of the castaway kelp heaps. Little groups of Audubon's warblers, small yellow and black land birds, hunt among these drying piles for the abundant insects now thriving in place of marine animals.

Though many shorebirds closely resemble each other, their differences become readily apparent with careful observation. Gulls are easy to identify, particularly while standing as they often do on one leg facing into the wind, their satiny gray and white plumage sleek against firm, fat bodies. While in flight, they can be confused with terns, elegantly slim close relatives. Gulls have a dignity about them and are rarely guilty of anything more frivolous than a proprietary interest in the garbage and refuse of dock and harbor. Sanderlings, on the other hand, collect in fussy little flocks as the small white birds scamper up and down the beach with the precision and unity of a corps de ballet. They spray out and converge in wonderful rhythm, moved this way and that by the attack and retreat of breaking waves, feeding just along the fringe of the surf.

A variety of probers enriches the bird life of the shore. Marbled godwits, wandering tattlers, knots, dowitchers, and Hudsonian curlews work their way over the wet sand and exposed seaweed-rich reefs hunting for tiny crustaceans, worms, and insects. Snowy plovers and other short-billed birds pick over the sea wrack with its fly-infested seaweed and organic debris. The many kinds of sandpipers visiting California shores usually keep in flocks and often feed much like sanderlings, receding and advancing with the wave line, busily searching for drifting food bits or small organisms exposed by the ebb surge.

Though large numbers of birds are supported by the shoreline's bill of fare, aside from organic flotsam, beaches seem quite devoid of the rich marine life of intertidal rocky habitats. The substrate itself accounts for this paucity. Sand shifts constantly with wind and wave, and sessile animals such as sea anemones rarely get a foothold on this unstable flooring. Many burrowing marine organisms, however, find the wet sand of the intertidal beach zone a most acceptable home. It is easy to penetrate and provides an excellent cover for protection against predation, wave shock, and dehydration. What appears to be quite sterile harbors a variety of animals which in turn are food for the shorebirds so closely linked with the beach. Another type of natural community lives here though it may not be as spectacular and obvious as in the case of tide pools.

One of the most observable species is the sand or mole crab. Every habitual swimmer along the coast has had the experience of feeling prickles under his feet as he walked down into the surf, particularly at low tide. These are the antennae and heads of small egg-shaped crabs waiting for food to be washed to them by the incoming waves. Their dependence on the tide for food has resulted in a kind of migratory behavior. They travel up and down the beach slope always within reach of the wave edge.

Clamming is a common and popular beach sport. In digging for them one's spade may turn up many sand beach residents. The Pismo clam of southern California and the razor clam of northern shores are excellent eating. They feed by means of syphon tubes that extend to the surface enabling these bivalves to burrow deep in the sand. The razor clam can dig itself in very rapidly, using the strong muscles of its foot as a tool. Small crustaceans live here, too. Ghost shrimp are dwellers of sandy flats, and apparently get their food from the tiny organisms living in the mud they ingest while digging their burrows. Gray shrimp and the shrimplike oppossum mysids are often found in swash pools along the more open coast. Sea cucumbers may surprise the clam digger who associates these living lumps with the crevices of the lower tidal rocks. Bristle worms or polychetes are much at home here. Their large family includes the sedentary tube-building worms. Some secrete lime, forming tube masses underneath rocks along the shore. Others are dwellers of sand or mud flats and line the tubes with mucus; a few species, apparently, even construct a mucus net with which to catch food particles. One bristle worm, so named because of the spines along its body, is bright red. From one to two inches long, it is found about eighteen inches below the sand surface. This is too far down for the probing bills of shorebirds, but other marine worms are numerous enough to be important items in avian diets.

Out on the flats or on the lagoon side of bars and spits where the sand is clean and relatively free from mud, many-armed serpent stars, basket cockles, large white moon snails, and sand dollars make their homes. Sand starfish, burrowing anemones, sand clams, and several types of crabs join them, appreciating the calm water behind the barriers closing off the open ocean.

Any discussion of how plants and animals live together leads quickly to the consideration of food sources available for the community and the various ways in which these are obtained. Food is present on the littoral in greater abundance than meets the eye. A vast network of eaters and eaten is woven from the strands of interaction among the organisms of the shore. This food web, as it is termed, is an extremely important aspect of any natural community. Its designs are determined by what species are present, meeting conditions imposed by both physical environment and the biological complex. It is a series of endlessly repeated feeding patterns consistently characteristic of the community.

The organisms of the shore are but part of the larger marine world, its fringe actually, adding to and taking away from its great supply of nourishment but having little impact on the total oceanic ecosystem. Here as everywhere, green plants initiate the strands of the food web as they are the only organisms capable of making food. From another point of view, they form the base of a numbers pyramid (see Figure 2). An explanatory word about these two terms is in order. Food webs stress the feeding relationships among species—who eats what or whom. Numbers pyramids show the comparative number of organisms involved in specific food energy transfers.

Phytoplankton (plant plankton) is a major basic component of both food web and numbers pyramid. For the most part it consists of bacteria, microscopic algae such as diatoms and dinoflagellates, and other tiny free-floating organisms. Dino-flagellates give rise to the red tides that poison oysters, mussels, and fish in epidemic proportions. Whole shorelines are strewn with dead animals during major outbreaks. The summer peaks of these organisms, called "blooms," are responsible for the prohibitions against eating shellfish in this season. California mussels are often under quarantine for much of the year.

Like most plants, diatoms and dinoflagellates make their own food through photosynthesis, the process of combining water and carbon dioxide to make simple sugar through the use of the sun's energy. They are the food factories of the open sea and are the most important source of plant-derived nutriments. Seaweeds, the other great crop of the sea, are decidely less significant, though some animals of the littoral do feed directly on them or their dead remains. Snails such as the midzone black turbans, various limpets, abalones, and chitons (or sea cradles) move out herdlike onto the village commons and upland mead-ows, as it were, feeding on the lush and prodigious growth of algae, both microscopic and larger forms. Sea urchins scavenge but also harvest seaweed. In contrast, huge numbers of animals depend in whole or in part on plankton. All the plant-eating forms feeding on the vegetative, or producer, base are first order consumers. They constitute the second level in the num-bers pyramid which, with them, begins to taper upward from the base, since there are fewer herbivorous feeders than plants. The food web, on the other hand, widens as more and more species get in on the feast, feeding on plants or preying on each other.

Zooplankton, the smallest of these first order feeders, in-cludes the larval forms of sea animals, and organisms such as copepods, other tiny crustaceans, worms, and one-celled ani-mals known as radiolarians and foraminifers. Most feed on phytoplankton and some on each other. Both types of plankton are consumed by larger organisms ranging in size and species from tiny invertebrates to fair-sized fish. It is often impossible to differentiate among those which eat plant plankton only, those dependent on animal material, and species which eat both. It is simplest to assign all to first order consumer rank.

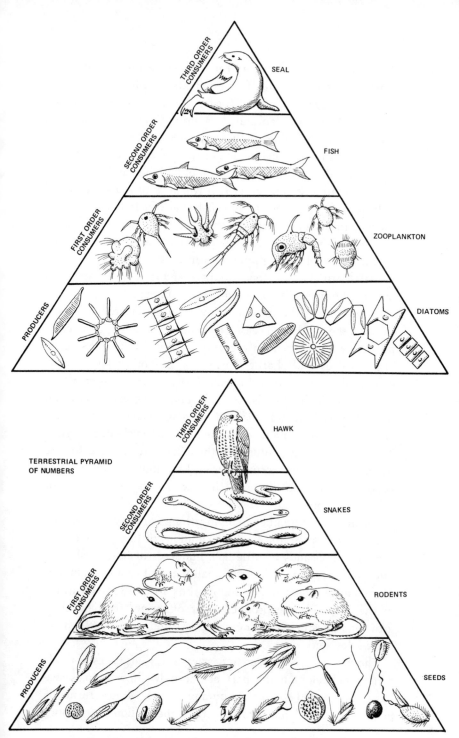

Figure 2. Marine and terrestrial pyramids of numbers

The next step is reserved for the second order consumers. They eat the animals that feed on plants. Starfish eat plankton-feeding mussels; gulls hunt for small fish, some of whom are dependent on the plankton "sea broth," sieved out by gill rakers. Many shoreline numbers pyramids end right here. Gulls and their fish-eating neighbors, brown pelicans, have very few predators. But other pyramids mount higher and higher, as small fish are prey for larger fish which in turn are victims of still larger fish. The carnivorous fish share the larder with other second, third, and fourth order consumers, such as the fish-eating birds to which we have referred, sea lions and others. The upper levels of the pyramid can only support a few individuals; attrition of food sources and strong competition among like size carnivores limit their numbers.

Occupants of the top level have few or no predators, and death is the result of disease or old age. Not many kinds compete with them; their only enemy is man. In the open ocean killer whales and sharks, barracuda and other large meat-eating fish occupy top positions. In coastal waters few creatures dare tackle elephant seals, sea lions, and true seals. Only when these imperial animals die and scavengers and decomposers work over their remains does the nutrition cycle begin again. Then the nutrients captured in their flesh are released for the use of other marine forms. During life, however, their nitrogenous wastes contribute to the ocean's vast storehouse of nutritious compounds.

An incredible number of living things are involved in the journey from plankton to shark: millions of tiny plankton organisms, thousands of little fish, hundreds of larger fish, and one shark. Its body is but the small remnant of a vast amount of biological intake and output on the part of all the creatures in the pyramid: the production of offspring, food hunting, growing, digesting, warding off disease and enemies, eliminating wastes, and so on.

Though we have alluded in passing to various types of food-getting behavior on the part of shore-dwelling animals, we have not covered the matter by any means. Minute forms of plant and animal plankton occur by the trillion in offshore waters. Many animals of the littoral feed entirely on plankton served to them by the surge and drift of tidal flow. Bivalved molluscs—oysters, clams, mussels, and scallops—open their shells and trap the tiny particles on mucous-covered gills. Sponges, tunicates, and barnacles also utilize the same food source. The seawater flooded internal chambers of sponges have cilia, or hairs, which help move minute organisms toward ingestion. Hydroids are small, sometimes delicately plumed animals living in colonies like coral. Each individual animal, called a polyp and usually indiscernible to the naked eye, weaves a set of stinging tentacles in a tiny dance for bits of food brought within reach. Such meals may include organic fragments resulting from predation or decay. Flower-resembling sea anemones make use of stinging cells at the tip of their petal-like tentacles. These capture and transfer food particles to the digestive cavity with a quick infolding action unexpected of such placid-looking creatures. Anemone congregations are often disguised by a blanketing of shell bits, sand, and gravel.

Many animals feed on the remains of other organisms. Rock crabs are notorious for being scavengers—that is, they will eat anything edible, alive or dead, including picnic refuse. This is almost as true for the little hermit and shore crabs so active in the higher midzones of rocky shores and the larger commercially valuable crabs of lower levels. They hunt about for any bit of plant and animal debris within their range. Beach lice, hoppers, and fleas forage in the wrack piles, eating the decaying seaweed or the detritus caught in it.

Starfish are outright carnivores. They clutch such shell-protected animals as snails, barnacles, and mussels in their many-armed embrace. Able to exert enough pressure to pry loose or open the shells of their victims, they need but the smallest crack in order to begin a remarkable process of feeding behavior. Everting its stomach, located in the middle of its body, the starfish slips this organ inside the opened shell to begin digestion. Nudibranchs, also aptly called sea slugs, often feed on hydroids, avoided by many marine predators because of their stinging cells. Sea slugs collect the "unpopped" cells in special tissue on their backs. A number of snails are predaceous and use a grinding organ called a radula to cut holes in the shells of clams, oysters, and other molluscs.

Though not of the shore communities, sea otters, one of California's most prized sea mammals, live in beds of giant kelp just along the outer edge of the surf. Frequently accused of depleting the abalones of the central California coast, research indicates a preference for purple sea urchins. They crack them open against rocks and eat the juicy insides. One of the more striking wildlife experiences of our coast is to see a group of these attractive mammals swimming or floating on their backs midst a tangle of bobbing kelp bladders.

It is perhaps apparent by now that seashores have several unique features. One is the presence of sessile, or stationary, animals that depend only on the bounty of the tidal currents to bring them nourishment. This particular way of being an animal is almost unknown on land. Any similar habit is largely confined to freshwater environments. Even there, very few species remain stationary for their entire lives. Terrestrial creatures must forage for their food; no kind current shoves the banquet table within their reach.

The vast numbers of animal species and individuals are impressive. Except for insect swarms or bird flocks, nowhere else do we see so many organisms in such concentration. The great beds of barnacles, mussels, and sea anemones, so characteristic of tidal life, have no land-dwelling counterparts. For the most part it is plankton, wave served and free for the taking, that is mainly responsible for such great abundance. The richness of this soup and its universality in seawater, though there is some variation in density from place to place, account for much of the profusion of sea life, serving as the almost inexhaustable support for broad and crowded consumer levels resting on it.

In any situation where dining goes on so lavishly, other creatures suffer. The young, nature's deposit in the evolutionary bank, have a particularly hard time of it. To compensate for the inevitable destruction of much of their progeny, most sea creatures reproduce in astronomical numbers. Their presence in the communities of today testifies to the survival of enough individuals to insure the continuation of the species. Many marine invertebrates have several stages of development, some of which are incredibly different from the parent animals. E. F. Ricketts and J. Calvin, in *Between Pacific Tides* (Stanford, 1952), a classic for anyone interested in intertidal forms, sum it up neatly: "It is a grotesque business, as bewildering to the average man as if he were asked to believe that rosebushes give birth to hummingbirds, and that the hummingbird's progeny become rosebushes again." One common jellyfish, *Aurelia*, produces as offspring a larva which looks like a small flattened oval blob with tiny hairs or cilia. It swims to rocks or seaweed where it eventually settles. After losing its cilia it develops tentacles and behaves like a sea anemone except that it builds layers of itself which break off and drift away to become jellyfish. In larval form it is merely part of the freely drifting bits and pieces, or plankton, and is available to any open mouth. The mortality rate is understandably high. Only a few individuals become large or developed enough to hunt for a toehold in the already densely populated tidal zone. Creatures die, making place for newcomers to the community, but competition is keen for the vacancies.

Consequently, many species are indiscriminate about the substrate upon which they come to rest or to anchor. Barnacles make their permanent homes on mussels as well as rocks. Many snails—red abalone, for example—carry tiny communities on their backs. Hydroids, bryozoans, other small forms, and seaweed live contentedly, not alarmed in the least when their homes occasionally move about. Indeed, some animals not only tolerate but welcome a disguising thatch on their backs. Masking crabs are famous for carrying about bits of seaweed or sponge as camouflage.

Among the marine plants well adapted to crowded conditions are epiphytic seaweeds, species with established footholds on larger forms. Common though this type of relationship is among plants, particularly in the tropics, one usually doesn't think of seaweed as being very much given to this habit. But in an environment where rhythms of moisture, temperature, and sunlight are fairly reliable, sea plants adjusted to such fluctuations thrive, and the inevitable crowding is the result of favorable conditions in general. Plants have taken to living on each other in an attempt to circumvent the limitations of specified space. Such seaweeds as delicate sea lace and tassel wing sprout in rosy fronds from the host algae. Some types actually do penetrate the tissues of the substrate plant in a kind of semi-parasitism, but these are few. Wrinkled, moderately branching algal "stems" support more epiphytes than those which are multibranched or smooth stiped. Bryozoans and other tiny sedentary animals are often in an "epiphytic" relationship to kelps and smaller seaweeds. Some form crusty or mossy patches, others a jellylike scum.

Defense from each other is, necessarily, a strong thread in the pattern of tidal life. Many of the safeguards against wave crash and desiccation serve to protect tidal creatures from predation. Strong muscles hold a limpet firmly to the rock or keep bivalves shut tight against danger. Snails merely retreat behind an unappetizing mound of lime. Food-getting devices such as stinging cells, claws, and spines are useful defensive mechanisms. A few tidal species are suspected of having unpleasant-tasting flesh. Sea spiders and kelp crabs, brittle stars and shrimp weave and scramble through the lush kelp patches, safe from the attention of larger predators which rarely penetrate such jungles. In the labyrinthian world of sea cliffs and rocks, there are crevices, crannies, and caves, some never uncovered even by the lowest tides. These provide excellent hiding places for shy animals, like octopi. They avoid their enemies by swiftly slipping into sheltering cracks or beneath overhangs. Rock projections protect many animals preferring the sandy or cobbled floors beneath them. Beds of sea anemones and mussels accommodate thousands of tiny organisms seeking to hide themselves. Sponges and other colonial animals take refuge in communal living. A large number, including tube worms, dig burrows in which they reside. Lime tube builders are quite secure, for a mouthful of rock is not pleasant eating.

With all of the perils and risks involved in living in the littoral, there is, as in all natural communities, a marvelous balance of success and failure. Take success to mean the ability of the individual to reproduce itself and the species to continue. California shares, with other shore-fronting lands, the oldest natural communities on earth. Life which we assume to have begun in ancient seas has changed less in this environment than in any other. We look back a hundred million years when we investigate tidal rocks and shores. That is not to say the individual aggregations of organisms of the littoral have undergone no change. California's coast is a rising one. Old wave-worn terraces occur high on the sea-facing bluffs. Erosion is constant along cliffs facing the open ocean. Softer strata are worn away. The undermined remains crumble into the froth-fretted surface below, destroying old habitats and presenting new homegrounds for tidal pioneers. Aside from these drastic shifts, many of the risks and hazards of life on land are missing. There are no threats from fire and periodic prolonged drought. But man, that most tireless, efficient, and voracious predator of all, has become a tide-zone invader. Abalones, spiny lobsters, and edible crabs, once common in the coastal waters, have decreased alarmingly; strict conservation measures are imperative to insure their survival.

Nowhere else in the natural world are two such richly different environments so close together. To seaward are fish and brown pelicans in measured flight just above the outer breakers; to land, cliffs or sand dunes with wildflowers and white-footed mice. Surf and bluff are natural fences bordering these strips of beach often no more than fifty feet wide, if that. The highest tide wave-line marks the last stronghold of the sea. From here on, cold and heat, rainfall and soil determine what will live.

The coastal dunes and cliffs are in themselves communities and have their own kinds of specialness. The sandy hillocks of dune country are found where the land slopes gently to the sea and are often stabilized with rushes, grass, and sea strawberry. Others are barren and shift and move with onshore winds. Almost as soon as one goes inland from the high-tide mark, the characteristic fleshy sea strand flowers appear—pink and yellow sand verbena, sea rocket, and sea fig. Salty sand is a poor substrate, and succulent plant tissue helps conserve what water is absorbed. Mock heather, beach morning glory, dune primrose, beach pea, coyote brush, and the silver-green feathers of beach sagewort reconnoiter the strand, pioneering to seaward as far as the waves will permit. The open spaces of sand between these clumps of vegetation are guide books of information about the animals that live here. The tracks of beetles and lizards, wild mice and other small mammals criss-cross over the fine dune sands. Even the lightest pressures by the smallest of feet tell stories of what went where, and sometimes why, as trail intersects trail in a revealing pattern.

Very few dedicated beachcombers of the California coast will top the last dune without pausing and looking westward once more—out to the restless horizon of breaker crest and trough, to sanderlings and kelp piles, to a beach perhaps already wiped clean of his footprints by that erratic housekeeper, the tide.

# 2. Sea Cliff

Sea cliffs form some of the great sceneries of the world—Côte d'Azur, Norwegian fiords, White Cliffs of Dover, and California's cliffs of the Big Sur country, Point Lobos, the San Mateo coast, the Golden Gate, Drakes Bay, Point Reyes, McClure Beach, Tomales Point, and the Sonoma and Mendocino coasts. Where headlands drop into the sea, there is a glorious pageantry of color and motion as wave follows wave, confronting the terrestrial outposts in endless procession. First comes the subtle shift in blue or green as the breaker is born. Then the infant swell slides toward land increasing in height until it crests and spills down upon itself in a white cascade. Now, when it is almost spent, tracelets of foam break away and eddy gracefully around the rocks and reefs at the foot of the cliff face, slipping seaward in the pull of the back surge.

Coastline near Big Sur

The greatest joy of a shore watcher is a curling wave breaking directly against cliff foot or tide rock. Then, in a sweep of aquamarine and indigo its fluid ice shatters in a shower of blue-white crystals. There are the marvelous sounds of impact, as well, in this crash and splintering.

California shorescapes would be far less interesting if they were all beach flats and dunes. Coastal mountains are responsible in part for such dramatic views as those along the Scenic Highway south of the Monterey Peninsula. The Santa Lucia Range drops sharply to the sea in an incomparable meeting of land and ocean. The actual sea cliff itself, the portion being eroded by wave action, is but part of a great downsweep of mountain. The highway, the only interruption of these plummeting curves, seems tacked on like makeshift decoration. This is not to quarrel with its being there. This country suffers little from being seen and admired. But conservationists cannot be less than grateful to the far-sighted citizens who fought inappropriate commercial development. Today California can claim one of the great unspoiled coastline drives in the world.

Whether natural seawalls are backed by steep mountain, coastal plain, or broad shelves and benches—common along much of the coast—they are under constant attack by the sea. Wavelet and comber bite and lick at their bases, nibbling out rock fragments which, surf-tossed, grind away still more rock. Compressed by the upslope of the shore, breakers hitting cliffs increase in volume and strike these faces, broadside as they often are, with tremendous power. The softer shales and sandstones of the coastwise sedimentary series erode quickly. Whole chunks drop away undermined by the constant gnawing. The harder rocks persist in headlands such as Point Reyes and Bodega Head. The Farallon Islands, thirty miles west of the Golden Gate, are made of the same ancient granites as those two famed promontories and have resisted untold centuries of battering.

Straight-sided islets known as stacks enrich the shorescape. They, too, have been successful in withstanding the attack. Either tougher rock or protection from exposure to full wave strength has enabled them to remain. Uncountable rocks and reefs are scattered around them and along the cliff base. In Sonoma and Mendocino counties, coves circle around to break into stacks and rocky clusters connected by arches that hover over breakers tumbling back and forth through the spanway. Such an inlet on a golden summer day is enchantingly lovely with a gentle wind nudging the needles of the firs and pines along the cliff tops, the silver of splash and slide-off, the turquoise of surge and swell.

Many coves are usually friendly places, and no better sites for picnics exist if they are accessible and open to the public. The larger inlets have beaches built by currents traveling along the curve of the cove head and endlessly working over the sand and pebbles of the little strand. In narrower coves the waves, confined as they are, crash into each other coming and going. These little pockets, or surge channels, are extremely dangerous for human exploration and are best left to be viewed from above.

Beaches also occur on the more open cliff-faced shorelines lacking cove indentations. South of San Francisco, in San Mateo County, wave attack against the foot of coastal hills has resulted in some remarkably straight cliffs with long beaches between the few and scattered headlands. North of Point Reyes, the west side of the peninsula is bordered by broad straight strands and inshore dunes around Abbotts Lagoon. The rocky slopes of the ridge have been partially smothered in sand dredged up from the sea bottom. Prevailing currents are parallel to the shore, and cross-current action which would aid in creating indentations is negligible.

The cliffline is broken at points along the coast, particularly where river valleys enter the sea. Frequently their mouths are semisealed across by bars, stretches of beach, or dunes that separate the open sea front from the lagoons and tide flats to the rear. California has a predominantly rising coast. One can deduce this from such topographical features as wave-cut terraces on the hills above the present shoreline and ancient stacks now standing as isolated remnants on the coastal plains that were once strands and beaches. Very recent subsidence, however, has drowned the mouth of the major river system of California and created San Francisco Bay. This estuary contains vast acres of mud flats rich in bird and invertebrate life. Tomales and Bolinas bays and Drakes Estero are also prime examples of tide marsh shorescapes in striking contrast to neighboring palisades. The first two are drowned mouths of rift valleys formed by the famous, or infamous, San Andreas Fault. Drakes Estero is a typical valley system flooded most probably by the same subsidence that made San Francisco Bay.

Some cliffs are mere bluffs with easy access to the beach. Others like Duxbury Point, at the outer end of Bolinas Bay, are practically unscalable, and their beaches and reefs are lonely places where only seabirds congregate. But all along the coast, people have managed to wear footpaths, often overgrown by vegetation and hardly discernible, that wind down these steep faces to disappear in the talus and boulder heaps of the cliff base. Sea-edge precipices are by no means always sheer or perpendicular. They may have ledges, gullies, knobs, and slopes where plants establish themselves and seabirds create a world of their own.

A cliff is not an easy dwelling place. Water even in this climate of relatively high rainfall is scarce for several reasons. Shallow soils cannot hold much moisture, and runoff is particularly rapid on steep gradients. The cool winds constantly blowing inland from the ocean are in themselves drying; they carry away buffering particles of moisture from leaf surfaces. Salt-burdened soils and atmosphere are additional hazards likely to be encountered by plants attempting life on a sea cliff habitat. Such conditions amplify any tendencies to dryness on the part of the environment.

Many forms simply cannot manage such a site at all. They need more water or deeper soils, less salinity or less wind. One or several of these limiting factors prevent many of the plants usually found near the coast from even a reconnaissance on sea bluffs. Some, however, do very well. They germinate in cracks where soil has begun to accumulate, rain water lingers longer, and there is shelter from the wind. In time the shrubs force a network of roots through rock joints and breaks, maintaining a tenacious hold on life. Or they find toe space on a barren ledge and proceed to build a soil base, often with the debris from their own discarded parts such as leaves and flowers. An existing clump of plants is an invitation for seedlings to try to establish themselves in the same place, if there is enough soil to go around. Gullies with their catchment hollows are host to many plants whose careers may end with the next great storm as they are torn out and tossed into the sea below.

Among the specific forms frequently found growing on sea cliffs are the carpetlike sea figs which conserve water in their thick triangular leaves, and hang in untidy masses from the cliff edge or spread over the bluffs in coarse friezes. A close relative, the naturalized ice plant, is also succulent. Tiny blisters cover the surfaces of leaves and stems to give them a jeweled look. Live-forevers have reddish rosettes of fleshy water-storing leaves. Their near relative, stonecrop, retains moisture in much the same way. In gullies along canyon sides and even on the more open bluffs, ocean spray feathers out in plumes of creamy white. Coastal forms of ceanothus, coyote brush, and bush monkeyflower are other typical cliff shrubs and have many of the drought-resistant features discussed in more detail further along in the book. Up to six feet tall, tree lupines have corn-kernel yellow or more rarely lavender blossoms. Though preferring sandy soils, like their shorter cousins the equally lovely dune lupines, they occasionally cluster in the gravel of road cuts and gully sides. Where the bluffs fold back along canyons and river valleys, the more protected locations may encourage low-growing masses of stunted sword fern, horsetails, berry vines, paintbrush, cow parsnip and other umbels, yarrow, and ceanothus.

Small flowering plants are not uncommon: rock cress, poppies, seaside daisies, goldenrod, evening primroses, buttercups, and wallflowers are small flares of yellow or orange often found among the quieter grays, whites, and rusts of coastal buckwheats. These last look like awkward handfuls of dried twigs and half-dead flowers even when they are in full bloom. Dock is the same rusty color and is another dweller of rocky outcrops overlooking the sea.

Though full-grown bushes away from the coast, many

shrubs are stunted, almost to prostration, on sea bluffs. Wind is responsible for the natural pruning and keeps exposed thickets in hedgelike form. The drying power of salty winds kills any pioneering twig daring to venture above the protective mass of compacted foliage. It is interesting that many of the adaptations typical of alpine and desert plants are present on this relatively moist and comfortable coast.

A prime reason some cliffs, offshore islands, and rocks are devoid of plants, or almost so, is the continuous congregation of seabirds, to a spectacular degree in some places. One of the best known such rookeries is the Farallon Islands, those last pieces of California where begins the immense loneliness of the open sea. Exposed and storm scarred, their aged granite is broken and cracked. There is hardly any covering vegetation except for a few low-growing plants such as the succulent Farallon weed and some introduced grasses and other non-natives. The result is a ceaseless weathering of rugged terrain. Though now they serve as a navigational facility with a Coast Guard station, beacon light, radio signal transmitter, and radar equipment, at one time they were major contributors to the markets of San Francisco. It seems that there were not enough laying hens around this thriving city in the 1850s. So the Farallon Egg Company was formed, and at one time 120,000 seabird eggs were gathered in two days and sold for a dollar a dozen. The practice finally came to an end when the islands were declared a bird reserve in 1909, but by that time the bird population had decreased considerably. Fur seal and sea otter skins were another source of income for early-day exploiters of this tiny outpost.

Many of the birds that nest on these and other coastal islands north and south of the Golden Gate, such as the Channel Islands off the southern California coast and those of British Columbia and Alaska, are truly seabirds. That is, they spend most of their lives on the open ocean, coming to shore only during the summer breeding season. If they could have evolved ways to incubate eggs out at sea, they might conceivably have done so. Birds such as Cassin's auklet, ashy petrel, and California murre behave as though land is to be avoided whenever possible except for the period of reproduction, which, however, may extend for several months. On the other hand, cormorants, western gulls, and oystercatchers are true shorebirds in that their activities are never far from shore the year around.

Though the Farallones are the most famed of these California seabird rookeries and have a large number of species and a great number of individuals, some coastal cliffs—on Point Reyes and Año Nuevo Point, for instance—have well-developed nesting colonies. Offshore islets, like Seal Rocks close to San Francisco's Cliff House, are frequently used. These natural communities differ from most others in being almost exclusively the homes of birds, either nesting, or nesting and roosting; there are few mammals, except for sea lions and seals on skerry or beach. Plants are extremely scattered or non-existent in the crowded rookeries. Seedlings would soon be trampled or buried by nesting activity. Guano accumulations, up to a foot thick, preclude the successful establishment of vegetation except perhaps for lichens, those hardiest of plants. Birds such as cormorants and western gulls use plant materials for their nests and depend on dried seaweed, twigs, or grass brought in or washed ashore. Bare ground nesters—murres, for example—if they make any preparation at all, line the nest depression with rock fragments or pebbles, harsh substrate for something as fragile as an egg.

Few nesting sites are as crowded as those of seabirds. The great gannet concentrations of Newfoundland and islands of the North Sea are so congested during breeding season that it is difficult to walk through them, if the birds remain stationary, without stepping on some offspring or parent. California murre colonies on the ledges of coastal promontories and islands are often equally crowded. To the enterprising bird watcher they appear as a solid mass of gurgling, restless gray. On the Farallones, in their avian heyday, they most probably outnumbered the neighboring species also nesting here. Though the islands never quite regained the bird populations of pre-egg-company days, they still support large colonies. One would suppose that much competitive struggle takes place as the birds arrive from the open sea in March and April looking for nest sites. It is hard to believe that there is little or no fighting for nesting space which is so limited.

Natural communities have their own laws of supply and demand. Desert regions are short on water, and desert dwellers must compete successfully for their share or die. Most communities have limits on the supply of food available to their animal residents. Each species has its own requirements and preferences, and competition for food is primarily between individuals of a species in any given environment. Any severe limiting of the supply intensifies competition, and ultimately the individuals competing for the diminishing food source die of hunger, change their diet, or move to better feeding grounds.

For the seabirds along the California coast, however, food is relatively abundant. Upwelling cold offshore currents carry nutrients which support a rich plankton population, attracting fish in heavy concentrations. Both for their own use and that of their offspring, the birds prefer nesting close to this abundance.

Ample though the source may be, many seabirds have developed additional ways to increase efficiency of food finding. Such birds as auklets, guillemots, loons, puffins, murres, and cormorants are divers and need not depend on surface feeding. The double-crested, or Farallon, cormorants have carried this a step further. They have been observed feeding cooperatively in San Francisco Bay. Flocks form closely packed lines and advance with some of the birds diving all the time. The fish are steadily driven forward, and escape is unlikely as up to a fourth of the flock is underwater on the attack. Pelagic cormorants, another local form, dive deeper than the other two resident relatives and will go to considerable depths in search of food, so A. C. Bent reports in *Life History of Petrels, Pelicans, and Their Allies* (Dover, 1964). Such interspecific division of the habitat allows a more efficient use of its resources.

Thus food is rarely a problem, nor is water, for these birds are adapted to drink seawater. What is scarce, however, is nesting space on the smaller islands and where suitable sites are limited. Over the thousands of years that these places have been host to seabirds, patterns of behavior have developed tending to lessen the burden of competition for breeding room. A basic ecological tenet states that species occurring in the same community cannot have identical sets of life habits, that is, they cannot live in precisely the same way. One type of mouse might be night active, its cousin diurnal. One sparrow species looks for seeds on the ground, another forages in shrubs. Each form operates in certain ways that may be slightly or largely different from every other possible competitor in the community. It has adjusted to fit one of the many variations in the shared habitat. This functional status or role of a species is called its ecological niche.

A physically limited community such as a rocky, barren seabird colony or collection of colonies would appear to offer little in the way of nest site diversification or, in other words, not many niches for various breeding site requirements. There is a range of accommodation, however, more than one would suppose.

Three closely related cormorants live on the California coast: pelagic, Brandt's, and the Farallon or double-crested. Each species has a slightly different pattern of nesting behavior, with enough diversity so that the three forms avoid getting in each other's way. The first cormorant prefers very narrow ledges on sheer seawalls. It appears to nest later than the Farallon and earlier than the Brandt's, both of which choose less steep slopes and broader shoulders.

The demure Cassin's auklet and the harlequin-billed tufted puffin, or sea parrot, dig burrows often three to four feet long in grassy banks and slopes. These tunnels occur by the hundred; and rather incredibly, no tunnel ever seems to intersect another, though they may be in close association. Many birds breed in these tunnels, most of them being used year after year, and there is evidence that some individuals wait until later in the season when burrows are being vacated by earlier nesting couples. Western gulls, California murres, and ashy petrels seem to take what surface space is left—any crevice or ledge, rock slide or debris resulting from human activity. Some birds, like murres, occasionally use old puffin burrows. Guillemots— stubby little black and white birds—seek great sea caves, fea-

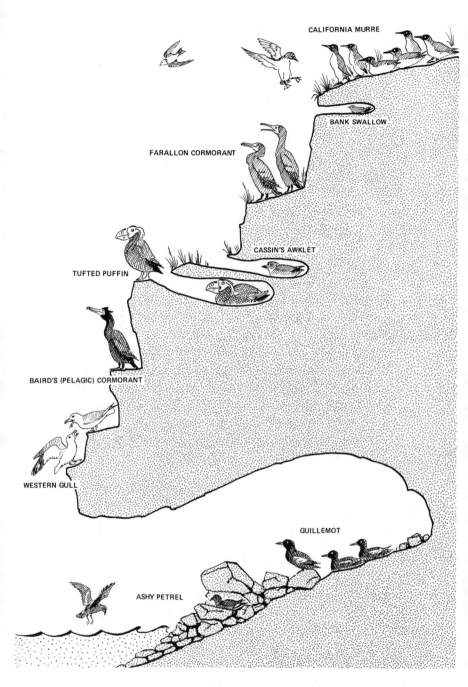

Figure 3. Typical nest-site preferences of some California seabirds

tures of shoreline cliffs which have been carved by wave action in weaker rocks at surf level. Here they huddle by the hundred on ledges and in crannies under arched ceilings sometimes sparkling mosaics of rich color. These crystalized mineral deposits, incidentally, result from seepage percolating down through cracks in the rock above.

Thus even tiny islands and severe cliffs provide more types of nesting niches than one would suppose, and competition for breeding sites is considerably lessened by differences in breeding habits. Other factors are also at work. When conditions are at saturation point, there is evidence for some colonies that the nest site area is used in shifts, one species succeeding another as the season progresses.

Each bird when finally settled has defenses against over-aggressive and impatient neighbors. Territoriality is a strong pattern of bird behavior. Crowded though these colonies might be, each owner defends his nest vigorously against theft of material or usurpation of space. Swift stabs or bites with sharp bills warn intruders against invasion of territory which, in such congested conditions, is the area within reach of the nest owner's bill. The same action is used in defense against predation from western gulls, ravens, crows, and other potential enemies.

There are other protective devices against predators. Some species seek shelter in more inaccessible nest sites—hard-to-reach-into cracks, burrows, and similarly restricted places. The massing of colonially nesting birds is in itself a deterrent to harassment. But threatening situations, approaching human beings, and the like will drive many seabirds from their nests, leaving them and their contents open to various hazards. Cassin's auklets and ashy petrels are nocturnal and confine their feeding and brooding exchanges to the night hours when danger is less.

Close association may have additional positive features. It is suggested that colonial birds are stimulated to breed simultaneously, thus hatching their chicks at about the same time. This supposedly confines predation to a short interval and does not allow prey-predator relationships to strengthen into what would be leisurely exploitation if the food supply were continuous. In many ways cooperation for defense is simplified by colonial behavior.

Birds breeding close to the surf level must be wary of another predator; young sea lions can develop a taste for eggs, though older ones seemingly are not interested. Sea lions, elephant seals, and true seals are the most important mammal members of sea cliff communities. Because of their awkwardness on land and bulky size, they inhabit the lower cliff ledges and reefs. From time to time, smaller mammals make their home here. Rodents, rabbits, and predators such as weasels and foxes, which often patrol sea bluffs, are found on some of the nearer islands, including the Channel group off southern California. Regardless of the presence of some predatory species, the fact remains that isolated bluffs and islands are the safest places for colonial seabirds. Difficulty of access helps protect the vulnerable throng, where little or no concealment is attempted by ground-nesting birds and whose equipment for defense is somewhat limited.

The larger sea mammals have their own breeding rhythms. Among the sea lions and elephant seals, competition is less for space than for mates, the females of the harems. The battles between mature males are famed in natural science literature as adventurous souls have looked in awe through the fog of desolate coasts on these violent struggles. The male northern fur seal, a migrant species along the California coast, exhibits an intense territoriality during breeding. He truly fights for space when he defends what he considers his ground, that is, where his pups will be born and he will mate with his harem. Any newcomers will be challenged and driven off, unless he is past his prime and gives way to stronger youngsters who must win their territories through the defeat of older bulls.

Like bits of foam on wing, flocks of gulls curve and circle past the cliff face. Long throated and slim, cormorants pause on a perching point before taking off for their feeding grounds. Oystercatchers investigate likely looking limpets and mussels as they patter over the reefs and rocky shoals on salmon pink feet. And the black swifts that also share the crannies of these battlements flash by in fleet arcs hunting for flying insects of little interest to their fellow cliff dwellers. They are busy places, these rough, inhospitable looking precipices, particularly when rookeries are present and it is breeding season, and noisy, too, when a shrill cacaphony breaks through the colony as something disturbs the compacted throng. Life is zestful here, out on land's edge, with winging, calling birds and spindrift blowing off a swelling sea.

Tide flat, Bolinas Lagoon

# 3. Salt Marsh

To many people, tidal mud flats are unattractive, particularly where man has used them as dumping grounds. Californians have been guilty of this practice, allowing unsightly fills around the southern edges of San Francisco Bay and on the shores of Richmond and Berkeley, where discarded tires and other such repulsive flotsam are strewn about in abundance. A kind of "we-just-drive-by-them, we-don't-notice-they-are-there" attitude enables the more insensitive to be ignorant of these awkward landscapes. However, this wasn't so easy some years back when the famed "East Bay Perfume," an overpowering mixture of sewer smells, crouched in wait for those commuting on the shoreline highway. Fortunately, much of this essence has now succumbed to modern technology. Only the faint memory of those heady days lingers in the air.

Ecologically, these too often despised acres are of deep interest. They are among the world's most productive. One plant species alone, cordgrass, produces five to ten times as much nutrient material and oxygen per acre as one of our most prized crops, wheat. It is doubtful if cordgrass will ever become a widely used commercial food crop, but in the economy of the salt marshes it is of tremendous importance. Few herbivorous forms eat it fresh; but when decayed into tiny particles, it is the main dish on the banquet table for the invertebrate feeders of the baylands. In even smaller fragments, it is useful as fertilizer for the beds of algae that help link these backwaters with the sea.

By all standards, San Francisco Bay is the state's largest and best known estuary. Most every young geography student, if asked what is California's most striking and scenic feature, will answer either the Golden Gate or Yosemite Valley. Historically it is unequalled, as much of California's story begins here, ends here, or passes by. Geologically it is the state's prime example of a drowned river mouth, whose topography prior to flooding was such that a north-south trending valley was already in existence. It is this basin which gives it a butterfly shape. The northern wing, or embayment, is technically San Pablo Bay and the southern is San Francisco Bay proper. The combined Sacramento and San Joaquin rivers flow into this huge backwater at Carquinez Strait, and Suisun Bay behind it is where the two great streams converge as they flow toward the bay. An enormous amount of sediment has been deposited on the bay floor and is exposed by low tides draining off the shallows and gently sloping shores around Palo Alto, San Leandro, San Pablo, and the flatlands north of Vallejo. There are several places, however, where rocky hillsides drop abruptly into the waters of the bay—for instance, around the bridge terminus at Richmond, the Golden Gate itself, and the Tiburon Peninsula. It is this fringing of hills that gives beauty to this inland sea; and patterns of island, cove, and headland, particularly on Marin's bay-facing shores, are charming daughters of this meeting of Coast Range and ocean. In less dramatic places, great expanses of mud flat and marsh gently ease out to permanent water. On a foggy day when the tide is in, one can become totally confused over what is land and what is water. Then gray floats over gray, and only ship whistles and the muted thunder of traffic on a nearby bridge enforce a reality of their own.

Four other central California tide flat areas are well known: Bolinas Lagoon and Tomales Bay of Marin, with Drakes Estero between the two, and Elkhorn Slough of Monterey Bay. These coastal flats have more or less the same features. Some have sandy beaches along the barrier bars separating their lagoons from the open ocean. Many have deep channels and basins that are never drained completely even by the lowest tides.

The two major types of water-logged environment found here are mud flats and salt marshes. There are differences between them, though we often loosely interchange the terms. Marshes are the higher of the two and generally have much vegetation adapted to the peculiarities of their not-quite-water, not-quite-land home. When soil conditions favor its development, this cover is broken by a network of meandering creeklets that accommodates the flood and runoff of both tide and freshwater streams flowing in from the surrounding hills. Marshes are usually above the average high tide level; and their plants, though adapted to prolonged feet wetting, are limited in the length of inundation they can endure. In general, mud flats occur between mean high and mean low levels; and the vegetation present is mostly composed of unicellular and larger forms of algae, with the major exception of eel-grass which, though common in saltwater shallows, is not universal along the California coast.

The deeper channels are permanently flooded. The eel-grass-algae habitat is usually under water, that is, below mean low tide. Cordgrass and pickleweed are by and large intertidal, but the former is able to withstand up to twenty-one continuous hours of submergence. Pickleweed begins its best growth at the average high tide line. Conditions vary, but one can generalize by saying that cordgrass growth is the deciding feature. Below its coarse and tangled masses are the tidal flats. Where it begins and above, the landscape takes on the characteristics of a marsh.

Flat or marsh, these bay shallows are home or favored resting place for many living things, harsh and problematic though they appear. Certainly they are inhospitable to most of the native plants of California. If one should drop seeds of bush monkeyflower in among the pickleweed, though they might germinate, it is doubtful they would ever mature. They simply are not adapted to life in a salt marsh.

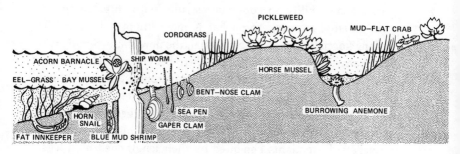

Figure 4. Tidal mud-flat zonation

Adaptation, or the successful meeting of environmental conditions, is the main business of life. It is one of the central themes in the story of evolution, that great and grand unfolding of the potential in the living organism. Adaptation does not happen, species-wide, overnight. It takes place within the framework of species survival, within the slow spiraling of evolutionary history through what is known as natural selection. Those best fitted to meet certain conditions survive; those less so do not, or have a harder time of it. These conditions are both physical and biological or, in other words, involve terrain and neighbor. Such features as temperature range, exposure to sun and wind, soil variation, and amount of available moisture are primarily physical in character. Residence in biotic communities also means interaction with other living things. Competition and predation are two of these interrelationships upon which we have already touched. Both types of environmental impact are of equal importance to a living organism. A limpet, to remain alive, must avoid being eaten as well as avoid death from dehydration.

The earth's history is one of inconstancy. Seas have invaded and withdrawn; ice masses have pushed forward and retreated; volcanoes have erupted and subsided; temperature ranges have widened and narrowed. Biological change is a key process in the ability to survive these fundamental habitat variations, and its major mechanism operates within the germ cell itself. Abrupt changes, or mutations, cause organisms to differ from their parents. Most mutations have no survival value; indeed, they are often detrimental. But some of them increase the organism's ability to cope successfully with threatening environmental factors. And what is most important, since the change occurred in genetic material, the new characteristic will be transferred to offspring for their benefit as well. For example, a forebear of a certain strain of rabbit developed hind legs that were longer than usual and, being able to better elude its predators, survived, while its shorter-legged cousins succumbed, moved away, or developed some other means of escape. Its descendants benefited by their lengthened hind legs, and today the jackrabbit is legion in the wild areas of the West. Natural selection favors the transmission of beneficial mutations, but weeds out those that are harmful. Animals can adapt in several ways: changes in behavior, in anatomical structure, and in physiological processes and functions. The same is true of plants, if we use the term "behavior" in a broad sense. Most broadleaf trees living in climates with severe winters lose their leaves during the cold part of the year, and their metabolism slows down to wait the season through in a kind of hibernation.

To return to the salt marsh habitat, what are the conditions this environment imposes on the members of its community? Certainly, they must accept tidal ebb and flow, once a day two highs and two lows with occasional springs and neaps. Part of it will always be under water in sloughs and channels and part above the high water mark, occasionally dampened by high highs and at times thoroughly wetted by wind-driven waves, freshwater floods, rain, and changes in water level. Variations in salinity are to be expected. The percentage of salt content in tidewater near stream and river outlets drops considerably in the winter and spring months when storm runoff increases. Out in the marsh pans and shallow pools, temperature ranges are broad. Organisms living in these pools not only must survive abrupt changes in salinity—during rainfall, for example— but must also withstand a possible rise or fall of $50°$ F.

Muddy and sandy substrates also pose problems. Waterlogged, salt impregnated, and lacking in oxygen, marshes and mud flats appear unable to offer much in the way of homegrounds. Nor is this all. They are unstable and constantly rearrange their drainage sloughs, filling in here, slumping there, particularly during the wintertime when high waves, tides, and runoff slosh and splash over these lonely looking flatlands. Where banks have been built up along the channel sides because of root accumulation, undercutting can occur. Plants act as silt traps, and the masses of vegetative tissue in themselves are responsible for sediment deposition, especially during floods. Denser, more cohesive mud tends to remain in place, particularly when stabilized by plant concentrations. Then the drainage ways shift more slowly. Sand flats rarely develop well-defined, more or less permanent channel systems. This accounts for their absence from a part of Bolinas Lagoon.

It is indeed testimony to the tenacity and resourcefulness of life that not only do organisms live here, but they thrive to the point of being the world's most productive species. How, in what manner have they adapted themselves to these pans and sloughs, where men seldom venture except to fill them in or alter them completely?

*Zostera*, or eel-grass, is probably one of the most interesting species of coastal lagoon vegetation. A seed plant, it lives a life of submergence, neighbor to sea lettuce and other algae such as various primitive unicellular species. Blue-green or golden brown, the latter vividly stain the dark gray tidal muds. Sea lettuce and eel-grass are both a brilliant green; so color is by no means missing in what is often thought of as a very drab environment. *Zostera* is a hydrophyte, or water plant. It is found only in bays and saltwater sloughs. The surf grasses of the rocks of the outer shore are different, though they too are real seed plants and are adapted to life in the wave zone. In the calm shallows of lagoons there is little need for structural rigidity, since the water itself provides a supporting medium. Instead of stiffening tissue, eel-grass has air spaces in its blades and stems to take advantage of the bouyancy of water and to store oxygen needed for metabolism. Anchored in the sands and muds of bay floors, it supplies a relatively stable habitat for many invertebrates, some of which could never be at home in bay waters otherwise. Eel-grass, particularly when dead and decomposing, is a source of food. In addition, many species of small algae are epiphytic on its blades, sometimes covering them until the original leaf surface can no longer be seen. These in turn are homes for microscopic algae such as the diatoms so abundant in plankton. Its thickets shelter many other organisms. The tiny white "flowers" of certain hydroids blossom on the blade tips. Nudibranchs and little snails such as the fragile bubble snail slowly maneuver through the interlacing stems. Transparent, skeleton, and pistol shrimp share the micropolis with marine worms, some of them tube building.

Once above the weaving ribbons of this little community, plants and animals must make their peace with a world that is rained on, tide flooded, sun warmed, drained off, and mud stuck. There are noticeable vegetation patterns as well as drainage systems. The more salt-tolerant plants bow out to those less so as the land slopes up to the surrounding hills. Cordgrass has already been introduced as a plant unique to the upper tidal zone, where it helps stabilize new mud deposits. San Francisco Bay is filling in naturally as well as artificially. Though parts of its shoreline have subsided due to the pumping out of underground water, thousands of tons of silt are constantly being dumped by the rivers and streams entering the bay. As the floor builds up, the land is elevated above the critical submergence level for cordgrass (about 4.5 feet above mean lower low tide) which then moves in. Even without human interference it is estimated that it will not take long, geologically speaking, for much of the bay to become first a marsh and then a meadow.

Cordgrass has several adaptive devices that allow it to survive prolonged submergence. It is equipped with hollow passages in its leaves and roots so that air can move readily throughout the plant even while underwater. In general, oxygen levels are low in the dense sediments of a salt marsh, though by no means is the vital gas completely absent. All tidal lagoon plants able to make food take carbon dioxide from the air and give off oxygen during the process of photosynthesis which then returns to the water, soil, and air to be available for the other great life process, respiration—the oxidation of food to produce energy.

Only a small number of plants can tolerate soils of high salt content. Called halophytes, these species have modified in various ways to cope with the substrate. Cordgrass and its distant cousin, salt grass, which lives at a higher level within the marsh, excrete excess salt by means of special glands. Films of salt crystals often cover their leaves in little white patches. That cordgrass thrives is indicated by the three- to four-foot-tall stems and rank growth. In places it gives the flats much the appearance of an upland meadow. A perennial, it spreads by runners which produce very hardy youngsters. The new spring shoots are almost certain to be inundated by high tides.

Pickleweed, the most widespread salt-marsh plant, is another story. It, too, is a halophyte; and its fleshy, segmented, leafless stems exemplify an additional modification to saline soils. Storing water in tissue, it uses a device employed by cactus and other succulent desert plants. At first glance, it seems somewhat absurd to imply any similarity between the two habitats, for certainly if a place is a marsh, it is not a desert. To understand this peculiar state of affairs, it is useful to know something about osmosis, the movement of water through the membranes that enclose living cells. Water generally moves from a less concentrated solution to a more concentrated one. Cell sap is usually more concentrated than soil water. Therefore, the flow is into the plant until equalization is approached. But, when the outside water is loaded with dissolved salt, as in a salt marsh, it is more concentrated than the cell water, and osmosis is reversed. Ordinary plants will wilt and die under these circumstances of losing water to the soil rather than taking it in. In effect, a salt marsh is a chemical desert with conditions as severe, if not more so, as those of a climatic desert. Halophytes have the ability to selectively concentrate certain salts in their cell fluids and so maintain the imbalance necessary for osmosis. However, this is at the expense of extra energy on the part of the plant. It is advantageous to store some of this water in its tissues since it has labored so hard to get it.

Pickleweed is less tolerant of submergence than cordgrass and grows on higher and drier soil. Therefore, the two species seldom overlap. Though pickleweed may have water storage tissues, it lacks those for air storage. It needs better drained soil than cordgrass does. Crab burrows and decaying root masses let some air into the thick sediments of the higher banks where pickleweed is dominant. Arrow-grass is another salt-adapted companion, and dodder, a ubiquitous parasite, often drapes tangles of orange-colored string over the shrubby cover. The swollen little segments of pickleweed remain green and juicy during spring and summer, but turn an attractive scarlet in the fall and then dry into woody looking twiglets. Its root masses are of great importance to the tortuous channelways as they give stability to slough banks and sides.

Widespread though pickleweed may be, it gives way to other halophytes when the salt content of the soil drops below a certain percentage. *Jaumea*, also a succulent, and salt grass are the dominant plants of the next higher zone, which is better drained and slightly less saline. Adaptations in plants are often so specialized that very small differences in substrate—soil substances, moisture content, and so on—will determine the floristic composition of the community. Up on the dikes are plants occasionally visited by extreme high tides, but most moisture results from precipitation or runoff. They must live through a long dry summer in salty, dehydrating soils. Saltbushes and their succulent relatives, sea blite and saltwort, grow with *Frankenia* and dock. Gum plant, sneezeweed, *Lasthenia*, fleabane, and one or two goldenbushes are members of that large and cheerful family, the sunflower group. Several potentillas and marsh rosemary occur here, along with peppergrass, fiddleneck, and coyote brush, one of the most common seaside plants. A native plantain is present; but many species of the same group are escapes—weeds that have run wild after sneaking in from Europe and other areas. They include species that were purposely planted to control erosion. One uninvited dike dweller is a dreadful thing. Called furze, or gorse, it has wicked spines up to 2 inches long. For people who only see the unpleasant aspects of a tide marsh, it is no doubt a fitting invader. Finally, a more hospitable environment for most plants is encountered in the grassy stretches on the upper shores. The usual weeds and more common natives of central California— mustard, wild radish, cheeseweed, scarlet pimpernel, filaree, wild oats, goldfields, and others—green up in spring and dry to straw in the fall.

We have already become acquainted with many of the animals for whom the lagoons and their intertidal flats are home. In the deeper waters of San Francisco Bay live fish, jellyfish, and other swimming forms. Some of the most readily observable organisms have small communities of their own on wharf pilings, concrete docks, and boat slips. In and among the sea-weed clumps one can see creatures often thought more typical of the tide pools out on the reefs and rocks of the surf-splashed littoral. Sea stars and sea cucumbers are by no means uncommon and may even prefer these quieter waters. Several anemones join them; one is an unusual and striking combination of orange and green. Tiny hydroid colonies fan delicate feathers through the food carrying currents. Various bristle worms compete with barnacles for tasty particles. Sea spiders, small crabs, and amphipods hunt for edible debris that may have settled on the sessile forms. Concentrations of moss animals spread brown fuzz over pilings and barnacles. Pouchlike animals known as sea squirts wait along with the hydroids for dinner. Among the host of gastropods—by and large the snail group—traveling up and down the stained dock sides are file limpets, checkered periwinkles, and unicorns. Several bivalves are very much at home here, often to the detriment of their man-made substrate. Bay mussels, originally from Europe, form brittle, dark purple masses. The arch enemies of all who have to do with the maintenance of shoreside installations are shipworms, in reality boring clams. Their long thin bodies appear more worm- than clam-like; but the boring tool, a small shell at the front end, establishes their relationship. Not only are there native borers, but one of the most destructive, a foreign *Teredo*, appeared on the West Coast some years back and added its efforts to the thousands of dollars of damage these pests cause every year. Gribbles, wood-boring isopods, also attack untreated wood.

Recent research on tidal marshes and mud flats has turned up some surprising data. These desolate-appearing stretches are very fertile in that nutrient flow through them is greater than in adjacent and apparently more prosperous natural communities. Several factors account for this. Tidal currents not only deliver food and oxygen to residents of the flats, but remove wastes. Many kinds of nourishment are produced in the lagoons themselves, plankton, large and small algae, various grasses, and other plants. All of these forms not only contribute fresh vegetation to the menu, but they add to the organic enrichment of the muds and sands when their dead remains are broken down by the anaerobic bacteria living in the oxygen-poor substrate.

A third reason for the fertility of this environment can be found in the presence of what are known as nutrient traps in many estuaries. Salinity differences between incoming fresh-water on one hand, and seawater on the other, are responsible. Ocean water, being heavier, sinks to the bottom, and fresh-water floats above. Vertical and horizontal turbulence is created by the meeting of these two water masses with resultant eddies that mix the nutrients, diffusing them and making them more available. Other factors contribute to the high fertility of baylands, and one specific to San Francisco Bay should be mentioned. Mussels occur here by the thousands. They excrete phosphate-rich fecal pellets which are excellent fertilizer for marsh plants.

Because of the types of food offered, molluscs here are either filter feeders or deposit feeders. The great beds of bay and horse mussels, clams, and cockles depend on tidal currents to bring them sustenance in the form of tiny particles of plankton, decayed vegetation, and so on. During the incoming tides they open their shells and strain out tidbits with cilia on mucus-covered gills. Deposit feeders actually ingest the rich oozy mud, and nutrient material is extracted from what would be an un-savory mess to human consumers. The unwanted sediments pass out as waste. A common "slurp" feeder, as Joel Hedgpeth calls it in his very useful little book, *Seashore Life* (University of California Press, 1964), is the California horn snail, the most abundant snail on the mud flats.

Scavengers such as the hairy hermit crabs and the little mud-flat crabs (*Hemigrapsus*) hunt about as their tide pool cousins do, looking for edible flotsam. The latter are the common larger crustacean of tidal shallows. They scuttle along the channel beds like swiftly moving shadows, popping into their burrows which often honeycomb the slough banks. Mussels form great congregations on channel banks. These shell-studded masses are bound together by the same sticky strings that fasten the tide pool mussels to their substrate. They are crawled over and lived upon by many smaller lagoon-dwelling species. But tidal mud, that surprising source of food, is the best home of all to the burrowers which make the most of this easily penetrated material. Burrowing anemones, sea pens, boring clams and piddocks, sand clams and gapers, bent-nosed clams and bristle worms are safe under the inches of sticky overburden they put between themselves and their would-be predators. One of the most famous burrowing tube worms is the fat innkeeper. This odd creature can be up to a foot in length and its permanent U-shaped burrow several feet long. A filter feeder, it has a funnel of mucus and strains its food through that device by pumping water through its burrow. So efficient is this sausage-shaped animal that there is plenty for other organisms as well. A pea crab, a worm, and a small fish live in the tube, dependent on the bounty. Such a relationship is called commensalism, where one organism feeds from the efforts of another or derives some other benefit, without harm to the host. It is adaptation carried to a remarkable degree.

Crawling around on top of the sediment floor and ready to return into their shells are horn snails and the predaceous moon snails in company with dog whelks, and purple snails. Basket whelks, which generally prefer clean tidal flats, share a device with other species of their group, a natural siphon through which these animals can take in clean water while rummaging about in bay mud. Like the fat innkeeper, ghost and mud shrimp are also burrow dwellers. Where oysters are bedded, both native and introduced, oyster borers and oyster drills are never far away. Some of these predatory species came along with their transplanted hosts and set up shop close to oyster colonies now supporting an active shoreline industry.

When the tide is in, the creatures of the salt flats are busy opening shells, waving antennae, sucking up mud or waiting hopefully in their burrows for the food drifting by. Watching for low water just behind the dikes and pans are the "second table" feeders, the waterbirds. As the hours pass and the tide makes its inexorable way out the Golden Gate or past Stinson Beach, the waiting birds flock on the newly exposed flats, for now it is their turn. Pintails and mallards, coots and gulls work their way over the squishy surface hunting for worms, shrimp, and little molluscs. Clapper and black rails are shy residents of pickleweed and cordgrass jungles and forage along the slough sides ready to disappear into the marsh if startled or disturbed. Avocets with orange flushed heads and precise markings of their cousins, the black-necked stilts, reflect neatly patterned images in the mirror of the marshlands. Stepping along, they swish back and forth with slender bills wonderfully adapted for feeding in shallow water.

Many birds are less concerned about waiting for low tide levels. Egrets and great blue herons stand sentinel in the shallow water of the marsh edge at all times of the day with eyes watchful for fish, shrimp, and other swimmers. In winter a legion of diving and fish-eating ducks gathers here during high water—canvasback, golden-eye, greater and lesser scaup, ruddy ducks, and mergansers. Kingfishers, looking like little figures out of some Bonapartian campaign with their jaunty cockades and rust, blue, and white uniforms, perch on bayside wires. Terns flash and hover, competing with the herons for the fish of high tide.

Many avian winter visitors settle here for a prolonged period of rest and feeding in preparation for the strenuous summer breeding activities inland and north. Divers such as grebes and loons, those birds of folklore with their ringing, haunting calls, winter here. Glaucous-winged gulls, dunlins, pectoral and least sandpipers, long-billed curlews, and black-bellied plovers share these teeming flats with western willets, dowitchers, greater yellowlegs and whimbrels. Some are migrants and do not intend to stay long. They use these marshlands of the Pacific flyway system as a major wayside stop. Others settle in, much like the northerners who flock to Florida to escape the cold of winter.

As these mud flat feeders investigate the now uncovered bill of fare, the algal colonies stretched over pool and bank sides are also in action. Using the unimpeded sunlight, they photosynthesize, producing the nourishment needed for more plant tissue. As on sandy beaches and in tide pools, food chains, single-strand associations of food webs, are building. Examples of typical linkages taking place at times governed by tidal rhythms are: in tide, fish and swimming crustaceans/diving birds; out tide, molluscs and worms/mud-probing birds.

Another rhythm superimposes itself on that of the tide, day and night periodicity. Coons pad down to the shores and hunt for tasty shrimp during the darker hours. Meadow mice and salt-marsh harvest mice, patter through runways confining their more adventurous feeding to nighttime. Shrews though furred and small are not rodents, but are insectivores. They join the many nocturnal predators such as owls and skunks.

Someone has suggested that an answer to the "tide flats are ugly and uninteresting, let's fill them in" way-of-thought would be a handsome book illustrated by inspired photographers. In color they could present the exciting vignettes, the telling details of life in this rich and varied community. Perhaps a November twilight with a pink-washed sky reflected on a pool in which a stilt is feeding in all his elegant charm; or a closeup of the scarlet tips of pickleweed just before winter turns them into dried wisps. Then there are the feathering "plumes" of hydroids on eel-grass, and the exquisite shells of the bubble snails; cordgrass, harvest-gold and frost-spangled on a December morning. Even the reticulation of a dried mud pan has its own austere but striking design.

And there are the groups of ash-gray and white gulls, facing the wind on piling tops, or one legged on the wet and shimmering flats of low tide, waiting for the slow and subtle inundation, the gradual, almost undetectable water lift along grass stem and slough side.

Serpentine ridge on Mt. Tamalpais, Marin County

# 4. *Patterns on the Hills*

Anyone driving the 118 miles between Dubuque and Cedar Rapids, Iowa, on a summer day will see the following: some towns, several rivers, livestock, crop fields, other cars, people, billboards, buildings, and woodlots. They add up to a pleasing, prosperous looking landscape or a deadly bore, depending on one's viewpoint. Central Iowa has its seasonal changes, but it does not have scenic variety. Considering its enviable position in the farming world, it probably doesn't care. Corn is King, and healthy stands of this crop are the best views possible to their owners.

In contrast, anyone drving the fifteen miles from Mill Valley to Bolinas Lagoon (via Panoramic Highway) in Marin County, just north of the Golden Gate, will pass through or alongside seven of the natural communities found in California: chaparral, coastal scrub, grassland, coniferous forest, broadleaf evergreen forest, beach strand, and salt marsh. This mosaic of plant associations is quite bewildering to the casual observer. Why is grassland adjacent to a dense redwood forest? Why is there a patch of scrub here and a magnificent stand of Douglas-fir there? Common sense would suggest a reasonable uniformity of natural vegetation in the five crow miles between these two points. Marin County, however, is only a segment of many square miles of similar coastal landscape.

Two of the seven have already been discussed, salt marsh and coastal strand. Their most important determining features are obvious: the salt floods of the tide and the nature of their substrates. The other five are not as clearly self-explanatory. This chapter will deal with coastal scrub, grassland (or coastal prairie), chaparral, and broadleaf evergreen forest. The major coniferous forest types of this part of the transect deserve chapters to themselves as do the other outstanding formations —oak woodland, freshwater marsh, and streamside vegetation.

This crazy-quilt arrangement is characteristic of many California hillsides, not only sea-facing flanks. The inner Coast Ranges, those east of San Francisco Bay, for example, may have slightly different floras, but they share many species and communities with the fog-hooded mountains to the west. In many places man has seriously disrupted this natural patterning, and it is difficult to guess what the native vegetation was like. Eucalyptus and Monterey pine—the first from Australia and the last, though a California native, was once confined to isolated groves immediate to the sea—replace natural tree and shrub growth. Orchards and crops, to say nothing of urban sprawl, have all but obliterated any hints of the original plant cover. But enough wild country remains throughout much of central California, making it possible to surmise what was once there and bring it into ecological focus.

This part of the state, hill-and-valley California, engenders its own special kind of love and loyalty. To most people acquainted with the region the phrase "rural California" means tree-sprinkled hills and ranches snug in valleys reached by wandering dirt roads. Unless they are really familiar with the geography of the West, few people will think of the flat farm acres of delta rice or Fresno orchard. Popularly, countryside California is pastoral California, the gentle topography of coastal range and foothill slope. Before we begin to discover some of the answers to the puzzle of their occurrence, it is appropriate to describe each of the four communities that lie in such curious patterns on the hills.

*Coastal Scrub.*—To someone without botanical training this low-growing shrubby cover looks much like true chaparral, which often occurs above it on coastal bluffs. Many species are common to both communities, yerba santa, coyote brush, and poison oak, for example; but coastal scrub is characterized by the predominance of subshrubs, one to five feet in height with semiwoody stems growing from a woody base. Because of the flexibility of both branch and leaf, in contrast to the stiff twigs and leathery foliage of true chaparral, this community has also been called soft chaparral.

Two types of coastal scrub have been described. The northern association, found from the Monterey area to southern Oregon, is an often dense cover of coyote brush, blue blossom ceanothus, salal, bush monkeyflower, shrubby lupine, prickly snarls of blackberry, thimbleberry and salmonberry, and a number of herbs, frequently rank in growth, including cow parsnip, paintbrush, and goldenbush. It shares a few species with the southern type—coastal sage scrub, whose black sage and California buckwheat continue north to the Bay Area. Our Lord's Candle, lemonade berry, laurel sumac, and white and purple sage, however, are strictly components of the southern community, most typically developed from Santa Barbara County south.

The coastal scrubs occur in two rather sharply contrasting environments. One is maritime, a narrow, windswept, sea-edge strip; and the other is a much drier habitat in the inner Coast Ranges from Mt. Diablo south. What can be termed interior sage scrub is composed primarily of California sagebrush, black sage, yerba santa, and bush monkeyflower; California buckwheat joins them as far north as Mt. Hamilton. The interior form is characteristic of thin-soiled, somewhat steep slopes; and like its seaward counterpart, it is usually found below the chaparral.

Sagebrush and sage should not be confused. The sagebrush species belong to the daisy family and include the Great Basin sagebrush spreading over many miles of the arid West. The sages are in the mint family. Both groups usually have pungent, spicy odors. Everyone has personal tastes about smells, but to some the sagebrushes are more biting, almost acrid. The true sages have more a perfumelike essence just as their distant cousin lavender does. One of the delights of wandering through coastal scrub is its fragrance, as a number of plants of this community have leaves containing aromatic oils and resins. Whatever its local variations, coastal scrub is one of the typical vegetations of road cuts lining the hairpins of Highway One, in Marin County and south of San Francisco Bay, climbing over the bluffs above the beach, crowding in brushy fields between stands of evergreen trees.

*Coastal Prairie.*—These balds of the outer ranges contrast greatly with the shadowed groves of cone-bearing and broad-leaf trees that are also a part of the coastal mosaic. In summer they look like scarves of gold velvet artfully draped over ridgetops and between the dark folds of redwood or fir. For the most part they are grasslands, but sedges and bracken occur here too. Fescue, reedgrass, velvetgrass, hairgrass, wild oats, and oatgrass are tawny tangles by late spring, unless cropped by livestock; and they blow in the onshore wind with grace and delicacy. Native bulbs such as the Douglas iris, blue-eyed grass, and mariposa lilies, and other wildflowers enrich these open slopes. Though most of the original coastal prairie grasses are perennials, many nonnative annuals such as soft chess and wild oats have encroached since livestock introduction, some-times shouldering aside the old-timers and thoroughly altering the floristic composition.

Like most meadowlands, these fields are tunneled by rodents. Meadow mice, sometimes called voles or field mice, are at home in the turf. They tunnel elaborate runway systems through the grass roots. Harvest and deer mice are plentiful in prairies. Harvest mice weave sheltering balls of dry grass; deer mice nests, lined with dry vegetation, are usually tucked in burrows or buried under logs and rocks. All of these small rodents eat seeds, berries, and other nutritious plant parts. Meadow mice are fond of green stems and leaves, and where the animals occur in large numbers they can be very destructive to crops and native vegetation alike. Mice are juicy feasts for keen-eyed and sharp-eared predators. Night-active habits protect harvest and deer mice somewhat, though owls and bobcats are constantly alert to their presence. Voles are busy at all hours. They are safe in runways, as long as their activities are undetected; but snakes, hawks, weasels, and the larger carniores such as coyotes and gray foxes watch or listen for telltale movement and noises.

*Chaparral.*—This is the typical brushy growth of the hillsides that means wild California to many people. It is the dangerous community in that so many destructive wildfires originate in its highly flammable vegetation. It is also one of the most effective plant barriers against ground travel by the larger animals. Man and deer alike find mature chaparral with its profusion of stiff twigs almost impossible to enter. One can crawl through it, but this means of getting somewhere is fatiguing and painful. Imitate the deer and follow their trails if you go exploring.

The word *chaparral* has an interesting history. It comes from the Spanish, *el chaparro*, meaning the evergreen scrub oak. This in turn has a Basque root, *chabarra*, which also refers to scrub oak. The *-al* suffix is common to many of the Spanish place names throughout the West, being added to the root word to indicate the phrase "the place of." We get the cowboy's chaps from the leather pants or *chaparajos* he used when riding through this dense prickly cover. It must have been very gratifying to the Spanish settlers in California when they discovered a land so much resembling their own, even to the same type (though not same species) of shrublike oak.

Chaparral consists for the most part of what can be considered either short trees or tall shrubs that are admirably adapted to a summer drought–winter rain climatic pattern. Its most active season is late winter and spring, when rainfall and temperature curves meet for optimum growing conditions. Then it sprouts and flowers. Summer and fall are the resting seasons, unlike regions having summer precipitation and cold winters where the frost season is the time of inactivity. The small leathery leaves of the dormant shrubs transpire sparingly—that is, emit little water vapor. Evergreenness is of real survival value to these plants; the growing season is so short, often just two or three months, that it is to the plant's advantage to retain its foliage. It does not have to expend energy in producing a whole new crop of leaves annually. These features are of great importance to the plant when dry years hit, and rainfall is less than normal. Brushy hillsides may suffer but are not put out of business; most healthy shrubs manage to remain alive until the next rainy season.

Chamise, the most typical shrub of the community, sometimes covers drier knolls and ridges with the uniform texture of broadloom carpetry; its tiny, needle-thin, water-conserving leaves are well adapted to drought. Other chaparral plants have leaves grading from the thumbnail-size foliage of mountain mahogany to the three-inch-long spear points of toyon and osoberry. There is a rough correlation between leaf size and dryness of site. Larger leaved shrubs such as creambush tend to remain on moister ground, while the small-leaved species of manzanita and ceanothus can cope with drier areas. Other common chaparral shrubs of the region are redberry, tree poppy, chaparral pea, hollyleaf cherry, coffeeberry, silk tassel, and scrub and other shrub-size oaks. A number of shrubs preferring more mesic (moist) sites are winter deciduous—snowberry and hazelnut among them—and drop their foliage during the cool season, but most of the species typical of xeric (dry) places are faithful to the evergreen habit.

In addition to the water-conserving features discussed above, other adaptations are characteristic of xerophytic (drought adapted) plants. Many send down long roots to tap moisture sources deep under the soil surface. Leaves of some species have a waxy coating or are cutinized, that is, have a varnish-like covering which serves to waterproof the surface. Scrub oak foliage is shiny; by reflecting sunlight, such leaves would tend to reduce solar radiation. A number of manzanitas have leaves of light color for the same reason. Much water vapor escapes through stomata, tiny openings in the leaf surface, during the gas exchange necessary for the plant's life processes. Small leaves have proportionately fewer stomata than large leaves, possibly accounting for the correlation referred to above. In many xerophytic plants the openings are tucked down in pits in the leaf surface, protected from drying air flow. A few chaparral shrubs have leaves so oriented that the edges of the blades receive more insolation rather than the surface.

By no means is chaparral always the olive green of the dry period. Ceanothus blossoms in puffs of blue or white. Toyon is aptly called Christmas berry. The clusters of its small bead-like fruits ripen to a brilliant scarlet in winter. Tree poppies have yellow flowers that closely resemble those of herbaceous cousins. Vines like wild rose and morning glory spread pink blossoms over fence and road banks. Wild currants have sprays of rose and white. Pale lavender bells hang from yerba santa stems. The justly dreaded poison oak is one of the few coastal plants to turn a lovely crimson in late summer and fall, before it loses its leaves completely.

Herbaceous plants are not absent. These are usually what is meant by the term "wildflower" which has juicy, in contrast to woody, stems. On the tops of road banks and in the more open slopes, light and space encourage yellow mariposas and tidytips, star lilies, blue dicks, shooting stars, globe lilies, and the little pink and purple pagodas known as Chinese houses. In the rich wet soils of seepages and marshy places, look for yellow monkeyflower, miner's lettuce, yellow-eyed grass, cow clover, and speedwell. Lupine, fiddleneck, purple nightshade, bird's-foot trefoil, and tar-weed grow in roadside shoulders, while locoweed, clarkia, chia, paintbrush, several pentstemons, and fairwell-to-spring—that poetically named harbinger of summer—are at home in cracks and soil pockets of steep canyonsides and road cuts.

Though these brushy areas appear forbidding and formidable, they shelter a surprising number of animals within their concealing thickets, many with night-active habits. One well-known but seldom-seen mammal is the dusky-footed wood rat. Its stick-and-twig home may be several feet high and just as broad, containing a complex of runways and living quarters which it leaves at night to scout for house material and food such as leaves, bark, and fruit. Then it is interesting to nocturnal predators—owls, skunks, and ringtails. The wood rat's nest at times is more of an apartment house than a private residence. Lizards, insects, amphibians, and the so-called California parasitic mouse—a white-footed or deer mouse type— find the wood rat's construction efforts very convenient, and the mouse often robs its stored food. Gray foxes dig into wood rat lodges, tearing them apart with their front paws. Running skillfully through the stiff-twigged maze, these attractive members of the canine family are on the lookout for other small dwellers of the coastal shrublands. Heermann's kangaroo rat, California ground squirrels, brush and pocket mice, the Sonoma and Merriam chipmunks, and brush rabbits are among their victims. Gophers, rodents of more open country, rarely expose themselves to such attentions and are careful to plug the holes of their feeding tunnels. But gopher snakes and weasels are only too successful, from the gopher's point of view, in entering.

Reptiles are extremely common in the brushlands, partly because of the large number of rodents. Pacific rattlesnakes, racers, and gopher snakes slip through leaf litter and other debris. Alligator lizards, skinks, and fence lizards are frequently encountered by hikers in brushy country. One can readily startle them out of their hiding places or from sunning spots while poking about rocky outcrops and under fallen limbs.

Several birds are so much a part of chaparral and scrub that they occur nowhere else. The wrentit, a shy bird with a long wrenlike tail, has a bouncing ball whistle that accelerates cheerily through the thickets. Scrub jays rasp raucously while diving in long bright blue glides from one vantage point to another. California thrashers sound like less talented students of their virtuoso cousin, the mockingbird, as they fuss about in the underbrush along with brown and rufous-sided towhees. A large number of birds typical of chaparral are neutral gray or brown in color. Thus they match the dull tones of the vegetative cover, which increases their chances of escaping predation. Goldfinches, rufous-crowned sparrows, kinglets, and bushtits work over the scrubby growth for tidbits on their way to other communities. California quail are common companions on a sunny morning hike through the chaparral.

*Broadleaf Evergreen Forest.*—Though lacking the imperial stance of an old-growth redwood grove, these thickets are delightful. While not deciduous, they resemble in many ways the hardwood stands of the East. The streamside jungles of interior California valleys share many of the genera present in the eastern woods, but the broadleaf evergreen forest has the same sun and shadow interplay as groves of deciduous trees in Pennsylvania or Ohio.

A digression here, for a moment. The word *genus* refers to the first of the two words of a Latin name of a plant or animal. It specifies to which branch of its family tree the organism belongs. The plural of genus is *genera*. A family of living things is made up of genera and their species, for example: family, Pinaceae (pine); genus, *Pinus*; species, *ponderosa*. This is the yellow pine so familiar in the mountainous West. No other plant in the world is named *Pinus ponderosa*. A specific name, such as *ponderosa* (heavy) or *albicaulis* (white stemmed), may be repeated without limit; but the names of genera and higher groups are unique. The word *species* is both singular and plural. The word *specie* refers only to coin, not to an organism. One speaks of a species of ground squirrel as well as many species of ground squirrels.

To return to the forest trees, their leafy masses look as though they have been cut from a rich assortment of fabrics in every shade of green. The madroño has large dark green leaves of satin in pleasing contrast to its red and chartreuse bark. Tanoak, chinquapin, and the coast and canyon live oaks spread out swatches of dull green homespun. The leaves of bay or California laurel (Oregon's myrtlewood) are cut from deep-green brocade. Black oak foliage is fashioned from spring grass-hued taffeta. It and California buckeye are the deciduous members of this largely evergreen plant community, but they lose their leaves at slightly different times. Buckeye leaves begin to wilt, turn golden brown, and drop toward the end of summer. Black oak waits until fall. Where moisture concentrates in canyon bottoms and gully floors, four other deciduous types—dogwood, willow, big-leaf maple, and alder—frequently occur.

Most of the trees of this community are broad sclerophylls, the technical term for plants having broad, evergreen leaves (in contrast to the narrow-leaved conifers) with a stiff, leathery texture. They occur in groves distributed in patches in the coastal ranges: on moister slopes, as islands surrounded by brush or grassland, or tucked away in the innumerable gullies, draws, and canyons of broken relief. They often edge redwood forests, where the giant trees give way to vegetation of a more drought-resistant nature, and occasionally appear on ridge tops.

Elements characteristic of specific communities are present in varying amounts in other associations throughout the coastal hills. Shade-tolerant shrubs of the brushlands mingle with the trees of both evergreen forests, coniferous and broadleaf. Blue elderberries grow in many communities and sites from road shoulders to open woodland. Grass is not only long and lush in forest clearings, it is scattered through broadleaf thickets except in the denser groves or those with heavy underbrush. Grass is also present in chaparral, filling in the gaps between shrubs, coming in after fires or clearing.

Shorter trees beneath the canopy of the dominant species form the understory. They are usually young individuals of typical canopy level trees or those requiring or tolerating shaded conditions. The broad-sclerophyll forest itself is often understory to the taller conifers such as redwood or Douglas-fir, although its status is sometimes temporary. In addition to the canopy and understory, most forests have three other layers or levels of plant growth: shrub, herbaceous, and floor or ground cover. Poison oak, western azalea, salal, snowberry, hazelnut, and jim brush are relatively mesophytic (requiring somewhat moist soils) and commonly occur in the shrub layer of coastal forests, while, shade-enduring grasses, bracken, California polypody, sword, wood, and goldenback ferns are plants of the herb level. Such horizontal subdivision of a forest is referred to as stratification, a major feature of the community structure.

The animal inhabitants of the wooded areas are much the same as those of the chaparral, with some differences. Mule deer readily move from one community to another, but tend to avoid the solid masses of thick chaparral. They prefer the more open brushy slopes. Favorite foods include the juicy tissues of herbaceous plants and spring-new sprouts of shrubs. They drift through the forest and along game trails, browsing as high as they can reach conveniently or nibbling at the grasses and forbs of the herb level.

Certain animals such as the gray squirrel are restricted to an arboreal life. One of the pleasures of exploring a patch of coastal forest is to see the down-feather tail of this tree squirrel flipping from side to side, or a bright eye peering over a limb. Since acorns are preferred food, oak trees are paramount in the life of this attractive animal, and its bulky nests are usually built in their limb crotches. A characteristic three-step food chain in oak groves is acorn/gray squirrel/hawk, but the tree-based life of the squirrel protects it from severe predation. If it eats the eggs of the black-headed grosbeak, common and typical bird of the broadleaf forest, a four-step chain ensues: seeds/grosbeak (in the form of eggs)/squirrel/hawk. The squirrel then moves to the rank of a second-order consumer.

With this background of introduction to four of the many communities of the outer Coast Range, it is possible for us to pick up some of the pieces of our puzzle and attempt to fit them together, keeping in mind that five types of coniferous forest also flourish here: closed-cone pine, redwood, mixed conifer, yellow pine, and relict cypress. It should also be restated that no one really knows exactly why all these peculiar patterns exist where they do. There are many research problems still remaining for future ecologists.

Any understanding of the factors governing the distribution of biotic communities begins with climate, and California has several climates; the state's relief features and its position with regard to neighboring land and ocean have resulted in a series of climatic spectra almost as varied as its topography. Because of its latitudinal range, California experiences a gradual increase in rainfall from south to north, from the near desert conditions of San Diego to the temperate rainforest of the Pacific Northwest. Its mountain ranges have heavier rainfall on their seaward sides and lighter precipitation on their eastern flanks because of what geographers call rainshadow (see Figure 5). Winds are forced to rise when confronted by a mountain barrier in their path. Any moisture-laden air masses they may bear become cooler during the upward journey. Such chilling increases condensation, and higher slopes are often soaked by resulting downpours. On descent the clouds are warmed and, already relieved of much of their moisture, may dry to the point of complete evaporation. Some major storms, particularly in winter, do continue on across the mountain ranges of the Far

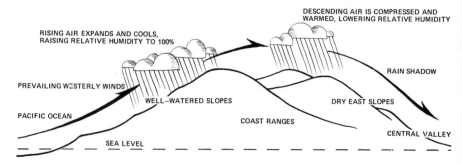

Figure 5. Precipitation pattern of central Coast Ranges

West, but by no means is this true for all. Most of California's winter rainfall comes from storms generated over the Pacific Ocean and carried east by winds known as the westerlies. The Coast Ranges are the first physiographic or relief barriers they meet; and rainshadow accounts for the fact that Santa Cruz, on the shoreline, receives roughly twenty-four inches of rain a year while, across the ridge, San Jose may have only thirteen.

So placed, maritime central California has what amounts to a moderate rainfall with many local differences based primarily on topography. Of equal if not greater importance is seasonal distribution. California shares what is termed the Mediterranean-type climate with four other regions in the world experiencing summer drought and winter rain. The extreme northwest corner receives occasional summer rain from storms that manage to slide down from Oregon, and higher ranges throughout the state have their share augmented by local thunderstorms. Masses of warm moist air occasionally wander in from the southwest, bringing rain to the eastern desert and even coastal areas in late summer. In general, however, vegetation must adapt to dry summers which are longer in the south and shorter in the north. Not only that, the Pacific High, a great midocean pressure hump, may deflect winter storms traveling down from the Gulf of Alaska. The Pacific High usually weakens or moves south in the winter, following the sun, but sometimes it remains strongly in position and blocks off needed rain. Then California can have a series of dry years to worry farmers and forest rangers alike. During the summer the Pacific High's presence bars from most of the state the rains that keep coastal Oregon and Washington green the year around.

Another factor complicates matters. A current of cold water upwells off the coast. During the summer the Great Valley bakes in furnacelike heat. Hot air rises, and cool air from the ocean is pulled into the valley to fill this partial vacuum. As the moisture-heavy air flows landward it passes over the cold water offshore. Enough condensation takes place to cause fog or drizzle, but not real rain. These summer mists, so disheartening to those who hope for a sunny day at the beach, are of extreme importance to coastal plant life—cropland and brush,

Eucalyptus grove and redwood stand. This natural air condi-
tioning forces many San Franciscans to wear coats in July while
Bakersfieldians swelter in sports shirts. Anyone driving in one
June day from Market Street to Bishop, east of the Sierra, could
have this temperature and weather schedule:

```
9:30 AM . . . . . San Francisco . . . . 55° . . . . . . . . fog
11:30 AM . . . . . Manteca . . . . . . . . .95° . . . . . . . . cloudless sky
3:30 PM . . . . . Tioga Pass . . . . . . .40° . . . . . . . . rain and sleet
6:00 PM . . . . . .Bishop . . . . . . . . . . 90° . . . . . . . . mostly clear skies
```

By now it will be obvious that there are many California climates. They account for much of the variety in its natural
landscapes. Brushlands owe their scrubby growth and appearance to the summer drought experienced by most of the state.
Such features as small leathery evergreen leaves and bushy
habit are adaptations to regions of cool wet winters and warm
dry summers. The same characteristics help the brush species
live through periods of less than normal rainfall when the Pacific High is in stubborn command. The shrubs of the coastal
scrub have many of these modifications. Some species, such
as California sagebrush, have the ability to go dormant to the
extent that their leaves desiccate and fall off during the dry
season.

The evergreen trees of the coastal forests enjoy the same
type of protection as chaparral in that they do not have to produce new foliage each year. One common species, buckeye, is
deciduous, but to balance the energy needed for growing new
leaves each year it loses them in late summer and remains in-
active for the rest of the dry period. Its large thin leaves are ill-
equipped for dry season dormancy, and their loss is another
way to limit life processes during this critical time. Other trees
of the broad-sclerophyll forest have many of the same evapor-
ation-retarding leaf features as the brush species: waxyness,
"water-proofed" leaf surfaces (cutinization), and stomata sit-
uated to cut down on water loss.

Grasses have their own adjustments to the climate. Shallow
rooted, they make use of surface soil water. When this disappears during drought, perennial grasses die back to under-

ground runners and root masses, and the annuals live through the time of tension as seed. Most grasses are more xerophytic than brushland or forest plants and, in the coastal areas, often occur where conditions are dry. In like situations, forbs—herbs, or green plants, minus grasses—react in much the same way.

In general, extensive chaparral is confined to summer-drought regions with an annual rainfall range of from ten to twenty-five inches. Desert occurs where the precipitation range is roughly from eight inches downward. Forests need more moisture than either brushland or desert, but there is a fair amount of variation. Areas supporting redwoods can receive as little as twenty-five inches per year or as much as a hundred. Thus, rainfall accounts for the overall pattern of California's vegetation: fir trees on the Sierran slopes, creosote bush on the flats of the Mojave Desert, and manzanita on Mount Tamal-pais. But it does not explain why a fern-carpeted tract of Douglas-fir should abruptly open out to the scruffy confusion of chaparral, nor why ponderosa pine, one of the dry-climate conifers, appears in the middle of a redwood forest. These sharp community shifts occur over and over in a region re-remarkably uniform in climate. This section of California en-joys moderate rainfall and maritime influences that keep tem-perature ranges small. Logically these sea-edge slopes should have but one type of vegetation, perhaps brush adapted to the lack of summer rain and making use of the summer fogs. If one were to envision a hypothetical vegetation diagram based solely on central California maritime climate, its moderateness and uniformity might indicate something like that shown in Figure 6.

Figure 6. Hypothetical uniform chaparral-type vegetation

There is a vegetation type admirably suited to coastal climate, the famed redwood forest, but this is by no means universal. In fact, in the San Francisco Bay region, these giants are held to pockets here and there. The extensive groves come into their own farther north. Man's inroads on the redwood stands in the transect aside, there are local restrictive climatic differences, more—and more influential—than one would realize. San Francisco is notorious for having its foggy streets and its sunny streets. The sea mists swirl in through natural draws and along channels formed by the valleys of this hilly city. In the warmer and more protected sections, housewives can garden in cotton dresses. In others, shoppers must button into wool coats against the chill and clammy winds. All along the coastal mountains, warm sheltered valleys huddle against exposed ridges, and a drizzly morning in Sausalito does not necessarily mean fog in Palo Alto.

Fog plays no unimportant role in central California's climate. According to Harold Gilliam's handbook, *Weather of the San Francisco Bay Region* (Berkeley and Los Angeles, 1962), parts of the Berkeley Hills receive moisture equivalent to ten inches of rainfall each year from fog drip alone. Fog not only lowers air temperatures and raises humidity, it eases the effect of summer drought by forming drops that build up behind veins and other tiny dams on leaf surfaces. When heavy enough, they fall in sparse but noticeable showers.

There are local differences in rainfall even in a relatively small area. Mount Tamalpais creates its own small rainshadow. Its northeastern slopes receive less precipitation than its southwestern flanks which directly confront the storm-bearing winds. This is also true of many individual peaks and hills in the coastal ranges and accounts for some of the variation in natural plant cover.

Sea-facing hillsides seldom support thick tall forest in California's latitudes if they are harassed by wind, particularly if it is salt-laden. Strong constant winds are essentially drying. Stunted scrub or grassland is typical of very exposed positions. What woody plants are present have the twisted and tortured habit of wind punishment. Clumped here and there on the sea bluffs of Marin are hedgelike mounds of California bay and other broad-sclerophyll trees in more sheltered hollows or behind rocky outcrops. The appearance of these thickets is due directly to wind. It trims by dehydrating any branchlet or twig venturing outside the dense rounded masses of leaf and stem.

But in the fog-visited and wind-sheltered canyons of the coastal hills, trees stand proud and straight. Just as mountain barriers cause rainshadow, passes and ridges channel and deflect wind which, when persistent in strength and consistent in direction, modifies the vegetation in its path. Where canyons open out to the sea, the benevolent bath of fog tempers the heat of summer. Such localized climatic units (microclimates) are due to the varied topography typical of many regions of California. Land and the great weather forces operate together in significant partnership.

In addition to affecting climatic patterns, features of the land exercise considerable control upon natural cover. The coastal hillscapes are rugged, broken by faulting and erosion. Ridge and gully succeed each other the length and width of the range system. Canyon bottoms are forested not only because of their sheltered positions; rainwater drains off the steep slopes above them and collects in permanent or seasonal streams on the ravine floors. Even where there is no visible flow, underground moisture concentrated here supports trees unable to live on drier substrates. We must now modify our hypothetical hillside to accommodate these additional situations (see Figure 7).

Another local variation of humidity and temperature must

Figure 7. Exposed and sheltered sites in coastal hills

be taken into account. It, too, is due to rugged relief. In non-tropical regions, slope face or aspect, as it is sometimes called, is of great importance. As California is north of the Equator, its southward-facing slopes get the benefit of the direct light of the sun, and those facing north are slighted. Solar radiation striking perpendicularly to a surface is more powerful in its effect than that which is oblique or glancing. Therefore north-ward-facing slopes are much cooler and damper than those facing south and commonly support forest or heavy growth of moisture-needing shrubs which in itself creates more mesic conditions. Wind is slowed and soil temperature and evapo-ration much decreased by the dense growth. Our diagram now undergoes another change; the shaded, humus-rich north-facing slopes are cloaked with forest, and the warmer, drier south faces have brush or grass (see Figure 8).

These basic moisture patterns are further complicated by other influences. What ecologists call edaphic conditions are very much involved with the coastal mosaic. These have to do with the specifics of soil and are responsible for some of the abrupt changes in vegetation. Two such local substrate cir-cumstances are noteworthy—outcrops of serpentine and ex-posed beds of ancient marine sands. The former occur in many places in California, particularly in the Franciscan rock series of the Coast Ranges where intrusions of molten material, at one time, forced their way into the earth's crust. Some of these, peridotite for one, were transformed into serpentine, a red-

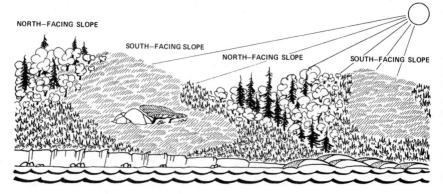

Figure 8. Differences in slope-face direction

dish or greenish rock which usually weathers to very infertile soils. The outcrops are high in magnesium and poor in enriching substances such as phosphates, potassium, and calcium. In addition, these soils are often too thin to hold much moisture. Such conditions mean poverty for most plants and result in semibarren hillsides with widely spaced, starved-looking bushes or trees. Those that survive are short on branches and long on moisture-seeking roots. Many species found on serpentines seldom occur elsewhere. By enduring the unfavorable chemical ratio, they benefit from the absense of competing plants. There is evidence, moreover, that certain harmful soil organisms avoid serpentine sites; consequently, tolerant species such as leather oak and certain types of manzanita have several advantages in addition to their ability to live on a hostile substrate.

"Fossil" sand dune areas in the Santa Cruz Mountains are comparably infertile. Much eroded, these old loosely consolidated sand deposits have become badlands, and their coarse soils are poor water holders. Where they occur, the surrounding evergreen forest immediately changes to open woodlands of dry-climate pines such as knobcone and ponderosa. Manzanita and live oaks provide a sparse and casual understory.

The broken bedrock of the hillsides has encouraged another adaptation on the part of broad-sclerophyll shrubs and trees. Interstices or cracks allow roots to penetrate deep beneath thin soils typical of these communities for water that has percolated into the fracture system. With a crowbar and a little energy one can pry apart the exposed root-sundered rock slabs of a roadcut or gully side and get an idea of the extent of this living network. Where ridgetops and hillsides are steep and heavily eroded, they may be too thin-soiled for either the larger trees or lush grassland. Then the aggressive brush with its moisture-miser leaves and enterprising roots comes into its own.

Talus faces of fractured rock are uneasy substrates and along with outcrops of bare rock account for barren patches appearing here and there on the hillsides. Only very hardy species such as digger and knobcone pines or the most drought-resistant shrubs can struggle along on the poor terrain. At the other extreme, seepages, springs, and local surfacing of the underground water permit more mesophytic species to intrude among those more spartan.

Soils differ in their ability to hold water because of texture. Sand, gravel, or cobble soils take in moisture quickly, but it rapidly sinks through these natural sieves, leaving the upper horizons relatively dry. Fine-grained soils, on the other hand, tend to take up water more slowly but retain it for a longer period of time. Soils of valley floors commonly contain much fine-grained clay and silt. Though deep, when underlain by impervious layers through which water is unable to percolate, these poorly drained basin bottom soils are waterlogged in the wet season. Since moisture is confined to upper horizons, however, it readily evaporates in summer, leaving baked surfaces, crisscrossed with cracks, where it has stood the longest. Chaparral shrubs rarely venture out onto these fickle substrates. They do better on the rocky soils of the steeper slopes where, with long exploring root systems, they can make use of reliable water sources deep in fractured bedrock. Shallow-rooted and quick-growing species such as grasses and weedy forbs are well suited to heavier soils of gentle slopes or valley floor, as they can take rapid advantage of water held close to the surface by the nature of the substrate. Some of the best soils in the area are thick, well-drained accumulations in the bottoms of ravines and canyons. When sufficiently moist a good part of the year they support forest or woodland incapable of growth on drier, thinner soils.

Soil organisms and chemical nature account for many specific plant associations. The rate of decomposition, or reduction of plant and animal debris to nutrients necessary for the growth of living things, depends on many factors—climate, the presence or absence of organisms responsible for such decay, vegetation, and the parent rock itself. If the process is slow because of the type of plant cover, drought, or long cold winters; if the bedrock resists disintegration; if certain soil elements are hostile to decay or if the substances so released are drained away through leaching or erosion, fertility suffers. Not only are pH values (acid-base ratios) of great significance in controlling decomposition rates, they determine the distribution of certain species. Some plants tolerate acid soils, whereas others can grow only on those that are basic or neutral. Because of the evergreen nature of chaparral, duff accumulates slowly. Not only are the leaves small in size, but they drop infrequently. Decomposition progresses quickly only when the soil is warm and has plentiful moisture, in other words, spring. Decay rates are slow the rest of the year. For these and other reasons, chaparral soils tend to be infertile. All of these features play their part in community placement, and our hillside should indicate an example or two (see Figure 9).

California's natural vegetation has another unusual aspect—its ability to survive the plant kingdom's most spectacular enemy, fire. Shocked and distressed as we are to hear of a disastrous fire, it is some comfort to know that the brushlands and forests of the state have built-in defenses against total destruction; it is poetic justice of a sort, because they are very fire-prone. Volatile oils, responsible for the pungency of scrub and chaparral, are highly flammable. Tinder-dry accumulations of discarded branches and other debris litter the thickets. Natural fires from lightning strikes have swept through the shrublands since their establishment far back in geological time (paleo-botanical history, important to the understanding of the coastal mosaic, will be discussed in chapter 5). When the American Indians entered what was to become California, they came as users of fire. With it they opened brush for hunting and seed gathering. It also escaped from campfires, as it still does today.

OUTCROP OF
INFERTILE SANDSTONE

Figure 9. Edaphic influences

Through millions of years a kind of equilibrium was reached between the native plants and fire. Fire is useful to chaparral because it clears out the dead wood and deposits ash, which is a rich source of nutrient material previously locked within living plant tissue as well as the slowly decaying debris. Not only is there evidence that upper soil oxygen is increased by fire, but it removes substances released from certain plants tending to inhibit growth of possible competing species.

A number of adaptations to the ravages of fire have evolved ensuring the survival of brushy species. Many of the most typical chaparral plants crown sprout after burning—that is, they start new stems from buds on the root crown which remains viable underground. Such species as toyon, poison oak, redberry, scrub oak, chamise, and mountain mahogany are flourishing shrubs again several years after fire has reduced them to black and leafless snags. Others, such as some of the manzanitas and types of ceanothus, seed sprout; their seeds are so adjusted to periodic burning that in many instances they readily germinate only after being heated to the proper degree. Then water easily penetrates the seed coat following such injury. These plants are commonly shallow rooted and short lived, in contrast to the deep-rooted and long-lived crown sprouters.

Grasslands are little damaged by most burning. They recover about as readily as they go up in flames. Annual species, by their very nature, assure renewal after fire. If the seed crop has fallen to the ground by the time of the burn, chances are it will escape injury and be ready to begin new growth in the next rainy season. Perennial grasses are almost as immune to fire damage. Their root masses are safe underground, and they will resprout as soon as weather conditions are favorable.

According to scientists who have studied the coastal mosaic, much of its seemingly inexplicable character is due to fire. Species and even communities may be shifted about when a vegetative cover is so destroyed. Each type of vegetation has its own route and rate of recovery. Forests may take a hundred years to return to former magnificence; brushlands can regain their previous aspect in a decade.

Almost all of the regenerating scrub and chaparral regions of California have an herb interval when quick-growing grasses and forbs, uncommon in developed brushland, dominate the postburn landscape. In many instances, the pioneering herbs are strictly fire types. The seeds have lain dormant underground since the previous burn, sprouting only when stimulated by heat or some other condition dependent on fire. Many spectacular wildflowers, including the delicately beautiful flame poppies and pale yellow whispering bells, belong to this unusual group of plants. At any rate, newly opened brush areas with their ash-rich soils invite invasion by quick growing plants requiring sunlight and space.

Coastal scrub elements are frequently in or near areas of chaparral. Most of these species are somewhat weedy in nature. They propagate with ease because numerous seeds are readily dispersed by wind or other means. Once established, the semi-woody branches grow rapidly. Yerba santa, lotus (bird's-foot trefoil), bush monkeyflower, California buckwheat, coyote brush, and black sage are common invaders of recently burned chaparral, sometimes creating as dense a cover as chaparral itself. Several light-seeded chaparral shrubs—tree poppy and chamise, for example—also pioneer in areas of recent burns.

Throughout the herb and subshrub stages, shrubs of the chaparral are slowly recovering from root crowns and sprouting seeds. Eventually they reign supreme, having shaded and crowded out the temporary species whose seeds now lie dormant or whose offspring have retreated elsewhere to disturbed sites scattered through the brushlands where they wait until the next great sweep of the fiery broom. Most trees of the broad-sclerophyll forest crown sprout, but after a heavy fire the length of time necessary for complete return from herb and shrub domination is much greater than that for brush.

The fire-induced herbaceous stage, under certain soil conditions, can be prolonged indefinitely by frequent burns. Many prairie balds exist for no other reason than recurrent fires staving off the reinvasion of shrubby growth. Any woody sprouts and seedlings attempting life in thick grass are subject to destruction in the next dry season. On the other hand, in the absence of burning, brush often invades grassland, extending its domain at the expense of the prairie.

The interested observer sees California's hillsides from but one point in time when he first asks about their puzzling vegetation patterns. A beginning student of plant ecology, given an introductory assignment of driving along Skyline Boulevard from San Francisco south to Santa Cruz and attempting to explain the hill-land mosaic, is able to base his opinion only on what he sees during that drive. He does not have as yet the background to interpret the landscapes from the point of view of passing time. After study and research he will gain this ability and remember that what he sees today is not necessarily what will be there in ten years (if man leaves it alone), nor what was there before disaster removed the stable community adjusted to meet certain conditions. Some of the prairies and brushed slopes, looking so out of place in the midst of a Douglas-fir or redwood forest, may be initial stages in the recovery, after destruction, of wooded landscapes.

This change in the landscape fits another piece into the puzzle. We must now amend the diagram to include the effects of fire, adding patches of coastal scrub and grassland that have replaced chaparral and forest burned some years ago (see Figure 10).

The animals of these burned communities are much affected by the holocaust that has flamed through their homes. Since this type of catastrophe occurs more often in the less humid

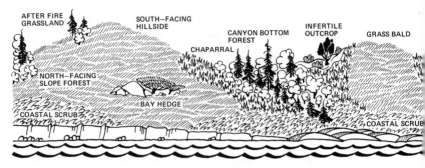

Figure 10. Typical vegetation mosaic

interior of California, a discussion of what happens to them during and after a fire may be found in chapter 11.

Man, himself, has many ways of controlling the natural landscapes over which he has assumed jurisdiction. He can alter their composition and change their appearance, using such methods as deliberate burning or the bulldozer. He can plow a grassy field and bring a piece of Iowa's uninspiring but money-making cornland to California valleys. By introducing livestock or encouraging herbivorous wildlife he can prevent the natural shift from temporary meadow to brush or forest. Mule deer relish acorns and nibble here and there on tender shoots of shrubs. By such feeding preference, large mule deer populations maintain grassland which would otherwise revert to woody vegetation.

Lumbering can be as disastrous an upheaval in the life of a forest community as fire or flood. If left alone, the normal transitional stages will return the cut-over land to the type of community for which it is best adapted. But man, the ever-active meddler, insists on manipulating nature, promoting those species most useful or worthwhile to him, eliminating those less profitable or desirable. By accident or on purpose, by carelessness or with considered reason, he has completely disrupted much of the orderly progression of cause and effect that for millions of years has played its drama upon forest and rangeland. Where the wilder areas are still tolerated, management has been substituted for the living world's own long evolved controls—competition and the struggle for survival. To fire, climate, relief, and substrate we must add man as a determining factor in California landscapes which reflect a complex of interacting components, each exerting its influence, each contributing its answers to the puzzle of the patterns on the hills.

Bishop pines on Inverness Ridge, Marin County

# 5. The Fire Pines

A good introduction to California's coastal pine trees can be found in John Steinbeck's *Tortilla Flat*:

A high fog covered the sky and behind it the moon shone so that the forest was filled with a gauze-like light. There was none of the sharp outline we think of as reality. The tree trunks were not black columns of wood, but soft and unsubstantial shadows. The patches of brush were formless and shifting in the queer light. Ghosts could walk freely tonight, without fear of the disbelief of man; for this night was haunted, and it would be an insensitive man who did not know it. . . . The wind rose as they walked and drove the fog across the pale moon like a thin wash of gray water color. The moving fog gave shifting form to the forest so that every tree crept along and the bushes moved soundlessly like great dark cats. The tree-tops in the wind talked huskily, told fortunes and foretold death.

There is no place more suited to ghost-haunted nights and wandering shadows than a grove of California's coastal pine trees. Unlike their upright inland brothers, the yellow and sugar pines, many older individuals of these species lean and twist, throwing out tufts of foliage here, pulling in gnarled old branches there. The words "pine tree" often bring mental images of trees that are straight and tall and tapered. Many of the ninety-odd species of this genus, however, do not grow that way. They are crooked, almost arthritic in appearance, and deliquescent, that is, the trunks fork into limbs which in turn branch out to boughs and twigs. This is a habit commonly associated with such trees as oaks or elms but not conifers. However, the Aleppo, stone, and Japanese pines of gardens and parks are deliquescent, branching and rebranching into picturesque poses. Not all of the pines of the western interior, for that matter, have a central polelike trunk and tapered shape. The digger pines, pinyons, and timberline species such as bristlecone and limber pines have as spreading and irregular crowns as many broadleaf types. The coastal kinds often combine the two habits. A relatively straight trunk with the characteristic side snags of tapering conifers will suddenly umbrella into spokelike branches that angle off in all directions, supporting rounded rather than pointed tops. Young trees are usually of traditional conifer shape. Wind and salt spray may be responsible for picturesqueness of habit, as dense and more sheltered stands of Monterey pines are usually straight boled and isolated individuals in exposed sites are prone to irregular shapes.

The engaging interplay of line and texture and the subtle gradients of color from the rich green out at needle tip to the dark inner heart of old and matted foliage endear them to their admirers. Place these old fellows on headlands and bluffs, back them against the tapestry of the sea, enshroud them with fogwisp bits of lichen—and they grant you a striking landscape.

California has a rich representation of pine types. It has as natives almost one-fourth of all the species in the genus, *Pinus*. Many forms from the Orient, the Mediterranean, and central Europe have also been introduced as ornamentals. Not only that, but by stretching the term "Californian region" to include the upper half of the peninsula of Baja California, the state can lay claim to eight endemic species; these are species restricted to a particular locale and occurring natively nowhere else. By no means is this the end of California's bid for forestry fame. It has a truly remarkable group of cone-bearing trees including three world records: the tallest, coast redwood; the largest in diameter, big tree; and the oldest, bristlecone pine. In addition, it has a large share of all the coniferous trees in the West.

The lists below might prove helpful in stressing just how extraordinary is the story of California's conifers. One asterisk indicates which of these western coniferous species occur in the state; two show those endemic to (found naturally only in) the Californian region. Not included are species restricted in the West to Canada and Alaska, only those growing in the continental forty-eight states, in other words, below the forty-eighth parallel. Also excluded is Texas, east of the Pecos River.

*Pines*
whitebark*
limber*
western white (silver)*
sugar*
bristlecone*
two-leaved pinyon*
one-leaved pinyon*
four-leaved pinyon*
yellow*
Jeffrey*
beach*
lodgepole*
digger**
Coulter**
Torrey**
bishop**
Monterey**
island** (species status unsure)
foxtail**
knobcone*
Southwestern white
Mexican pinyon
Chihuahua
Apache

*Firs*
lowland (grand)*
white*
silver
noble*
red*
Santa Lucia**
subalpine

*Junipers*
creeping
common*
Utah*
red-berry
drooping
Ashe
California**
Sierra (western)*
alligator
one-seed
Rocky Mountain

*Spruces*
Engelmann*
blue
white
weeping*
Sitka*

*Cypresses*
Macnab**
Modoc*
Arizona
Piute**

Arizona smooth
Tecate**
Monterey**
pygmy**
Abrams**
Sargent**
Gowen**
Cuyamaca**

*Odds and ends*
redwood*
big tree**
incense cedar*
western larch
alpine larch
western hemlock*
mountain hemlock*
Douglas-fir*
big-cone spruce**
western red cedar*
Port Orford cedar (Lawson
    cypress)*
Alaska cedar*
western yew*
California nutmeg**

Of the seventy-three cone-bearers in the West, fifty-four occur in California, and twenty-one are endemic. The neighboring state of Arizona has thirty-two coniferous species, but only one is endemic. It would be no exaggeration to conclude that the Californian region is an outstanding world leader in its number of cone bearers, both endemic and wide-range species.

Its twenty-one endemics are dispersed sporadically throughout the state. Some are confined to very small specific locations; others have wider distributions. Not all will be covered in this chapter which features three fire pines—Monterey, bishop, and knobcone (the latter is not endemic to California in that it also occurs in Oregon)—along with five of the native cypresses —Sargent, pygmy, Gowen, Monterey, and Abrams.

The three pines have far more in common than membership in the yellow pine group, occasional deliquescence, and residence in coastal California. Often referred to as closed-cone pines, they, along with the broadleaf evergreen shrubs and trees of the sunburnt hillsides, have adjusted to the inevitable presence of fire. The three species bear tightly closed, somewhat lopsided cones that cling to trunk and branch. Solitary cones or pairs are not unusual, but these pines are unique in that several are often whorled around the supporting stem. Clusters of a dozen or so have been collected that look for all the world like a colony of prickly gray barnacles that has renounced its tidal home and exchanged a wharf piling for a tree trunk. Here the cones remain year after year, unable to release their seeds unless one of two things happens: fire melts the resinous coating that glues the scales together or heat of summer sun, age, or insect damage finally relaxes them to the point where they open of their own accord. Of the three species, knobcone has the most persistent cones. Hanging onto trunk or bough, the clusters weather to driftwood gray, looking drier and less alive with each passing season. There are many examples of the growing trunk slowly incasing its attached cones, burying them deep in woody tissue. Only sawing open lengths of felled timber reveals these nurseries, some still stubbornly closed. Once released, the seeds readily germinate and produce hardy offspring. In no way do the seedlings indicate that the parent seeds may have waited for years, locked up by a habit that is fire insurance as good as any in the plant world. When burning has been the instrument of release, the new plants receive an additional benefit. The soil is improved by the removal of litter and the consequent deposit of nutritious ash.

Knobcone pines are the least maritime of the three. They grow on dry, rocky slopes of the inner Coast Ranges and Sierran foothills from Oregon to southern California, tolerant of many adverse circumstances but not shade. Serpentine soils, infertile to plant life generally, are often host to these xerophytic pines. Bishop and Monterey pines have a more restricted range. Never far from the ocean, their striking bluff-top groves seem designed by Japanese printmakers. The two-needled bishop pines frequent swampy places as well as ridges and slopes and, in widely separated stands, are found usually with-

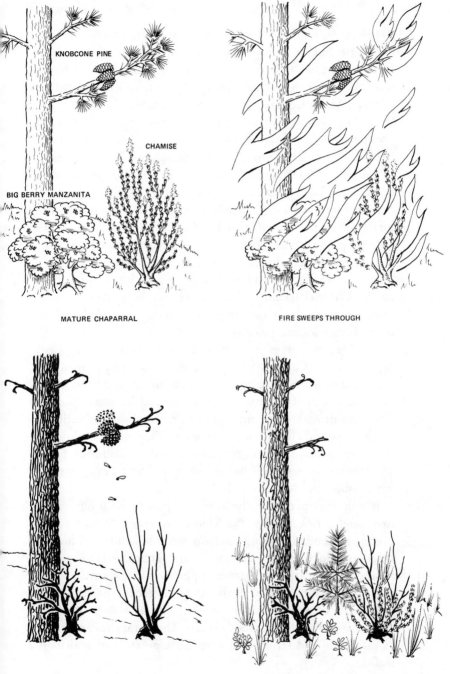

Figure 11. Stages in return after chaparral and knobcone pine fire

in several miles of the ocean. With what is termed a discontinuous distribution, they occur here and there from Trinidad Head in Humboldt County, to Mendocino County (where they mix with beach pines and pygmy cypress), and to Inverness Ridge in Marin County. South of San Francisco they neighbor their close relative, Monterey pine, on Huckleberry Hill near Monterey. Bishop pines also occur in the San Luis Range near Point Buchon, in the Santa Inez Mountains and Purisima Hills in Santa Barbara County, on the coast of Baja California, and on offshore Santa Cruz and Cedros islands.

Monterey pine, a three-needled form, is the most limited in home site of all three. It is confined to hills and slopes around Monterey, to scattered groves near Año Nuevo Point, to tracts at Cambria Pines, and to Guadalupe and Cedros islands off Baja California. (Some authorities place a variety of this pine on the Channel Islands.) Both coastal species have been extensively planted in parks and gardens, along roadsides, and in re- and afforestation projects.

All three fire pines have typical shrub layers. Salal, wax myrtle, toyon, California hazelnut, more mesophytic manzanitas and ceanothus, coyote brush, huckleberry, poison oak, and chinquapin often grow under bishop and Monterey pines. The more drought-resistant types of chaparral such as various manzanitas and chamise are frequently associated with knobcone pine. One often sees madrone, live oak, California bay, and other members of the broad-sclerophyll forest in company with bishop and Monterey pines.

It is difficult to discuss the Monterey pine without reference to a neighboring conifer, the Monterey cypress. This tree is even more limited in range, as its home is the cliffs and headlands around Cypress Point and Point Lobos, a state park. Monterey cypresses are extremely photogenic. Exposed to the salt sting of the western winds, they have been harried and driven, forced to bolster their position with buttress roots that twist and curl into great woody snarls. Their branches are quite as grotesque and struggle to keep aloft parasols of scalelike leaflets.

Gowen cypress is the fourth native conifer found on the

Monterey Peninsula, enriching this scenic elbow of California. All of them have settled into limited locations. Monterey cypress has taken possession of the granitic sea cliffs on two famous points; two small groves of Gowen cypress occur close by. One is a mile and a half from Point Lobos; the other grows inland on the same Huckleberry Hill where the two coastal fire pines meet. Here they are mixed with bishop pine on thin, acid, sandy soils in an "island" surrounded by Monterey pine. This last species fills the gap between the two cypresses, growing up-slope from Cypress Point to the summit of what must be one of the most botanically interesting hills in the entire state. It appears to mingle with bishop pine only around the edges of the island and does not penetrate into the latter's stronghold.

The other three native cypresses of coastal central California have more or less limited ranges. The pygmy cypress, often called the Mendocino cypress, characteristically lives on substrate having an unusual edaphic condition. These are the white beds of true podsol-type soil which are patchily distributed on ancient marine sandstone terraces along the Mendocino coast, notably near Fort Bragg. An impervious iron hardpan layer prevents roots from extending to any depth, and consequently they are incapable of obtaining subsoil moisture, in spite of a relatively heavy yearly rainfall. The surface soils are dry in summer but are waterlogged in winter. As they are also among the most acid and nutrient deficient soils found in California, these beds form an extremely poor substrate. These conditions are reflected in stunted pygmy forests of cypress, and beach and bishop pine. Abrams cypress grows among the shrubs of dry shallow-soiled hillsides on three sites in the Santa Cruz Mountains. In one of these locations—ancient marine sand deposits—it mixes with knobcone and yellow pine. Sargent cypress has the widest distribution of the five. It is found on the serpentines of Mount Tamalpais and is scattered through the inner, middle, and outer ranges from Mendocino to near Santa Barbara often on similar substrates. It is very much a member of the chaparral.

Only the wind fighters tie themselves in knots. When young

or in more protected localities, the cypresses are the familiar pyramids or spires of coniferous tradition though some species tend to become broad crowned with age regardless of location. Individual cypresses of the pygmy type have been found growing as tall as a hundred feet where better soil conditions permit. In color they vary from the rich dark green of the Monterey cypress to the soft green of the interior Sargent groves. All appear to be adapted to drought, climatic or edaphic—as in the case of Mendocino County's white flats and the serpentine outcrops of Marin. The tiny evergreen scales are water conserving. As the small round cones tend to persist, remaining on the tree for some years, most of the California cypresses have been described as closed-cone types. Evidence indicates that fire hastens their seed dispersal, and vigorous germination takes place after burning.

Of these eight trees—three pines and five cypresses—seven are endemic, all are conifers, all are drought resistant, all are fire adapted, and all occur in scattered sites on coastal hills. Again, it is appropriate to ask why. Why are some of these species confined to two or three tiny pockets and grow naturally nowhere else in the world? Why doesn't California have just one or two kinds of cypress, like Arizona, instead of this flock of cousins, most of them poor relations living on their little plots of serpentine or other dry infertile soils? Why are the fire conifers, with their marvelous adaptation, often confined to some of the worst real estate in California, from the point of view of plants?

Remnants of once widely distributed populations or floras are termed "relicts." They are the last remaining descendants of forebears that occupied larger territories. To fully understand our eight conifers we need to probe a bit into California's geological past. Some of the state's native plant species owe their remote origins to a flora centered in the tropics. A neotropical plant association moved northward from tropical latitudes during and following the Dinosaur Age. Such tropical plant types as avocado, wild fig, palm, tropical almond, and cinnamon were characteristic of this forest. They grew well in a gentle landscape and warm humid climate extending as far north as southeastern Alaska. But two trends began to influence the climatic pattern. It became cooler and drier. The neotropical flora largely disappeared in California or reconstituted itself. During the same geologic period, close relatives of modern alders, birches, oaks, and maples and cone bearers such as pines, redwoods, and firs invaded from the north where a flora adapted to the increasing chill was evolving. This has been designated the Arcto-Tertiary because of its Arctic base of dispersal. The word *Tertiary* refers to the geological period in which the invasion took place. Concurrently, pockets of xeric, or arid, environments appeared here and there in the mountains and high plateaus of Mexico and the nearby Southwest. Rainshadow, soil peculiarities, and local air pressure systems most probably stimulated the beginning of the Madro-Tertiary (Madro refers to the Sierra Madre Mountains in Mexico), a xerophytic flora destined to become increasingly important in California's vegetation, particularly in response to developing summer drought and lower rainfall averages.

As the worldwide climate complex moved into and through the Ice Age and subsequent warming up and drying out, much happened to California's landscapes. Mountain systems came into being, glaciers and ice caps formed and melted, and rainfall averages fluctuated through alternating wetter and drier periods. It was as though two great hands were at work, one pushing the northern elements south along the rising and, therefore, cooler and moister mountain chains, and the other shoving the summer drought adapters north and west from their southern bases. Eventually, all of these forces at work—geological, climatic, and biological—sorted out, shifted, and shuffled the species a generous nature had put at their disposal.

A number of forms with a wide tolerance range for many climatic and environmental variations continued their universality. Various types of currant, ceanothus, and manzanitas flourish almost all over the state. Each of these three generic groups has representative species at timberline and on the seacoast, and from desert hills to redwood groves. Other genera, however, have restricted distributions. The big tree grows only between certain elevations on the western slope of the south and central Sierra. Those with more rigid requirements remained in places where conditions were congenial or died out. The dry climate species of the central outer Coast Ranges survived only in battlements unassailable by the wet climate types. They settled on the sandy barrens, the steeper, often unstable slopes, dry exposures, and infertile serpentines. Among the more successful were those having tolerances for conditions avoided by other species: soil hyperacidity or alkalinity, mineral deficiencies, and so forth. Unique endurance features are the mainstay of their defense.

As conditions became drier along the coast, those needing moisture either retreated to the northern third of the state where rainfall was more dependable or kept to the higher elevations, north-facing slopes, fog zones, areas of seepage, and drainage bottoms. Escaping the turbulence of changing times, the relicts stayed behind in hospitable niches—the refuges so numerous in the broken, climatically complicated country of coastal California. They remain conservative, cut-off, the diehards of the plant world. How does this explain the star-billed eight? The two great elements of California's flora, northern and southern, have a pronounced and dramatic meeting ground in the complex relief of the central coast. Bays and estuaries thrust themselves deep into the heartland. Mountains poke up here and there. Faults cut across hill and valley indiscriminately. In the period of the major north-south confrontation, inundations created an archipelago, an island chain, out of what is now the central coast. Any isolated area, such as an island, is favorable to the production of endemics. Mutant species, unable to spread, remain imprisoned. The crossbreeding of such "sports" gives rise to more diversification, particularly where there is a variety of ecological niches to accommodate them. For example, the ancestral pair of Darwin's finches gave rise to a whole congress of new types in the Galapagos Islands, all still finches but each species distinguished by its own special bill shape which evolved through adaptation to the feeding requirements of a particular ecological niche.

Geological processes reunited the scattered islands of the San Francisco Bay region, but left behind a potent combination of such relief features as the Golden Gate and mounts Diablo, Hamilton, and Tamalpais, all of which are barriers to plant distribution. Therefore it is not surprising that ninety-seven plant species stop in Marin County and do not occur farther south. Thirty-four reach their northern limits here. Many typical and common plant species of the central and southern parts of the state have never migrated north above the Bay area—for example, black sage, California walnut, Mojave rabbitbrush, and California buckwheat.

This topographical complex occurs where the coastal climate becomes increasingly cooler and damper. Nor is this all. The region is somewhat isolated, as the dry Great Valley, with its seasonal temperature extremes, lies to the east and the ocean to the west. This combination of isolation, transitional and varying climates, a multiplicity of soil types, broken relief, and traveling floras meant tremendous opportunities for the surviving species. Here were all kinds of corners for outpost positions. Though many species with wide ecological amplitudes, or tolerances, continued to have widespread distributions, those with limiting requirements remained in pocket environments where conditions were favorable to their needs. One community, the broadleaf evergreen forest, is a collection of remnant species from both northern and southern elements. It is a compromise, and it is frequently found where a moist community intergrades with a drier one, in this case where the humid coniferous forests merge with chaparral or scrub.

The closed-cone pines remained in ramparts where they successfully withstood competition through the years. The knobcones keep to limestone outcrops, sterile sand deposits, and serpentines which are edaphically dry, or to the exposed and southward-facing slopes of the inner ranges and foothills. These are conditions many trees cannot tolerate. The shore fire pines are able to thrive on infertile sites such as Mendocino County's white beds and sterile chert-derived soils near Lompoc only under certain climatic conditions. Where they grow naturally, bishop and Monterey pines are restricted to maritime regions. Temperature ranges are small, summer fogs are frequent, and precipitation is sufficient for their needs.

Recent evidence indicates that all three—with their much-disputed cousin, the island pine of California's offshore islands and possibly a few mainland sites—now occur in remnant or relict stands of a widespread closed-cone pine forest of ancestral species. Presumably this ancient forest—Madro-Tertiary in origin—flourished in a mild climate similar to the coastal conditions required by bishop and Monterey pines which continue to hold their own on climatically suitable if edaphically difficult sites. University of California geneticist G. Ledyard Stebbins makes an interesting point when he describes what could account for the fact that the three fire pines have not hybridized with each other to any great extent. Bishop and Monterey pine live side by side in several places, and though some hybridization occurs in the contact zone, they keep their identities distinct. They shed their pollen at different times. Bishop pine has a slightly more northern distribution pattern than its occasional neighbor and is therefore somewhat winter dormant. It sheds its pollen in April; whereas Monterey pine, restricted to the gentler climate of maritime midlatitudes, sheds its pollen in February. Obviously, the two species cannot pollinate each other's cones. This is a striking example of seasonal isolation which is just as efficient as geographic isolation in keeping species from merging genetically. There is evidence, too, that Monterey pine seems to take the better soils, leaving the poorer for its relative.

The cypresses have more or less the same story. Each species, long evolved from a common ancestor covering a great deal of territory in its time, has established residence in very specialized kinds of environment. There is indication, however, that their ecological amplitudes are narrow and diseases such as cypress canker play havoc with any experimental attempts, man-made or natural, for establishment elsewhere. The different Monterey and Gowen cypress habitats point this up nicely. Dr. S. Carlquist of Rancho Santa Ana Botanic Garden has come to the conclusion that a combination of fog, granitic substrate, and salt spray confines the Monterey cypress in its homeland to sea-bluff sites. Any attempt to move out of this narrow ecological niche dooms it to canker infection. In a way it has, as Dr. Carlquist says, "painted itself into a corner." Through overspecialization it may carry the seeds of its own destruction.

On the other hand, the Monterey pine, so restricted in California, is one of the most widely planted trees in the world and is constantly used in afforestation and reforestation projects. Huge plantations in temperate regions of South Africa, Australia, and New Zealand testify to its vigor. In these locations it grows tall and tapered, as classic a conifer as one could ask, when protected and away from wind harassment.

The aged pines of Steinbeck's tale may well have their own stories to tell: the demise of less fortunate relatives, the hardships of being paisanos, countrymen, native Californians who have weathered many ghost-ridden, moon-haunted hours through the long slow nights of geological time.

Redwood grove, Bull Creek, Humboldt Redwoods State Park

# 6. The Tall Forest

Many visitors to California redwood groves are depressed at
first by the dark and somber dignity of the forest, particularly
in rainy or cloudy weather. On bright days in spring and summer, however, the groves have color resources of their own.
The pink petals of oxalis (redwood-sorrel) open tiny whorls
among shamrock-shaped leaves. Sword ferns arch green fronds
over log and root. Orange-bellied water dogs paddle about in
the clear shallow pools of the streams and rivers draining the
coastal slopes, and the banks above are brocaded with five-
finger and maidenhair fern. As the early sun burns through the
morning mist, long shafts of light touch the flattened fanlike
foliage with silver fire. In autumn the leaves of the vine maple
blaze coal-red through the shadows of the understory.

A relict like the fire pines, the redwood belongs to California,
except for an eight-mile extension above the Oregon border.
In a state which boasts of twenty-one coniferous natives, two
have such outstanding features that they are the best known
California trees. The coastal species—*Sequoia sempervirens*,
or redwood—is the world's tallest tree, and its mountain relative—*Sequoiadendron giganteum*, or big tree—has the largest
base circumference. Both have enviable records of longevity.
The tallest redwood was discovered only recently. For years
Founders Tree near Dyerville in Humboldt County had this
distinction, but its 364 feet have been overtopped by a giant
367+ feet tall. Once on privately owned land near Orick in
Humboldt County, it and several others almost as tall are protected in Redwood National Park. However, the distinguishing
feature is not the unusual loftiness of several individuals but
that the species as a whole is characterized by great height.
Records have been claimed for Douglas-fir and Australian eu-
calypts, but none standing today can match the redwoods. Big
trees, whose sheer mass is most impressive, cannot come near
their coastal relatives in height; too often their tops have been

lightning blasted. But they outdo the redwoods when it comes to age. Though 2,200 years of life, a coastal record, are venerable indeed, much longer lives have been noted for the big trees; however, these apparently have been bested by the bristlecone pines of the White Mountains in eastern California and other Great Basin ranges.

Though the largest groves and most magnificent stands are in the three northernmost coastal counties of the state, redwoods occur as far south as southern Monterey County where little groups cluster in canyons opening out to the sea. At one time, they were part of the forest cover on most of the coastal hills from Santa Cruz north, but logging has removed them from many of their former habitats. The northern part of their range extends farther east than does the southern portion, which is confined to the western flanks and valleys of the outer Coast Ranges.

The beauty of their forests, their great height and long lives, their hardiness and the quality and durability of their lumber have put these giants into a very special category. They evoke a kind of reverence accorded no other American tree. Their groves have been called temples and their spires cathedral-like; every writer describing them is lavish with vocabulary borrowed from church architecture. But our task is to go beyond description and attempt to account for their lingering presence along the northern coast. There is fossil evidence that *Sequoia* and related genera were widespread over much of the northern hemisphere following the heyday of the dinosaurs. They flourished as part of the Arcto-Tertiary flora, the great plant group that thrived in the mild humid climate then prevalent even in the Far North. The family, Taxodiaceae, in which this genus is placed includes the baldcypress of the southeastern United States and Mexico, *Cryptomeria* of Japan, and a relict relative of the sequoia discovered not too long ago, the deciduous dawn redwood of China. California's two famed trees are not wholly alone in the world, ancient and isolated though they are.

If redwoods have died out elsewhere but continue to thrive in the coastal mountains, there must be some explanation why this is so, particularly since they have peculiarities. Their seedlings rarely survive in soils rich in the humus of undisturbed forest floors; fungi present in such soils are harmful to their roots. Instead they do well only on newly exposed soils where duff has been removed by fire or some other disturbance, or on recently deposited silt. A layer of topsoil is soon built, however, by decomposing needle drop. Redwoods as a species are relatively tolerant of shade. Seedlings apparently require full or partial sunlight; yet well-established youngsters flourish in the shade of the forest's interwoven canopy. This is not to say that the crowded trees do not respond to thinning. The increased light, nutrients, and moisture made available to the remaining trees result in growth spurts reflected by wider year rings of woody tissue.

One generally accepted characteristic of redwoods is their restriction to the fog belt of maritime central and northern California. Not only are the climatic conditions here most closely akin to the mild temperatures and humidity of the ancient Tertiary epoch, but redwoods, like all plants with foliage, lose water from their leaves by evaporation. The almost daily summer fogs are of inestimable value in reducing such water loss as they increase air humidity and decrease temperatures. An additional requirement limits the species. It does not fare well in soils having less than 18 percent available soil moisture in August, the critical month in California's dry summer climate. Fog drip contributes surprisingly large amounts of moisture to soil during the dry season, up to thirty or forty inches, it has been claimed, in some parts of the northern coast.

Despite its special needs, the genus *Sequoia* had tolerances enabling it to compete successfully with newcomer species. These began intruding when the climate settled down to summer drought and greater temperature ranges, seasonally and regionally. Such conifers as the cypresses and Coulter pine, whose close allies, if not the same species, are recorded from this period, are better adapted to a dry climate than the mesophytic redwood. Conversely, wet-climate species—Sitka spruce, grand fir, Port Orford cedar, and canoe, or western red, cedar—are descendents of old cronies from Arcto-Tertiary days. They are important elements of the Pacific Northwest rainforest from which redwood is absent north of latitude 42°. They cannot endure any prolonged summer drought, and though they mingle with redwoods up in Del Norte and Humboldt counties in a mixed-conifer forest, only grand fir and western hemlock, another conifer of mesic sites, appear as far south as coastal Sonoma County. Redwood has a well-defined climatic niche—too summer-dry for strong representation of many north coastal conifers but damp enough to edge out xerophytic species that are held to the drier pockets of these corrugated mountains.

All through its range, but more particularly in the southern half, redwood is part of the coastal mosaic. Its edaphic and climatic needs concentrate the species in canyon bottoms, along river flats, on north-facing slopes, and where ocean fog is a dependable summer visitor. It leaves the exposed, windblown shoreline bluffs and the serpentines, the steep, thinsoiled southward-facing hillsides and sterile sandy outcrops to chaparral, scrub, and grass, or more xerophytic trees. Broadleaf evergreen forest is typically transitional between the humid redwood groves and drier communities and often forms buffer stands between the two extremes. Man, however, has greatly interfered with these natural patterns because of the high commercial value of redwood timber.

A number of features of endurance help offset the requirements of redwood. Like the fire pines, it is adapted to fire. Not only do its seeds flourish in the bare soil left by fire, but it root- and trunk-sprouts as well. Sprouting is the characteristic method of propagation where the soils are rich in humus or in heavily shaded areas where seedlings probably would not survive. Rings or straight rows of saplings are typical features of all the Pacific Northwest rainforests. So-called nurse trees are downed logs which are fertile substrate for seedlings growing like well-behaved schoolchildren in line on the upper surface of the decaying trunk. More typical of redwood are the circles of young trees which started as sprouts around a burned or injured parent tree. Fire usually is not fatal, however. Thick, fireproof, nonresinous bark; wood of high moisture content;

and a humid environment limit its destructive ravages. Most burns heal over in time, and trees whose foliage and side branches have been destroyed may re-sprout as fire columns. The new shoots project from dormant buds as bushy twigs all along the tapered trunk.

One might say that the coast redwood seems disaster-proof, up to a point. Floods, short of the rare catastrophes that undercut roots and topple trees, add silt to its substrate, encouraging seedlings and even invigorating the mature stands. The finest groves are on alluvial flats. They not only survive the low oxygen levels of flooded soils, but extend up to the new soil surface vertically oriented temporary roots from the old roots. Shortly after, they begin to spread horizontal root networks from newly buried portions of their trunks. The giants of alluvial terrain characteristically have several such systems from each successive flood.

Cut or burn them, and seedlings and sprouts soon form thickets of vigorous growth. Insects and decay rarely trouble them because of chemicals in the thick bark. Though high winds can fell them as they have shallow root systems, they are considered by foresters to be relatively wind-firm. Diehards they are, in their fog-frequented, wind-sheltered canyons or hillsides, when they have sufficient soil moisture to tide them over the summer season. Foresters have referred to them as "disaster climax forests," meaning that if totally protected from the rejuvenating effects of near calamity the species would sooner or later suffer the consequences of its vigorous nature and degenerate under the decadence of soft living. Regeneration of the forest occurs only when new plants become established to replace the dead and dying. As noted above, sprouts grow from injured roots and boles, and seedlings thrive when fire or flood prepares the seedbed and opens the forest to fresh growth. It appears that the older a stand becomes, the more it is prone to extensive damage and destruction, with rejuvenation taking place less readily. Some researchers judge that a 300 year old grove is already entering senescence with accompanying loss of vigor.

Sequoia sometimes grows in pure stands, more often with

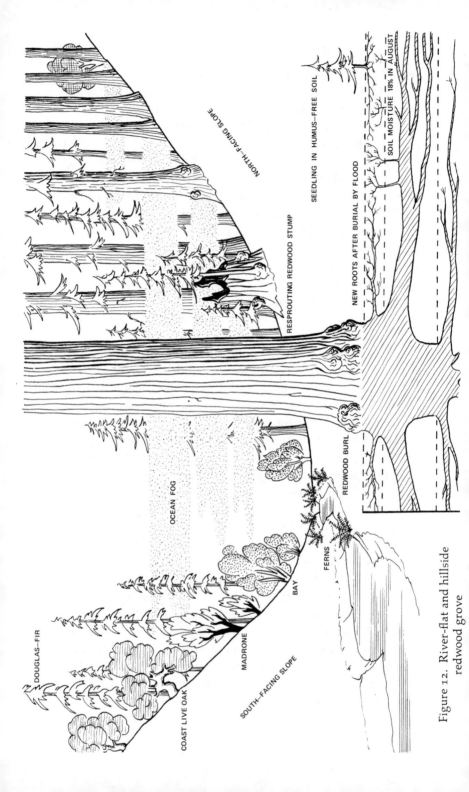

Figure 12. River-flat and hillside redwood grove

DOUGLAS–FIR

COAST LIVE OAK

MADRONE

BAY

FERNS

SOUTH–FACING SLOPE

OCEAN FOG

REDWOOD BURL

NORTH–FACING SLOPE

RESPROUTING REDWOOD STUMP

SEEDLING IN HUMUS–FREE SOIL

NEW ROOTS AFTER BURIAL BY FLOOD

SOIL MOISTURE 18% IN AUGUST

other trees. Douglas-fir is probably the most common coniferous companion to redwood throughout its range. It has an
extremely wide amplitude, for it thrives in the wetness of the
Olympic Peninsula rainforest as well as on the drier slopes of
western mountain ranges and is the most common conifer of
the broadleaf evergreen forest. Requiring the same conditions
for seedling health, bare mineral soil and sunlight, Douglas-fir
is strongly represented in redwood forests. But as it does not
stump sprout and is susceptible to death from fire and flood,
its success as a potential competitor is somewhat limited. It
is also relatively unresistant to insect damage. Two less frequently encountered cone bearers, California nutmeg, an endemic, and western yew which has a wider range, are found in
redwood country. They look somewhat alike in having sprays
of large flat needles, but nutmeg has hard berrylike fruits which
keep it from being a typical cone bearer. It is often classified as
a semiconifer.

Several shade-tolerant members of the broad-sclerophyll
forest comprise a by-no-means ubiquitous understory and also
grow at grove edge. Tanoak, California bay, madrone, chinquapin, and in some areas live oak, black oak, and Garry oak
share the light filtering down through the crown canopy. So
hungry are some individual trees of these species for light that
they angle out over stream beds or trails, become off-balance,
topple over, and then continue to send up branches growing to
the light at right angles to the horizontal trunk.

Numerous shrubs fill out a second underlayer: rhododendron, hazelnut, dogwood, ceanothus, poison oak, salal, huckleberry, Oregon grape, wax myrtle, and various berries. Western
azaleas are shiny-leafed bushes with fragrant gold-and-white
blossoms. The startling flame-red fruits of the western burning
bush smolder by trail or path. Looking like a giant stalk of
celery, spikenard, one of the herbaceous ginsengs, looms ten
feet tall and seems taken straight from a tropical jungle. Many
of the old-growth cathedral groves lack these understories except for shade-tolerant ground cover plants, and only an occasional vine maple or redwood sapling brings the tracery of
foliage to eye level.

The herb layer is characteristically rich with ferns, spore-bearing plants whose antecedents have flourished since before dinosaur times. Sword, chain, and wood ferns spray out like small green fountains by pathside, on fallen timber, and at the bases of trees and stumps. Epiphytic ferns, mosses, and club mosses grow in a green plush over branches and root tangles, reminiscent of a tropical cloud forest where epiphytes cover every inch of woody tissue. Bracken often spreads between the boles of the forest. Lady ferns are streamside and nod under the impact of drops tossed from the little cascades of coastal brooks.

Except in openings such as in meadows, along stream courses, and by trail and roadside, the wildflowers of the redwoods are often inconspicuous. The blossoms of Solomon's seal, woodland star, sugar scoop, and alum root glow like small white sparks in the trailside shadows. Red clintonia has a long stem supporting a top-heavy cluster of rosy bells. Alaska fringe cups have delicate pink-edged puffs along slender stalks. Wild ginger, buttercups and violets, trillium and other members of the lily family appear in the springtime woods drying out from the rains of winter.

As in all California's coast and foothill country, trees growing along the river bottoms and beside the larger streams are often somewhat different from those occurring slightly higher. Few redwood trees are at river edge. Their place is taken by riparian (streamside) vegetation which includes many species also found along interior river courses: box elder, cottonwood, willow, white alder, dogwood, and big-leaf maple. One such species, red alder, is typically coastal and is never found very far inland. Individual trees of the broadleaf and coniferous evergreen forests drop down to the steam bank here and there.

A generalization often made about redwoods is that one seldom sees animal life deep in their mature groves. One may look and listen in vain for signs of birds and mammals other than *Homo sapiens*. When by oneself the silence seems to have small sounds of its own. It is as though by listening hard enough one could hear the multiplying cells, the flowing sap, the stretching roots—the countless processes going on and on in these great trees, and around them, too, for a redwood forest is not quite the zoological desert it is often assumed to be. It is an ecosystem in its own right; and though animals such as black-tailed deer come and go in their constant quest for food, many others are at home in these shadowed stands.

Crested jays are the most easily recognized of several birds occurring in the dense foliage of coastal coniferous woods. Their cocky black crests, bright blue plumage, large size, and abrasive call are unmistakable. In a place where life seems to go about on hushed tiptoe, their boldness is refreshing. Any camp or picnic table will be under the surveillance of one or more of these friendly neighbors perched on a nearby limb, hoping to freeload off some generous visitor. Sit on a comfortable trailside log and watch quietly. Brown creepers and pygmy nuthatches will resume their appraisal of the insect population, apparently never stopping to rest during daylight hours, constantly pattering up and down the massive trunks and along the larger boughs. Chestnut-backed chickadees are on the same quest and work over the needled foliage. They often hang upsidedown as they probe with their bills into likely places. A large robin-like bird with a broad black V across its orange breast moves about quietly under shrubs or sits on lower limbs of trees. It is the varied thrush and belongs to the same family as the western robin. Winter wrens are even more ground dwelling. They flit in and out of root tangles and rest occasionally to pour out the rivulets of song so typical of wrens. Golden-crowned kinglets flutter through the masses of limb and leaf pausing only to pick up a tasty insect.

Though mammals are harder to find in these dark groves, one species, the Roosevelt elk, has almost become a symbol of the northern redwoods. No doubt this is because of the fine herd maintained at Prairie Creek State Park in Humboldt County. Not mammals of the dark forest only, they browse their way in the more open glades and meadows, feeding on the vine maples and shrubs. Closely related to the Rocky Mountain elk, this particular subspecies is restricted to the humid forests of the Pacific Northwest. The Olympic elk of Walt

Disney fame belongs to the same group. Many of the parks in Washington's rainforest are supposedly kept open by the browsing of the elk, for they spend the winter there when the higher ranges are snowbound.

At the other extreme in size is the Trowbridge shrew, a tiny fellow whose insect prey may be almost as large as the captor and whose runways tunnel the duff. Two kinds of chipmunks, Sonoma and Townsend, are redwood residents; and the western gray squirrel of the oak groves is also at home in coniferous forests. One would suppose the gray squirrel to be in severe competition with the agile chickaree or Douglas squirrel, but the latter's diet of cones and nuts is very different from that of its acorn eating cousin. Chickarees often nest in woodpecker holes small enough to prevent entry by the larger carnivores, such as bobcats and mountain lions, and too high for gray foxes and skunks.

One of the most intriguing, if rarely seen, animals of the redwoods is the mountain beaver. It is not related to the true beaver except that it too is a rodent. Looking like an outsized gopher, it lives in a system of tunnels whose entrances are screened over with brushy cover, berry patches, fern fronds, salal, and the like. Plants make up its diet which includes needles and leaves. It digs efficiently, and its task is made that much easier when it chooses to construct its tunnel maze in the damp earth of streamside, which it often does.

The many creeks, moist places, and rivers of the redwood country are home to amphibians of more than passing interest. The rosy-hued *Ensatina* and the ocelot-spotted giant salamander are common, as are several newts and other salamanders frequenting this damp habitat. *Ensatina* keeps undercover much of the time, in rodent burrows and hollow logs, under leaf litter, and in other hidden places. The giant salamander apparently prefers being close to water, for it seldom goes far from stream or creek. On occasion, however, it takes to climbing tree trunks.

Other oddities of the sequoia woods are the large banana slugs, shell-less land gastropods unable to live in drier environments or expose themselves to the direct sun for too long a time. Any desiccation of their mucus-covered skin would be fatal. They ooze about on the duff, feeding on vegetation and litter.

As with all biotic communities, the redwoods have their share of animals that feed on each other. Owls and the giant salamanders watch for amphibians, small reptiles, and rodents such as red tree and deer mice. Various insectivorous birds, shrews, and smaller salamanders hunt tiny game. Raccoons forage about in their favorite streamside haunts for frogs and other water dwellers including the young of fish such as steelhead and cutthroat trout and salmon which begin mature life by spawning in these coastal rivers. Regardless of the species discussed above, these great groves, it is true, do not support the animal life so rich in many other communities. Lack of variety in diet, scarcity of grass seeds, and the absence of sheltering cover, particularly in the old-growth stands that are so impressive and dramatic, help account for the paucity of both individuals and species.

Very little is written about redwoods without serious concern for their future. We know they are some of the most valuable timber resources, and provision must be made for their most efficient utilization. Esthetically we may deplore the ugly scars and slash piles of their harvesting, but we will not be able to prevent this major industry from operating in these coastal forests. Nor should we wish to stop its activities entirely. The wood is too useful and of too fine a quality for abandoning sequoia as a timber crop. Wise forestry practices should ensure a continuing supply from maturing second growth.

Be that as it may, we are the custodians of one of the world's most wonderful natural heritages, the proud old-growth redwood forests. Through the activities of various conservation groups, the American people have had the foresight to set aside a number of the virgin stands which invariably call forth wonder and admiration from all who come to stand at the feet of these great giants. Not too much is left of the privately owned "cathedral nave" forest, and its acreage gets smaller each month as the lumber companies continue their felling.

A major victory in the battle for their conservation was won in 1968, when Congress passed an act creating a 58,000 acre national park in the Redwood Creek area of Humboldt County and in Del Norte County's Mill Creek section. A corridor connects the two portions which has 33 miles of beach. It includes three state parks which may be retained by the state, if California should choose to continue to own them. Lost Man and Little Lost Man creeks are prime old-growth areas long urged for preservation. Through a land-swap arrangement, private lumber companies received roughly 13,000 acres of Forest Service land in return for timberland given to the park. The remaining acreage is being acquired through purchase.

Over fifty years of unflagging effort are at last bearing fruit. The finest remaining specimens will be protected from the logger's chain saws. There is much question, however, about the possible long-term effects of complete protection. Many foresters and ecologists are doubting the wisdom of such a procedure. The total absence of fire and flood may bring about an eventual loss of vigor and even their demise, allowing competitive species such as tanoak and Douglas-fir to replace the redwood stands. We need to know much more about their behavior and life history before we can truthfully prognosticate their future. It may be that we will have to counteract the results of our interference with the processes of nature by further interference.

Oak woodland near Arroyo Mocho

# 7. Woodpeckers in Oak Trees

Time itself seems to yawn and take a nap in the long golden hours of a foothill summer day. Bees hum in the straw-dry grass, dipping into the curl-rimmed saucers of white and russet mariposa lilies, hovering among the purple trumpets of harvest brodiaea, both late bloomers and heralds of summer in the oak-dotted parks of the foothills. Scrub jays answer each other from thickets of buckeye and other brushy growth. Yellow-billed magpies swoop onto fence posts, ready for flight into nearby oaks on the hillside. Digger pines sift the sunlight through their sparse foliage.

Little country roads pursue circuitous routes, here reaching around grassy slopes, tawny-brown in late June, there keeping company with drought shrunken streams or hanging onto steep-sided roadcuts.

If one pulls off on many of these narrow tracks fenced by aging posts and the ubiquitous barbed wire, he should soon become acquainted with one of California's most typical foothill residents, the acorn woodpecker. His shrill JACK-A *jack-a jack-a* has all the forthrightness of a football coach giving hell to a losing team. With scalloped white-and-black flight he nips from tree to fence post and back again with a seemingly endless source of energy. His red cap glimmers back to the nape of his neck, and the white and ebony cowl around his face frames the pale circle of his eye.

Watching a *carpentero*, as he was called by the early Spanish settlers, fitting acorns into holes he has drilled for the purpose is an instructive experience. He positions the acorn, tip end first; then he drives it in with a few hard whacks until it is flush with the surface. His drum major costume becomes him as he clings to the side of the tree, head back, eyes alert, and feet and tail firmly braced.

Once central California slides down the eastern slope of the outer coastal mountains it buckles into the accordion pleats of the middle and inner Coast Ranges. Though the interior ridges surrounding San Francisco Bay and the western Delta are influenced by the sea and its foggy winds, our transect at last is moving away from maritime California. Summers are hotter and of longer duration; winters are colder; and rainfall averages drop considerably in many places. However, most of the biotic communities to which the book has already introduced the reader remain familiar—chaparral, coastal scrub, broadleaf evergreen forest, streamside vegetation, and fire pine—but with variations. This inland mosaic is somewhat different from its maritime counterpart. A few new dominant species and three new communities must be added: northern oak woodland, foothill pine woodland, and savanna. Not that these are absent from the outer Coast Ranges—quite the contrary—but since they are best developed in the interior it seemed advisable to leave them for this chapter. One community disappears, the redwood forest with its dark dignity; and the coastal closed-cone pines and cypresses must also be left behind on their picturesque bluffs and headlands.

Some features are approximately the same in both environments. There are the grassy balds which summer-bronze ridge-tops and sides. Chaparral still covers many southward-facing slopes and steeper crests with its rough homespun. Live oaks, bay, buckeye, and madrone thicken on north-facing slopes and mingle with the typical trees of canyon bottoms—willow, alder, cottonwood, and big-leaf maple. Sage scrub spreads gray-brown chenille over dry hills swelling above grass-carpeted broad valleys to the east. For the most part, a casual glance reveals little that is different from the ranges neighboring the sea. A number of species, however, are absent. Salal and wax myrtle, for example, are gone and will not reappear. Other mesophytic shrubs and trees such as ninebark, tanoak, California nutmeg, western yew, and Douglas-fir, though missing from mounts Diablo and Hamilton, reoccur on the Sierran slope. Yet many members of the chaparral are as common here as they were on the more humid coast: toyon, hollyleaf cherry, chamise, poison oak, silk tassel bush, coffeeberry, redberry, mountain mahogany, and scrub oak.

Two outstanding species of the southern sage scrub—black sage and wild, or California, buckwheat—range as far north as Mount Hamilton. Together with California sagebrush and bush monkeyflower they form a thin cover on the drier hills. All are subshrubs; and two, sagebrush and black sage, are deciduous in summer. During the hotter months this sage scrub community has a very different aspect from its coastal scrub counterpart which is thick with bracken and sword fern, umbels of many kinds, and berry brambles. It is in great contrast to the half-dead-appearing similar formation of the dry interior hills which looks as though dried twigs have been thrust willy-nilly into the inhospitable soil. The inclusion of black sage and wild buckwheat, never very lush in growth anyway, helps account for the dissimilarity; but the increased aridity of the environment keeps out the more mesophytic species and threatens to dehydrate those shared in common. As in the outer ranges, elements of the scrub are often temporary, moving in after fire and then giving way to the reinvading chaparral or forest.

In place of the coastal conifers, drought-resistant species now enter the landscape. Though more common in southern California, Coulter pine occurs as far north as Mount Diablo. Not only is it distinguished for being one of the state's native sons, it has the world's heaviest cone; specimens 18 inches long and weighing up to nine or ten pounds have been collected. They have thick, coarse, clawlike scales. Unlike the gaunt and somewhat starved looking digger pine, Coulter pine, though also a xerophytic species, has a prosperous, well-fed and -watered air about it, particularly on better sites. Plants of the chaparral such as squaw bush, manzanita, redberry, and poison oak frequently consort with it, and small live oaks are not uncommon companions.

Knobcone pines keep to their sterile sites and pockets on these inner hills, associating with chamise and the more drought-tolerant manzanitas. The yellow pines have a spotty distribution in the coastal portion of the transect. From the Santa Lucia Mountains south of Monterey, they skip to sandy badlands in the Santa Cruz Mountains, go on to two rather confined localities on Mount Hamilton, and become more prevalent on the inner ranges in Napa and Sonoma counties to the north.

Sargent cypress has a widely scattered distribution in the interior, appearing casually on Mount Hamilton and reaching south to Santa Barbara County and north to Mendocino County. California juniper is new to the transect. Very drought resistant, it is the westernmost tree-size species of its genus in North America. One can find it on rocky outcrops on Mount Diablo and follow it north to Tehama County, east to the Sierra foothills, and south in the inner Coast Range. It forms a woodland of its own in the broken country west of Mount Pinos in Ventura County.

The most typical conifer of hot-summer California slopes is the digger pine—that awkward, off-balance excuse for a shade tree with its thin, long-needled foliage. It shares a derogatory and undeserved name with a group of California Indians who did much more than dig. They wove some of the world's most beautiful basketry, a type of craftsmanship that has never been surpassed. Their namesake tree has a precisely defined range: the dry interior from 200 to roughly 4,000 feet. It is never found on the outer coastal bluffs nor on the eastern slopes of the central Sierra Nevada. Truly a Californian, it does not exist in Oregon and is rare south of the Tehachapis, though a stand occurs near Gorman which extends east for some distance. Because it frequently accompanies the deciduous blue oak, one of the more drought-resistant trees of the interior, botanists speak of this partnership as the digger pine—blue oak association. In general, the characteristic conifer of this community is a lanky and unappreciated tree. However, it has a remarkable ability to withstand conditions imposed by the hot interior summer-dry hills. Infrequent on deep, fine-grained valley soils, its typical substrate varies from the coarse alluvium of foothill riverine beds to rocky slopes on both sides of the Great Valley. One of the most drought-enduring pines, its light gray, drooping needles reflect much desiccating insolation, and transpiration surfaces are reduced because of the sparse foliage.

Though there are parklike sites in the foothill pine community where one receives the impression of a random scattering of trees whose canopies seldom touch, there is a considerable variation in density of cover. In places, blue oaks combine with related species and other shrubs and trees of brushland or broadleaf evergreen forest to mass in heavy thickets or spread out on the more open hillsides typical of many oak-dominated woodland areas. Digger pines often sprawl in thin groves up through a cover of wiry chaparral. Elsewhere, diggers and blue oaks grow together on undulating grassy slopes which in early spring look as though they are carefully tended golf fairways.

Though savanna is the driest of the three community types we are discussing here, foothill pine woodland is one of the less well-watered California habitats. Rainfall ranges from 15 to as high as 40 inches; but long, hot, dry summers cancel out many of the benefits of the increased precipitation of more favorable sites. Northern oak woodland (to distinguish it from the southern oak woodland of Los Angeles County and south which has a somewhat different composition), on the other hand, enjoys a higher minimal rainfall figure of from 25 to 40 inches. This community is confined to the northern edge of our transect, phasing out in Napa County where foothill pine woodland takes over on the inner Coast Ranges and continues to the south. Northern oak woodland has strong affinities with the broadleaf evergreen forest as golden and interior live oaks are joined by big-leaf maple, black oak, and California buckeye. One species, the arboreal form of the Garry oak, is largely confined to this community, which extends from the redwoods on the coast to the savannas of the inner hills. Strikingly majestic in appearance with a large spreading crown, it is the only oak that enters British Columbia. A shrub form of this tree occurs south to the northern section of Los Angeles County.

One more community disengages itself from the vegetation mosaic of the inner Coast Ranges. This is savanna, a term commonly used for the tree-dotted stretches of the drier tropics. In California, it is the transitional community between the woodlands of the hills and the grasslands of the broader valleys. Where the original trees still stand, they are fewer in number and more widely spaced than those of the woodlands proper. For the most part they are valley oaks, with blue oaks and interior live oaks making an occasional appearance, as do buckeye and a few xerophytic shrubs clinging to footholds on roadcuts and rockier places. Where the trees cluster in arroyos and along stream courses, they are often joined by riparian vegetation typical of the dry interior. Characteristically, these sparsely wooded lands flow down out of the forest and scrub of the higher crests, slopes, and canyons of the Coast Ranges. Driving to Vacaville or to Tracy via Livermore, you can quickly note the dark mounds of the upper brush and tree-blanketed hills, and see how these separate into freckled slopes giving way in turn to cultivated fields, range, and residential tracts with an occasional old valley oak left standing here and there.

California's oaks are almost as exceptional as its pines. Sixteen species of *Quercus* (oak) occur here in contrast to Arizona's twelve; and only two, possibly three, are shared with the neighbor state to the east—Palmer, *turbinella* (which might be called desert scrub oak after the habitat), and golden, as some botanists contend that this species continues as far east as New Mexico. Three tree oaks—golden, black and Garry—and two shrub types—deer and huckleberry—are also found in Oregon. Thus the Californian region can claim nine for its own. The endemic tree forms are coast, interior, and Engelmann live oaks; and valley, blue, island, and Macdonald oaks. The last two are found on offshore islands. The shrub types are scrub oak and leather oak, one of the few species confined largely to serpentine soils. (Serpentine, incidentally, has been officially designated as California's state mineral—a distinction for one of the state's most infertile soil types.) A number of oak species do well on xeric sites inasmuch as they occur in arid regions of California and Arizona. Not only are they deep rooted, their foliage has many drought-resisting features, which is particularly true of live oaks. Though most of the deciduous oaks, in general, prefer mesic situations, some of them, notably blue oak, have leaves designed to restrict water loss. Most oaks are quite fire adapted as well, and readily stump sprout after burning.

The genus tends to hybridize with ease, and species intergrade with bewildering complexity. For this reason it is often difficult to determine a specimen's exact status, particularly one of the shrubbier forms. They may be dwarfs of generally larger types, examples of true scrub forms, or hybrids of just about any small oaks present in the area.

Because they are so much a part of this section of the state and vary considerably in their habitat tolerances and preferences as well as appearance and behavior, it might be useful to discuss each oak species of the mid-latitude Coast Ranges in some detail.

*Valley oak* (*Quercus lobata*).—This is the most impressive local tree of the oak group for sheer size and patriarchal demeanor. It bends its huge limbs over such diverse understories as shopping centers and chicken runs, where allowed to remain. A deciduous species, in wintertime it looks as though it had finally succumbed to insect infestation or drought. But after a month or so of springtime warmth, it leafs into great spreading crowns that bless the hot interior valleys with cool dense shade. Though found as high as 3,000 feet and on steep gradients, it is generally confined to foothills and stream courses of broad valleys, north to the Pit River and south to Los Angeles County, particularly where the water table is relatively high and floods were common in the early days. The Latinized name refers to lobes scalloping the leaf edges; thus the foliage resembles that of the white oak, a close relative and deciduous resident of the eastern half of the country.

*Coast live oak (Quercus agrifolia).*—As its name implies, it is mostly restricted to the outer Coast Ranges, though it occasionally occurs in interior sites, particularly in the southern part of the state. It is considered an evergreen as it does not shed all of its leaves at one time, but many old leaves are discarded when new foliage is produced in spring. The young leaves are a glistening, rich green in contrast to older leaves which are darker and somewhat curled under around the edges. Both young and old foliage has the sheen, crispness, and shape of holly leaves, prickles and all. Where the atmosphere has sufficient humidity, coastal oaks are often hung with "grandfather beards" of *Usnea* and *Ramalina*, pendant lichens.

*Tanoak, or tanbark oak (Lithocarpus densiflora).*—This handsome tree of the broadleaf evergreen, redwood, and Douglas-fir forests is not a true oak. Instead of flat scales its acorn cups look as if covered with patches of brown turkish toweling. That it has mesic preferences is evident from the communities in which it is commonly present. Though found on the west slopes of the Sierra, its typical domain is on the coast and not too far inland at that. The foliage, often larger and more spearpoint shaped than that of live oaks, when new is woolly in texture and delicately pink, changing to light golden-green before full maturity.

*Interior live oak (Quercus wislizenii).*—In appearance, it is much like its coastal counterpart, but its leaves are generally more leathery and less curled, and the tree is likely to be less massive. There is a major difference in behavior. Leaves remain on the branches for two seasons instead of one and begin to drop late in the second summer. The best way to tell them apart is by geographical ranges. The interior species takes over from the coast live oak, beginning in the middle Coast Ranges, and just about supplants it on the eastern slopes of the inner ranges. The inland species occasionally is found in what would be considered the territory of the coastal form, for instance, on Mount Tamalpais. Where they are both present, they usually do not mix, having somewhat different requirements. Interior live oak can stand lower temperatures and more xeric sites. If it occurs on moist northward-facing slopes, it grows above the coastal species. The latter seems to keep to canyon bottoms, more humid hillsides, and warmer pockets. Though appearing to be out-of-place on upper, southward-facing crests, when found there the coast live oak, presumably, is taking advantage of higher temperatures. Increased precipitation at these elevations may compensate for what would otherwise be a drier location. Both, in their own range, occur on rolling contours, on deep-soiled broad drainage floors, and even on the shallow soils of the higher ridges. Like coast live oak, the interior form may have a grassy underlayer or it consorts with such chaparral shrubs as yerba santa, manzanita, ceanothus, mountain mahogany, and coffeeberry. Blue oak, buckeye, digger pine, and bay are other frequent associates, occasionally crowding in patches of forest. When the groves are more open, the character and individuality of the tree's rounded masses are quite apparent.

*Canyon, or golden, oak* (*Quercus chrysolepis*).—With still a third name, maul oak, this is one of the more widely distributed species, ranging from Oregon down into Baja California, and, according to some authorities, extending into Arizona and possibly beyond. It typically occurs on canyon floors and sides, sometimes in narrow gullies, and often on rocky terraces where it seems about to lose its footing and topple to the depths below. It may form pure stands, but it is usually found with other oaks and conifers common to the area. There is great variation in leaf shape. The younger ones are often sharply spined; but older leaves, which persist the longest of the three evergreen oaks of the transect as they take from three to four years before dropping, are usually toothless. Distinguishing characteristics useful to the amateur naturalist are the color and thickness of the acorn cup. Though occasionally thin, it is more commonly heavy, woody, and of a golden color, hence a fourth name: golden cup oak.

*California black oak (Quercus kelloggii).*—This species with its brilliantly green, deeply cut deciduous leaves is certainly one of the most beautiful of its group. Frequently, though not necessarily, found with yellow pines, it seldom grows below 1,000 feet and usually keeps to areas having rainfall above 25 inches. In San Diego County, near the southern limits of its range, it grows in a rather peculiar woodland of its own; and the coniferous partner is Coulter pine, one of the more xerophytic cone bearers. Where conditions are favorable it may be quite large in size, but it rarely is as impressive as valley oaks of venerable age. Black oaks appear to thrive in a variety of environments, from scant-soiled rocky slopes to deep-loamed valley floors, and shifts from open groves where it may be alone to mingle with other trees of the same altitude preferences.

*Blue oak (Quercus douglasii).*—Without exception, this is a foothill tree. It rarely occurs above 4,000 feet and is most unusual near the coast. The common name refers to leaf color, though at some times the bluish haze on the deciduous foliage is less apparent than at others. Then it is difficult to distinguish from neighboring valley oaks; but in general the leaf is less lobed and smaller in size. Blue oaks seldom become as large as valley oaks, and they rarely venture out onto the broader floors where the latter is king. Though they integrate with appropriate live oaks, digger pine, buckeye, and xerophytic shrubs of the inner woodlands, they often sprinkle themselves about in pure parklike stands. They may crowd together, and the canopies touch and intermingle; elsewhere the trees dissociate from each other and push out cramped, awkwardly angled branches, surprisingly short for the height of the tree. At best, however, they are broad-spreading, good-looking trees and welcome providers of shade on a hot summer day. Another of their common names, rock oak, points up the fact that they are often found on rocky outcrops of the foothills rimming both sides of the Central Valley.

Though fire and man have been as active here as in the outer hills, climate and edaphic conditions, in general, account for these rolling parks, and for their inclusion in the natural landscapes of California. Where rainfall averages 10 inches or below, plants of the chaparral usually fail to compete with more xerophytic scrub and herbaceous species. Much of the extreme eastern inner range country, where the foothills flatten out beneath the floor of the Central Valley, experiences even less than 10 inches of annual precipitation because of rainshadow. Large portions of the woodland communities enjoy more rainfall, however, particularly those at higher elevations. Of great importance is the long summer drought with the added complication of high temperatures during the dry season. Additional factors too are at work—soil particle size, the presence of impervious hardpans and claypans, compaction of grassy root masses—which leads us to a close examination of the herbaceous partners of the trees which are such outstanding features of this gentle and charming landscape, and to discussion of how the trees themselves fare so well where many smaller woody species do not intrude.

The highly drought-resistant features of grasses are of prime significance in their sharing of this marginal environment, particularly the annuals, either native to California or introduced from elsewhere. By and large, they grow more quickly than the perennial grass species, which, though having drought-adapted features of their own, were driven from their home territories (see chapter 8) around midpoint of the last century. Rapid growth enables grass to use the available moisture of spring before it disappears under the powerful rays of the summer sun. The original bunchgrasses, of long residence in the foothills, included such species as needlegrasses, blue wild rye, various bromes, melicgrass, and deergrass. They were replaced by fast-growing annuals—downy chess, foxtail fescue, wild oats, and the like—opportunistic species able to mature quickly and head out before the harsh heat of summer.

The soils of the interior valleys and gentle slopes also influence the types of vegetation cover occurring here. Deep valley and terrace soils generally are accumulations of residual material washed down from higher slopes. The finer particles tend to be glued together, resulting in sticky clays which absorb water slowly and are difficult to penetrate. Soils on terrace benches often develop a hardpan close to the surface. This impervious layer tends to concentrate moisture in the upper soil levels resulting in water puddling and deoxygenation during the rainy season and rapid dry-off during drought.

The optimum growth period, therefore, is limited to a narrow time span between saturation and dehydration. Quick-growing, shallow, fibrous-rooted grasses and forbs are remarkably adapted to just such a situation, making the most of the few weeks allowed them before they succumb, leaving seeds or underground plant parts to which they die back during the hot dry months.

What of the trees? They forego most of the surface moisture, leaving that to their herbaceous companions, and instead probe for deeper water with long roots. Even so, valley oaks tend to remain close to drainage channels where moisture collects in permanent or ephemeral streams and where the water table is usually high. Blue oaks, though winter deciduous, have the small, leathery leaves typical of drought resistance. Live oaks share xerophytic characteristics to an even greater degree, as they are decidedly sclerophyllous as well as evergreen. One of the most effective means of successfully sharing a meager water supply is wide spacing: the drier the site, the fewer the trees. The roots of each compete vigorously for the available moisture. As the rainfall averages decrease on descent to the floor of the Central Valley, the point is reached where trees cannot exist at all, unless, as in the case of valley oaks and riparian species, underground or surface water is available for most of the year. Out on these rolling plains, grass and its partner forbs reign supreme or did until irrigation inaugurated the drastic changes which have so altered the aspect of many interior hills and valleys.

In regard to the distribution of chaparral within the realm of the drier woodlands, there are numerous islands of both chaparral and sage scrub, and brush species sometimes form a dense understory beneath the trees in more mesic sites. Low rainfall in the savanna precludes much brush growth, however, and it is rarely found on the lower approaches to the Great Valley. When chaparral occupies isolated patches within the oak groves, most probably edaphic conditions differ from those of the open woodland. Sclerophyll shrubs depend, not so much on surface water, as do the grasses, but on moisture sources in lower horizons and buried in bedrock but accessible to vigorously probing roots. Clay accumulations in dense subsoils of terrace and valley floor would prevent such root development. The shallow-soiled, well-drained, xeric hillsides and ridges with pockets of bedrock water remaining long after the onset of summer drought seem to be the natural home of brushlands, unless fire or man have interfered. Deep, well-drained soils with plentiful subsurface water can accommodate heavy woodland and even forest. Even steep slopes in the transect's inner Coast Ranges, if facing north and possessing the proper edaphic conditions, can be clothed with such vegetation.

Three additional factors are also active in maintaining more open natural landscapes. Root and stem masses of grass are sometimes so compacted that seeds of woody species cannot penetrate them or reach the soil beneath. If they were successful in germinating, chances are that the quick sprouting grasses would soon deprive them of water during the short growing season. For many prairies this is a possible perpetuating factor. Another influence is fire, destroying the seedlings of woody species but with little long-term effect on the grasses which readily renew themselves the following spring. The older trees of open woodlands seldom undergo serious damage as grass fires are relatively cool and, in the absence of brush, quickly burn out. Furthermore, most oaks crown- or stump-sprout. Unless severely injured by repeated fires or browsing animals, they eventually return to their former appearance. Stock and wildlife cropping, referred to above, is the third factor controlling the maintenance of open country.

These are lively communities, particularly in spring. Canyon oak and California hairstreak butterflies emerge from pupae, ready to lay eggs from which will come larval forms feeding mainly on oak leaves. California sister, silver blue, and tailed copper are the other common butterflies of the oak woodlands, bright flashes against the newly green hills.

Trees and grass offer more than food to their animal associates. The herbaceous cover provides shade and shelter for jackrabbits and many kinds of wild mice. The oaks serve as observation posts for hawks and other predators, and are rich sources of food for the acorn eaters—magpies, scrub jays, mule deer, and ground squirrels among them. The attractive pink-fronted Lewis' woodpeckers, western bluebirds, titmice, and black-headed grosbeaks call and carol, hunt and probe for insects or seeds.

Two bird inhabitants of the woodlands have rather more complex relationships with their arboreal neighbors. The acorn woodpecker feeds on their acorns but not to the point of preventing their replacement, nor does he seriously damage the trees in his hole drilling as he seldom penetrates into living tissue. Dead snags and other nonliving woody material may be actually preferred as they are more easily drilled. The scrub jay may even enter into a mutually beneficial association when he buries the acorns in the ground, unconsciously taking the role of a competent nurseryman as he places them in the substrate most suitable for their germination, mineral soil under duff. This activity is possibly of much value to the oaks, for their acorns without such aid often come to rest in tangles of dry grass stems where germination is improbable. The oaks feed the jays and the jays plant the oaks, a most useful relationship. Both birds use the trees for nest sites. The woodpecker excavates holes in dead trunks and branches; the jay uses living trees for support and to harvest the twigs as nest material.

Speaking of acorn woodpeckers, let us digress for a moment to appreciate a rather remarkable bird. Although it has some unusual patterns of behavior, described below, it shares many of the features distinguishing the group as a whole. Its tail is used as a brace. Bent at an angle and propped against the surface of whatever the woodpecker is climbing, it serves to support the bird as it hitches along. Like the rest of its tribe, the acorn woodpecker can drill into bark and wood with speed and strength that seem almost power tooled. Not only is the cranium unusually thick for birds in general, but spongy tissue takes up the pounding jar of hole boring. Most woodpeckers have a long tongue which fits into a sheath around the back of the skull. When extended, it projects some distance in front of the bill and serves to capture grubs living in bark and other tree tissue. Bristles on the tongue assist in the process of grub capture. Many authorities feel that the larvae which frequently infest acorns are the principle target. Others are certain that the woodpecker is primarily after the contents of the acorns themselves. Regardless, this particular species depends on acorns for the primary food source, though it may chase flies or hunt worms on occasion.

One of the attributes which distinguish this species from other woodpeckers, indeed, from many other birds as well, is a pronounced type of colonial behavior. It is social to the degree that it excavates large nesting holes for the communal tending of eggs and young. Any bird in the colony will feed any fledgling regardless of its parentage. Presumably, mates and food are shared in the same relaxed fashion. A well-developed colony is the place to look for the classic acorn storage places, trunks of dead or living trees, fence posts, and wire poles, often so full of holes and acorns that one can hardly see the wood between.

Such tight interaction between organisms of the same species is not too common, but close relationships between organisms of different species in a community are frequent. When there is an intimate association between two or more dissimilar species, this is commonly spoken of as symbiosis. The term includes three basic types of such a relationship with gradients from one to the other so that there is often no abrupt shift or hard line drawn between them. They are commensalism, mutualism, and parasitism. The first implies that one organism lives with another, deriving benefit from the relationship but without injury to the partner. The second, as the word indicates, means benefit to both organisms and danger to none. The third is more sinister; one organism lives at the expense of another, even to the point occasionally of killing its host.

The woodlands of the foothills have many examples of all three symbiotic associations, including degrees of each. Such variations in degree often reflect incomplete knowledge on our part of the exact relationship. It is difficult to know whether a certain interaction, or "coaction" as it is sometimes termed, is parasitic or semiparasitic when there is little data on the relationship involved.

The insect world is one of highly developed parasitism. In the foothills, bot flies prey on deer, chipmunks, ground squirrels, and wood rats. Aphids suck plant juices and in turn are utilized by braconid wasps. Oak moths defoliate their host trees and are sought by such insect feeders as bushtits and flycatchers. Gall insects are among the most fascinating of the oak-grove parasites. Small organisms known as cynipid wasps are gall makers; each species produces distinct forms of galls and is usually restricted to one type of tree. The story is by no means simple. Two generations are involved. Female wasps oviposit their eggs on leaf buds, young twigs or acorns, unopened catkins, and the like. The eggs hatch into larvae which feed on the plant tissue and make an irritating substance which stimulates the tree into producing galls. The round feather-light brown protuberances, or "apples," scattered on scrub or tree oaks are familiar to most of us (see Figure 13). They are really benign tumors in that large numbers of wasp attacks would be necessary to harm an oak seedling. Only female wasps develop in the large round galls. When the temperatures of spring force the oaks to bud, the wasps emerge and lay their eggs on leaf buds. Another set of galls is produced, and these are often bizarre in color and shape. Some are shiny little pink blobs bristling with antennae like the stalked eyes of snails. Others look like tiny champagne glasses. The larvae of these galls are of both sexes. Their adults mate and the females complete the cycle by laying eggs that will hatch into "apple" gall-making larvae again.

Not only do the wasps feed on the galls; bees, woodpeckers,

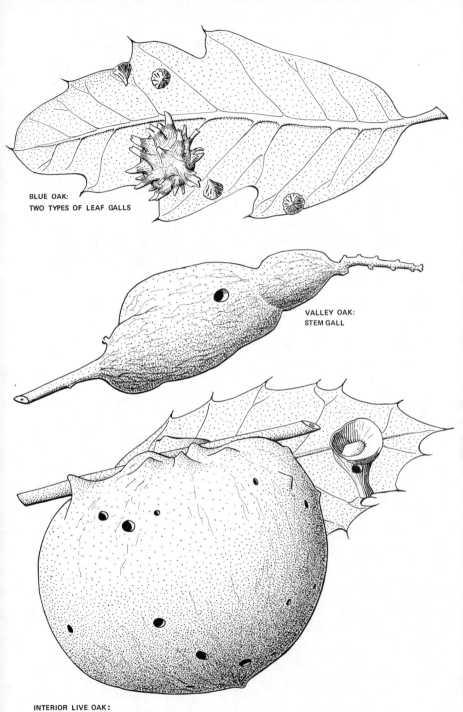

BLUE OAK:
TWO TYPES OF LEAF GALLS

VALLEY OAK:
STEM GALL

INTERIOR LIVE OAK:
ALTERNATE GENERATIONS OF SAME SPECIES OF GALL WASP PRODUCED THESE
VERY DIFFERENT STEM AND LEAF GALLS

Figure 13. Several types of oak galls

and ants also enjoy the sweet substance exuded from some of them. Guests, often other cynipid wasps, share the table with the original inhabitants. Both guest and host wasps are parasitized by a very pretty little irridescent blue-green chalcid fly which, disdainful of the gall itself, feeds directly on the tiny creatures within.

Where life has spectra and range, from grass stems to oak trees, from wasps to woodpeckers, the network of its patterns is complex in structure and rich in detail. Things live on things which live on things, combining and recombining in innumerable symbiotic associations, spinning out food webs and energy chains that reflect the great diversity life has enjoyed in Californian hills.

Sacramento River near Elkhorn Ferry

# 8. Riverlands

No natural landscapes of California have been so altered by man as its bottomlands. The grass-rich stretches of the great Central Valley are, for the most part, lost to orchards and vineyards, cotton and alfalfa fields. Many miles of curving green ribbon along its water courses have been eradicated, replaced by the sterile concrete of flood control and navigation channels. Most of the tule marshes of the Delta country are now neatly diked rice paddies. On the freeway between San Francisco Bay and Sacramento one forgets that this was once wild land with golden beaver going about their industrious ways and great blue herons on guard with that watchful immobility so peculiarly their own. To recreate this world of

slough, bank, and riverway takes more than the simple list-
ing of what can be recalled, or guessed, was there. It needs
imagination coupled with a persistent searching for the last
few remnants of the original river country. It means that the
bait-and-beer shacks and houseboats, and the ocean freighters
and bridges must retreat from consciousness, if one is to evoke
the past. Instead, walk as the Indians did on game trails
through the riverine undergrowth, where silence and birdsong
are complementary.

In a way, those times were harder for the Great Valley. It
was alternately soaked and shriveled as the floods of spring
were followed by the hot winds of summer. Then the Valley
knew a seasonal pattern it will never experience again as long
as man controls the rivers flowing into it. Enterprising as always, the first white men to arrive here knew a good thing
when they saw it, and the Valley did not disappoint them. It is
one of the richest pieces of agricultural land in the world today,
blessed with good climate, rich soil, and an irrigation potential
unequaled in the West.

To those interested in the natural landscapes of California,
the Central Valley of Indian days would have been far more
fascinating than it is now. None, not even the most enthusiastic
sugar-beet farmer, can seriously claim that State Highway 99
from Bakersfield to Sacramento is one of California's great
scenic highways. Little towns once broke the monotony of the
two-lane highway back in the 1930s; but by-passed as they are
by the multilaned throughway, they almost escape notice.

Two hundred years ago, the Valley had many features that
would have been most attractive to naturalists, professional
and amateur alike: great shallow lakes in the southern end with
staggering numbers of waterfowl and other birds, the many
rivers flowing from the Sierran slope, and the network of
woodland bordering these streams with tangles of welcome
green during the warmth of summer. The Delta, where the two
great river systems, the San Joaquin and the Sacramento, meet
to flow out through Suisun Bay to the Golden Gate, was a vast
complex of basin and island, natural levee and slough. Its
marshes were host to birdlife that must have numbered in the

millions, particularly in the season of migration. Roads then would have connected a series of cool shaded oases bordering riverbeds or skirted sloughs and lakes teeming with wild creatures making the Valley their home.

But history brought its changes; and after the discovery of gold in the Sierra foothills it was but a matter of time until the great potential of this flat-floored topographical oddity was recognized. The last noun is used advisedly, for the Great Valley is unique in the mountainous West. There is no other flat area of comparable size west of the Rockies. Elsewhere any level terrain, such as Oregon's Willamette Valley, is either much smaller or broken by intruding hills. Any good relief map of the United States will show California's Great Valley to be an outstanding feature. Geologically, it is simple. It is merely a trough between the Coast Ranges and the Sierra Nevada, filled with thousands of feet of alluvium washed down from the surrounding mountains. Lying in the rainshadow of the Coast Ranges, the Valley has a rainfall which varies from between 30 and 40 inches near Redding to less than 7 south of Bakersfield. Most of it is relatively dry, and its rivers are like the fingers of beneficent gods to the farmers living here. These streams ensure an underground water supply from artesian wells, and impounded behind dams, they become power and water resources without parallel in California.

The four southernmost streams, the Kern, Tule, Kaweah, and southern distributaries of the Kings, are not part of the San Joaquin river system; but irrigation has altered the original drainage patterns to some extent. Prior to reclamation measures, these rivers fed two lakes, Tulare and Buena Vista, locked in a basin by the huge alluvial fan which the Kings River system built during ages of eroding the Sierra Nevada.

The fifth of these southern Sierra streams, the San Joaquin, flows west until, deflected by the broad, alluvial plain fronting the inner Coast Range, it turns northward. The next five rivers —Merced, Tuolumne, Stanislaus, Mokelumne, and Cosumnes —feed one by one, at right angles, into the main, northward-flowing stream.

In the northern end of the Great Valley, the American,

Feather, and Yuba rivers join the Sacramento which flows due south from the junction of the Pit and McCloud near the base of Mount Shasta.

There are but one or two permanent tributaries to either the Sacramento or San Joaquin rivers reaching them from the west. The detritus deposits of the few intermittent creeks are small compared with the great fans on the flanks of the Sierra. As the Valley dips slightly to the west, the rivers all run to within sight of the inner Coast Range foothills before entering the main north- and south-flowing channels. Each of these major tributaries has its own delta. Collectively, in conjunction with the main bodies of the San Joaquin and Sacramento, they lace the west-central valley floor with veinlike systems of branching and rebranching channels and islands of higher land between.

Marshy areas were common in much of the Valley before agricultural reclamation. A number of federal and state wildlife refuges have been established in these once vaste wetlands and are hardly more than grainfields periodically and deliberately flooded. There are places, however, such as San Luis Island near Los Baños, where one can still see old slough channels, margined with woodlands, and shallow basins.

Near the confluence of the two great rivers, the land grades into several levels: the upper floor on eroded alluvial surfaces, the floodplain which is covered in times of high water, and seven basins—Butte, Marysville, Colusa, Sutter, American, Yolo, Sacramento—which lie between natural levees (known technically as *the* riverlands) and the higher levels. So-called islands are smaller land segments in the delta formed by the two rivers. Before agricultural development they were, for the most part, extensive marshland. This last landscape will be discussed in chapter 9, and chapter 10 will describe grasslands characteristic of the higher plains. In this chapter the primary concern is with the natural levees which, when undisturbed, support communities of towering woodland of a very special type. Such streamside vegetation has been given the name of riparian, a term in frequent use throughout these three chapters. Because it is so much like corresponding riverine woodlands in tropical savannas, or grasslands, it could be referred to as "gallery forest," though more commonly this term is used to describe the riparian woods of the tropics.

The levees are banks of flood-borne sediments some ten to thirty feet above the normal water level and extend several miles back of the river's edge. Where both levees and vegetation have remained undisturbed, a hummocky landscape borders the river, with more open swales where the levees slope down to the neighboring floodplains. The meandering rivers are often muddy and sluggish. A gradient of a dozen or so feet separates sea level from midcourse out on the valley floor. Too slow to carry rocks, unless in flood, their floors and banks are composed of silt. Sandbars detach themselves from the streams and are bare or covered with such quick-growing plants as mule fat, whose long limber stems bend with the swifter currents of flood time. During high water, the vertical banks erode into chunks which fall into the stream.

Riparian vegetation is often rampant in growth. Some of the temptation to refer to it as gallery forest is inspired by its junglelike appearance, particularly in summer when wild grape and clematis hang in thick green curtains reminiscent of the lianas in rainforest clearings. Unless one follows trails it is almost impossible to penetrate such profligacy of plant life. Not only are the trees so crowded that the foliage of one merges with that of its neighbor without interruption, but also the underlayers are savage conglomerations of fallen limbs and other debris, berry vines, wild rose snarls, poison oak patches, rank herbaceous growth, and saplings. Away from the river, the woods usually open out into more parklike stands.

It is still possible to find groves of well-developed riparian growth in certain state parks such as Caswell on the Stanislaus near Manteca, and Colusa which edges the Sacramento River eighty miles to the north. Here, as well as on private land, individual trees and thickets remain to give some idea of the overwhelming nature of this lowland arboreal landscape and its special character. By and large, the trees living here are confined to more mesic or riparian communities, with the exception of valley oaks which are also common on the rolling hills and in the valleys of the surrounding ranges. Fremont cottonwood, box elder, Oregon ash, and various species of willow are typical of the bottomlands. Where the streams course through the foothills, the groves include live oaks, sycamore, bay, black walnut, buckeye, big-leaf maple, white alder, dogwood, and other more or less mesophytic species. Many shrubs find such conditions favorable: buttonbush, honeysuckle, wild rose, coffeeberry, elderberry, and species of *Ribes* (pronounced rye-bees, a genus that includes both currants and gooseberries). Among the herbaceous and semiwoody plants are two considered most unwelcome by human visitors, poison oak and nettle, and three burdened with names singularly awkward—mule fat, the introduced horehound, and mugwort. The last, by the way, is an *Artemisia* (wormwood and sagebrush) and has the typical pungent odor of this genus. It is frequently bound with tangles of the orange string-stem parasite, dodder. All five have tall, shaggy-leaved stems in these densely shaded groves, and three—horehound, mugwort, and nettle—are nitrophiles. They are restricted to fertile soils rich in nitrogen, which are typical substrates of the community. Grass is but occasional and, where it does occur, has the long stems of shade-tolerant species.

No place is less typical of California. One can almost expect to see the fireflies of a midwestern summer evening when the hot wind of the Great Valley rattles the leaves of the cottonwoods and catches back the drapery of wild vines falling from the richly embossed canopy overhead. California's familiar evergreen natives—madroño, bay, digger pine, and the like—are missing on the bottomlands, and the observant visitor can make the acquaintance of a new assemblage of trees, all of them winter deciduous. This alone is unique behavior for much of the vegetation of the state, but there are even more unusual features. Not only do the same or kindred species occur widely throughout the West, but all are related to well-established broadleaf species of the East.

Most of the eastern tree groups are left behind when entering the Rocky Mountains. The West has no native elms, beeches, basswoods, or hickories, for example. The East, in turn, cannot claim California bay or madroño, tanoak or Douglas-fir. It is an intriguing question: What is this woodland doing here, with its deciduous oaks, its sycamore, willows, walnut, ash, alder, maple, and cottonwoods—all with kin in Ohio, Tennessee, and Arkansas?

Habitat provides the main clue—streambank. Not only are the deep silt soils rich and fertile, this is the one California environment in which the plants do not have to allow for summer drought or aridity in general. Permanent water makes evergreenness less useful. There is no advantage in having foliage ready and waiting to make use of the unreliable coincidence of spring warmth and sufficient moisture. There *is* usefulness in dormancy during the cold season. Not only are the winter temperatures lower in the Great Valley than they are on the coast, they also last longer. The lowlands and foothills of the upper Sacramento Valley can expect frost for six months of the year. In contrast to coastal scrub with its average winter low temperatures of 35 to 40 degrees, these interior woodlands may experience average lows of 32 to 38 degrees; and dips down to 15 degrees can occur. Long weeks of near-freezing tule or ground fogs intensify the winter chill. Rapid radiation of the earth's heat during long winter nights cools the air below dew point. Condensation results, and dense, persistent fog blankets the Valley floor with cold, clammy mist.

Since cold air is heavy, it drains downhill and along canyon floors opening into the Great Valley. Bottomlands often have lower temperatures than the surrounding hills and ridges. Moreover, any winding, narrow foothill gully will be partly shaded for much of the low-sun winter day, and north-trending canyons may have little or no solar radiation. Thus four features account for local pockets of colder air: northward aspect, steep and shaded gully sides, gravity, and interior or continental-type temperature extremes. Dormancy in this period has possible survival value for trees able to depend on summer warmth *and* water, a most unusual natural combination in California. No wonder that these types, left over from ancient landscapes and unadjusted to the climate of the rest of the state, remain only in river-edge refuges where local conditions resemble those of Mississippi bayous.

In its natural state, the riverbank community is startlingly isolated. The gradation from grassland to tree grove is about as abrupt as that from street curb to lawn edge, particularly now when so many of the valley oaks formerly dotting the floodplains have been cut down. Transitions from one biotic community to another are termed ecotones. In most instances, it is a zone containing various elements of both vegetation types, but it often has certain features of its own. For example, the mixed evergreen forest of the hills—Douglas-fir, tanoak, madroño, bay—is transitional temporally as well as ecologically. It came into being during the confrontation of the two great Tertiary floras, Arcto- (northern) and Madro (southern) and has elements of both. Today it is transitional, in other words, an ecotone between the mesophytic redwoods and the xerophytic brush or grasslands.

An ecotone, or meeting place of two communities, is likely to be rich in animal life. This "edge effect," as it is called, results from two habitats offering resources to shared populations; for example, one may provide shelter and the other food. There are inner and outer edges for both strips of woodland bordering a stream, making four altogether—two riverbed-grove ecotones, one on each bank, and two grove-grassland transitions. The outer ecotonal zones may be widened when forbs and grasses form an understory under extensive oak groves as at Caswell State Park. From another point of view, there are three habitats: the river itself, woodlands, and the surrounding prairie. Figure 14 illustrates what could be a typical habitat combination along the lower San Joaquin River.

Many animals use two or all three communities, though some confine most of their activities to just one. A kingfisher may choose a limb of a sycamore tree for a perching site but will restrict the business of food getting to the river. A family of raccoons may hunt for crayfish in a slough, hide in a tree-trunk hole, and raid a farmer's orchard in one twenty-four-hour period. Aquatic insects, on the other hand, tend to remain in water or near it. Some, like dragon- and damsel-flies, are water dwellers during the nymphal or immature stages, but as adults are flying predators. They usually are not far from water, however, and often pause to rest on some half-immersed log or aquatic plant. Water striders, back swimmers, and water boatmen rarely leave their aquatic home at any stage of their development.

Tent caterpillars and box elder bugs, which parasitize certain species of riparian trees, pay little or no attention to the river. The former weave webby shrouds filled with a nerve-unsettling mess of wiggling larvae feeding off the imprisoned leaves of such trees as cottonwoods. Whole branches can be defoliated by the voracious caterpillars. Attracted by the rich riparian vegetation and its food resources, many other insects are common—butterflies, day-flying moths, wasps, and bees among them. Such a wealth of insect life in turn attracts their feeders. Aquatic insect species are sought by the native and introduced fish of these lowland rivers—carp, squawfish and other local minnows, bass, bullhead, bluegill, and perch. Even though dams prevent their free access to the higher interior streams,

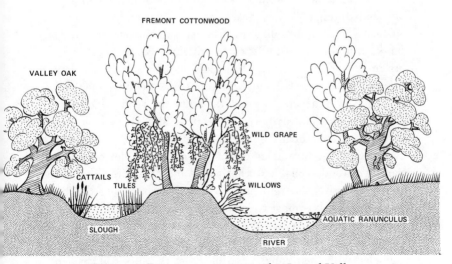

Figure 14. Riparian vegetation in the Central Valley

salmon, steelhead trout, and lampreys regularly use the Sacramento and San Joaquin riverways for spawning.

Flying insects are not only taken by the leaping fish such as trout but by insectivorous birds that find these riverine groves good hunting grounds. Wilson's and yellow warblers, yellowthroat and chat flit and flutter from tree to tree searching for insects. Vireos, gnatcatchers, and flycatchers are equally active. Downy woodpeckers tip-tap their way through the river-edge strip. Flickers call from snags, and yellow-billed cuckoos are seldom seen anywhere else. Bewick's and house wrens find the environment to their liking, and almost every knothole has a wren's nest. Each high snag seems to have a watchful avian predator—white-tailed kite and Cooper's, red-tailed, and red-shouldered hawks. They watch for movements of basking lizards or adventurous mice. Horned and long-eared owls take their places at night. Where the shrub and herbaceous growth is rich, seed eaters such as goldfinches, song sparrows, black-headed and blue grosbeaks, and towhees are constantly at work. Streamside growth is one of the preferred locations for lazuli buntings. Bullock's and hooded orioles hang their nests in cottonwoods and willows and are exquisite flashes of orange and black against the peridot green of the canopy.

In the backwaters of sloughs, western pond turtles look like suspended lumps as they float, nose out, just under the quiet surface. Tiger and California slender salamanders frequent banks and pockets of moist earth or debris. Being insect feeders in part, their riverine life should satisfy any tastes they have for such a diet. Though raccoons and the once plentiful golden beaver never stray too far from the river edge, gray foxes, cottontails, coyotes, jackrabbits, and striped skunks travel back and forth from river to grassland or, to be more accurate, to the farmfields of the present time. Not only is a variety of food available for herbivore and carnivore alike, but cover is handy in these dense thickets. The shade afforded by riparian growth is most welcome in the heat of the day. Small rodents such as harvest and deer mice tend to stay close to seed-rich areas for food; many of the ground layer tangles are tunneled with their runways. Moles find the silty soil easy to excavate, and dusky-footed woodrats are very much at home in all the litter and debris from profuse plant life.

At one time, golden beaver, a varient of the well-known aquatic mammal, were plentiful in the Great Valley. Today they are controlled to the point of occasional occurrence. Unlike their mountain-dwelling relatives, they rarely build lodges but prefer to dig dens in the banks lining slough and stream. For this reason they are also called bank beaver. When they do construct lodges they use tules as well as the boughs and mud commonly associated with the efforts of these intriguing rodents. They feed on the bark of riparian trees as well as other available vegetative material such as grass or even suitable food from planted crops. Though they seldom build dams in these lowland streams, their activities have resulted in damage to irrigation installations. They are considered a nuisance, and the Valley is one of the few places in North America where anyone may take beaver at any time in any way.

When fall nudges summer out of the way, these woodlands imitate, somewhat timidly, the color sequence of their eastern counterparts. The cottonwoods and willows turn butter yellow, and their leaves drift down onto levee tops and floodplains. The foliage of valley oaks bronzes before it drops. Box elder and ash leaves become light tan and look as fragile as charred paper. Then the sycamores expose trunks of mottled cream and white and massive boughs which bend and angle in all directions. Tufts of mistletoe are obvious now, unscreened by summer's canopy. The rain-gray skies of February wrap the bare twigs and branches in their own kind of melancholy. Juncos may pick in the more open glades, but the rich lushness of summer with its counterpoint of bird chorus seems very far away. Fourth of July picnics in the oak groves seem as unlikely as Roman orgies until April opens silky green leaf buds, and warblers return to the willows. Seasonal California tells a special kind of story in her riverlands.

# 9. Red-Winged Blackbird

He clung to the swaying tule, his left foot higher than his right, Through binoculars both legs looked like thin, dried twigs bent at sharp angles, particularly where his feet grabbed the stem in little knobby-cornered rectangles. Above his slender underpinnings, he was ebony and red. As he swung in the cool wind of a May morning, he flicked his tail and displayed the flame-bright shoulder patches that have given him his name. From time to time he clipped a short, crisp chirp. Then a dark gray female flew overhead and settled on the branch of a nearby willow tree. He immediately hunched his shoulders, bowed his head; and as the epaulets opened into elegant scarlet puffs, he flung out that ringing *kon-ka-reeeee!* that is the marshland's carillon of spring.

The couple was not alone. All around, black and red wings dropped to the tule and cattail thickets or rose to take off for fields and trees bordering the slough. The clucks and the calls, the comings and goings were those of busy, sociable creatures, flocking with their own kind in a habitat of their preference. Red-winged blackbirds have rather rigid requirements for nesting places, and they seldom choose any other environment than freshwater marshes, rich in the sedges, cattails, and reeds they need for shelter and nesting material.

Wet or damp places are not uncommon features of the earth's surface. In fiction, the three words, *bog, swamp,* and *marsh,* are used casually, often synonymously, along with terms inherited from dramatic fiction indigenous to the British Isles: fen, heath, and moor, where countless lovers have had misadventures in forbidding, treacherous, and often mucky wastelands symbolic of death. Many aquatic habitats, however, have a wealth of life. Though evolution has destined numerous species to arid environments, every living cell, plant or animal, is a microscopic puddle in which the genetic material determining what we are is suspended in what could be

Gray Lodge Wildlife Refuge, Butte County

called the liquid of life. Water in some form or another is absolutely necessary in the life cycle of every living organism.

Most aquatic habitats are potentially rich in living things. This is true of the sea and its littoral, and of the bays and sloughs of the saltwater world. Freshwater environments, such as swamps, bogs, and marshes, share this wealth. Though these words are often used interchangeably, they have definite and separate meanings. A freshwater marsh usually has shallow water clogged with dense masses of sedges, cattails, rushes, reeds, and other types of aquatic herbaceous vegetation. Pools of open water are commonly present unless plant material has accumulated to the extent of crowding them out. Bogs have a unique vegetation characteristic of poorly drained lakes and ponds. Sphagnum moss and other plants coagulate in floating masses or islets which sometimes loosely cover the entire water surface. Plants of the heather family are often present as they tolerate the cold, acid, waterlogged, and peaty soils characteristic of the true bog. Swamps are distinguished from marshes in that they have shrubs and trees, though they also may have vegetation typical of the other two environments. All three have two features in common which differentiate them from the freshwater habitats typical of streams and rivers. They have abundant, conspicuous plant life and have standing rather than running water.

California has few true bogs, as they tend to be confined to northern latitudes and the once glaciated midcontinental states around the Great Lakes. A cooler climate seems to be a requisite of their formation, but a number of small pitcher plant bogs are located in the northern part of the state. Swamps are plentiful in the South with its water-soaked baldcypress groves. Though some swamps occur in California—along the riverways of the lower Colorado River, in the delta of the Sacramento and San Joaquin rivers, and elsewhere—most of the state's native trees requiring large amounts of water are riparian in habitat. They grow in edge forests along the banks of rivers and streams where the substrate may be damp, but not covered with water except during floods. However, marshes are, or were, numerous in the Delta, up north in the

Klamath country, and in coastal and interior drainages where water slows down and accumulates.

Although we tend to employ the words *river*, *creek*, *brook*, *lake*, *pond*, and *pool* as loosely as the three we have just discussed, they have usefully different meanings. River, creek, and brook imply running water. The first is the largest of these three landscape features; the last is the smallest. Within a region of uniform climate they frequently share the same biota, that is, the inventory of living species found in any one community. Among the factors determining the biotic composition of California's stream environments are: amount of brackishness (significant in the lower Delta), water temperature, seasonal fluctuation, rate of flow, and in recent times degree of pollution. Cold and rapid streams contain more dissolved oxygen than those that are warm and slow. Consequently, aquatic organisms requiring ample supplies of this gas are limited to life in fast, cool water. California's sluggish lowland rivers are not well aerated. They are akin to marshes in the biota they support and, indeed, are often paternal to such soggy places—sloughs formed from water cut off in oxbows or spread in overflow basins. The word *stream*, incidentally, refers to any flow of water of any size.

Lakes, ponds, and pools are bodies of standing water, and like the terms for running water indicate a size range. They intergrade with other wetland environments. Intermittent streams dry into puddles that eventually disappear until the next wet season and are related to a special type of pool, springtime or vernal—"hog wallows," as they are called in the Great Valley. The biota of these evanescent pools, saline or fresh, depends on its ability to exist in some manner through the dry season. Permanent ponds and lakes, though these may be involved in a long-term successional change from a wet habitat to a dry one, have stable communities that change little from year to year. They are found in lowland sloughs where river water spreads into a sink or basin and in higher country where they are often the heritage of lava flow obstruction or where cirques scooped out by glacial action and other natural depressions collect down-draining water. Lowland lakes often have extensive marshlike or swampy areas around their borders and in bays and inlets.

After the initial open water phase, invasion by marsh vegetation begins, and chances are that time will gradually close out any remaining pool-like areas as living plants and their dead debris enlarge the ever-growing clumps and brakes. Man interrupts the process when he drains marshland, accomplishing in one year what would take nature centuries to do, that is, change it from wet land to dry.

The Delta and its bewildering waterways have their special terms—bypass, cutoff, cut, wasteway, slough, sink, tract, island, canal, river, channel, dike, levee, and aqueduct. The first settlers added their anxieties and needs to these words—Little Potato Slough, Whiskey Slough, Bacon Island, Disappointment Slough, Hope Trace, and Poverty Road. No doubt life, property, and economy were all somewhat precarious in the sometimes drowned, sometimes desiccated bottomlands until control from levees and dams imposed the dependability so necessary to the farmers of the Delta.

Before these reclamation efforts, there were many square miles of tule-choked marsh. When the problems were removed so was much of this wetland which, when drained, made an excellent place for crops. Today only a few sloughs and a basin or two still resound with the calls of red-winged blackbirds. Most of the original wetlands are now rice or produce fields, spreading out in tidy rectangles enclosed by dikes. If one really hunts for the last remnants of the marshes, one can find them: around Trapper's Slough west of Stockton, in Butte Sink, along the Yolo and Sutter bypasses, and in the quiet little side waters here and there, the cattails still grow tall and release their seeds to the westerly winds of the Antioch Gap. Look for these small watery worlds. Stand, perhaps, on a dike in the Gray Lodge Wildlife Area where a wealth of wildfowl pauses on migratory wanderings along the Pacific flyway to glean in croplands planted for its benefit. Or watch quietly beside some riverside pond. One can become an observer of life as rich as that of a tide pool, but often as unobtrusive as that of a decaying log in a lodgepole pine forest. Most of the organisms of a marsh go about their business hidden under the water surface or in the tangled screen of its vegetation.

The similarities of fresh or brackish water environments to the salt marshes and tidelands of the sea are apparent upon observation of their biota. Once again we meet plankton at one end of the size range, and birds and the larger fish at the other, with all manner of intermediate size organisms in between—crustaceans, molluscs, worms, coelenterates, sponges, and bryozoans among them. Salinity fluctuates from place to place, and tidal rise and fall occurs some distance upstream; but there are major differences. No great tidal surge brings food and oxygen to marsh dwellers. In compensation, they do not have to undergo the risk of low-tide exposure and desiccation, though flood and drought are possible risks. Insects reach an importance they never have in tide pools; on the other hand, molluscs are seldom found in large numbers in most freshwater habitats, but there are exceptions such as the alien Manila clam whose success in colonizing California's inland waters is phenomenal.

Every body of quiet standing water, salt or fresh, demands several basic adjustments on the part of its residents. In the first place, they must adapt themselves to inadequate oxygen. There are several reasons why marshes may lack this essential element. Running water aerates itself as it tumbles around boulders, down rocky stretches, or over waterfalls. A major source of oxygen in water is plant life. In the process of photosynthesis, oxygen is released. The tiny plants—bacteria, fungi, and the like—responsible for the decomposition of the dead material on the floor of the marsh have no green bodies or chloroplasts; therefore, they do not photosynthesize. They use oxygen in the process of respiration, as do all living things, but they do not liberate it. Instead, they release methane or marsh gas. Green plants in the aquatic biota add to the available store of oxygen. In addition, some of this element is absorbed directly from the contact surface between air and water; in general, however, it is scarce in these stagnant, often warm pools.

As a result, marsh dwellers have developed many ingenious

ways to make sure they obtain enough oxygen. Water boatmen, back swimmers, and a number of diving beetles capture
air bubbles from the surface of the pond which they wear like
silver cloaks or trap under wing covers. The bubbles slowly
shrink as the oxygen is used by the insect, and the nitrogen
dissolves into the water. Other small insects use air captured
in hairs on their bodies. Many aquatic animals have external
gills to absorb oxygen. Some are fingerlike projections; others
resemble small plates and are attached to the abdomen. Mosquito wigglers have air storage organs and breathing tubes that
reach up to the water surface. The larvae of certain beetles
penetrate directly into plant tissue to tap its oxygen supply.
Back swimmers ease up to the surface and head down, thrust
their abdomens to the air which enters and diffuses through
their suspended bodies. Fish must also adjust; and those, like
trout, needing a great amount of dissolved oxygen keep to
streams where it is plentiful. Sluggish stream fish such as carp
are often surface gulpers, and tadpoles have the same habit.
They must begin early in adjusting to life out of water.

Green plants also need oxygen for respiratory activity. Fortunately, it is a product of photosynthesis, and many marsh
plants have air spaces in their stems to store a surplus for future use. Aquatic plants have made many adjustments to their
habitat. Floating species have air pockets scattered through the
tissues of their leaves and stems for buoyancy. As water
screens out solar radiation, submerged plants must cope with
the diminished supply of light. Their stems and leaves have
thin "skins," that is, little or no cuticle, and the gas exchange
necessary to photosynthesis and respiration can take place directly and readily from water to plant and vice versa. The
chloroplasts, or food-making green bodies, are concentrated in
or just under the surface tissue to make the most efficient use
of their unique ability. Many amphibious plants simultaneously grow two types of leaves which differ markedly in
appearance. Those that are submerged are finely divided to
provide more surfaces through which gas exchange can take
place. Those reaching to the air are coarser, and the leaf pores
or stomata are more numerous on upper surfaces of floating

foliage. Emergent vegetation—tules and other bulrushes, cat-tails, reeds—is confined to shallow margins and hummocks as much of the individual plant is usually above water. Moisture is abundant in the substrate, making large root systems un-necessary. The stems often have connected air chambers as-sisting the transport of gases to the submerged portion of the plants.

Rank, coarse growths of such vegetation clutter the edges around open water, along with witch-caldron brews of thick green pond scum (filamentous algae), sheets of duckweed and attractive islets of such flowering plants as aquatic ranuncu-lus, water-cress, potentilla, loosestrife, and marsh pennywort. Small jungles of interwoven stems and matted leaves dis-courage mammalian predators and baffle avian enemies of nesting birds. Marsh wrens, rails, bitterns, and red-winged blackbirds seek and rely on the shelter afforded by the tangled vegetation. Even such sharp-eyed predators as marsh and duck hawks, watching with interest the progress of the breeding season, find nest raiding difficult in the concealing ranks of marsh plant cover. Western and eared grebes and coots often scorn such screening and use the plentiful plant material to build small floating masses on which they lay their eggs out in more open water.

Whistling swans and various geese—Canada, white-fronted, and snow—are winter gleaners in the grain- and croplands fringing many of the Delta marshes. Being visitors only, they need food, not nesting cover. Among the resident ducks, mallards, gadwalls, redheads, and the little ruddies make use of the diversity of both diet and nest site in the wetland hab-itat. The first two are primarily gleaners, feeding in crop fields or neighboring grasslands, though both often utilize aquatic plant and animal food. The last two are decidedly omnivor-ous. They eat plant material as well as any insects, tadpoles, and other animal life they can find. Redhead ducks either keep to the surface of the water, dabbling or "tilting"—that is, tip-ping the head forward until it is well under water with the tail high in the air—or dive on occasion. Ruddy ducks are divers and most frequently feed at the bottom of the pond.

Blue-winged and cinnamon teal are summer guests; but pintail, baldpate, and green-winged teal settle in marshes of the Central Valley during the cooler months, often in impressive numbers. Startled from their quiet feeding, they wing past by the thousandfold, riffling across the pink-and-gray of a winter's dawn or the freshly laundered sky left by a solstitial storm.

Most of the shorebirds with which we became acquainted earlier in the book visit the inland marshes: yellowlegs, avocets, stilts, sandpipers, curlews, egrets, and black-crowned night, green, and great blue herons. Glossy ibis, gallinules, and Virginia rails are partial to screening thickets of cattail and tule habitats.

Underwater plant material provides concealment or anchor base for fish, insect, and snail eggs; pupa cases; various types of larvae and nymphs; molluscs; and crustaceans such as crayfish. Stems, root masses, submerged leaves, and the undersides of floating leaves offer attachment sites and shelter, protecting numerous small residents of the marsh.

Many aquatic insects, adult and immature forms alike, are strongly predaceous, quick to hunt down and attack any suitable prey. Dragon-flies and damsel-flies, for all their gauze-winged elegance, are "hawking" as they hover over ponds and other quiet water. Such varying aquatic forms as back swimmers, water striders, and creeping water bugs are all classified as water bugs which also includes the fearsome-looking toe-biter, giant of its family. Much of the group is aggressive, assaulting all possible victims unfortunate enough to come to its attention. One diving beetle actually feeds on small fish.

A marsh and its surrounding feeding grounds form an ecosystem. The creatures found in it, with the exception of bird and terrestrial insect visitors, remain within its borders and seldom venture beyond. Energy, the capacity for performance, once it enters the marsh, cycles from the various plant producers to and through the consumers of the habitat's characteristic food webs.

All the energy powering the biotic world originates from the sun. Plants are the conversion factories changing solar energy to chemical energy through the remarkable process of photosynthesis. Such diverse forms as huge trees and single-celled green algae share this ability. One of the milestones of evolutionary history is the amazing capacity to use the energy of sunlight and, through chlorophyll, combine certain basic chemical elements into nutritious material. Not only useful for the food needs of the plant, these nutrients are basic for all the animal kingdom's energy requirements. Unlike plants, animals cannot directly utilize solar energy. They depend on food to power the activties of life. Food chains spin into food webs that enmesh the living world through interdependencies without number. As the initial "chunks" of solar energy, captured in leaf, root, seed, stem, and flower, are ingested into the bodies of the first-order consumers, or herbivores, part of this

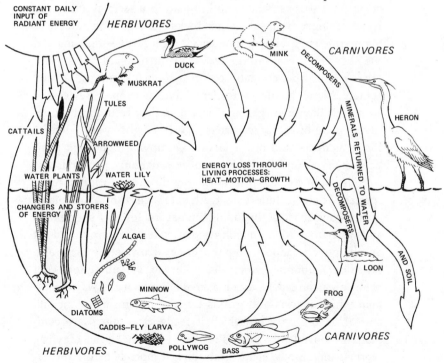

Figure 15. Typical freshwater marsh energy flow patterns

energy is used to build and repair animal tissue, part is discarded through elimination, but part of it is burned through activity and dissipated as heat. When the herbivores are consumed in turn by second-order consumers, or carnivores, more of the initial solar energy escapes as heat, though the efficiency of energy transfer increases with each step away from the plant base. So it goes until the last of the original energy is used by decomposers, as they in turn break up what matter is left into basic chemicals needed by plants. It is a remarkable cycle; none of the matter is really lost. At the end of what may be a long journey, the final organisms of decay sift back to the earth the basic nutrients needed for the nourishment of plants which then resurrect it in the form of their own tissue.

Energy flow routes, through food webs, are not too difficult to discover in the microcosm of a marsh. Some of the chains begin with worms, snails, and immature insects cleaning microscopic algae from submerged rocks and logs. Comparable to the marine environment, one-celled algal forms—diatoms and the like—are present in the waters of the marsh. Protozoa and other microscopic animals comprise zooplankton, also a food source. Many plankton feeders have developed devices to strain out the tiny organisms on which they feed. Fresh or decaying plant life of larger size is eagerly sought by such diverse forms as ducks and insect larvae. Occupying important positions in marshland food chains, rotifers, daphnia, copepods, ostracods, molluscs, and insects enlarge the menu for predaceous species. These include fish, freshwater jellyfish, amphibians, carnivorous insects (including immature forms), shorebirds, and waterfowl. Many marsh residents are omnivorous and eat anything from tadpoles to pond slime, arrowweed tubers (also called duck potatoes) to caddis-fly larvae. The ubiquitous coot is one of such feeders, as, on a smaller scale, is the water boatman which ingests and grinds up tiny organisms, plant and animal, in the ooze on which it feeds. Scavengers are common in the wetlands. Debris feeders—sandfly larvae, crayfish, worms, amphipods, etc.,—grab the last morsels before the decomposers reduce them to elemental ingredients.

As the potential energy within the last plankton meal of a hapless rotifer is transferred to its captor and on through successive and inevitable food chains, each progressive marshland consumer uses its share until all that remain of carcass and wastes are basic substances. They can only be reassembled by the indirect energy of sunlight acting on carbon, hydrogen, and oxygen pulled into plants of the wetlands and creating new food through the catalytic agency of chlorophyll.

It is no wonder that a marsh, with all its generosity of food sources, is a community rich in animal residents. It rings with bird calls and the sonorous honk of bullfrogs. Marsh hawks hover, hoping for a garter snake, but make do with a dragonfly. Wrens clutch bobbing tule stems, eyes alert for damselflies. Pools mirror grebes, ducks, and coots feeding, clucking, swimming with that effortless-appearing ease behind clumps of cattails as esthetically pleasing as though arranged by some artful human hand. Wilson's snipe and greater yellowlegs work over the mud, exposed where a pond is slowly shrinking under the summer sun, for small crustaceans and insects. Feet resting on dimpled pockets in the water surface, water striders dart about with incredible agility, hunting for any small animals they can capture, including others of their own kind. Red-winged blackbirds have many neighbors, large and small, which by the simple act of living, open their own accounts in the energy-nutrient bank and withdraw from them until death. What remains of them is transferred to other accounts in an endless cycling of resources.

Bunch grass near Rio Vista, Central Valley

# 10. California's Kansas

It must have been a living sea—brilliantly green in April and richly tawny in August as the glinting grass bounced back the sun. Early travelers marveled at the vast flat floor of the Great Valley, its *tulares* alive with wild birds and its rivers wandering through hedgerow woodlands. But most probably they viewed with keenest interest and speculation the great wind-riffled prairies. Only three vegetation communities originally occurred here; and their distribution was dependent on the available moisture. The riverlands with their dense riparian woods and navigable streams were both useful and troublesome to the first settlers. One could hunt the animals seeking shelter in the rank vegetation, cut down trees for construction or firewood, and use the waterways for transport; but the sloughs and channels imposed barriers to both foot and horse traffic, especially during the wet season. The marshes were, except for duck and geese hunting, largely useless. Indeed, their soggy interiors forced the slow travel of the day into wide detours. During the runoff, much of the Valley was a flooded wasteland that denied permanent use and settlement.

The prairies were something else again, particularly those on higher ground which, in normal years, stood above the flooded bottomlands. They were covered, for the most part, with perennial bunchgrasses which quickened and died in a seasonal rhythm changed but little since the present climate regime took over from that of the Pleistocene. The green of spring is followed by the gold of summer. In the open rangelands of the Central Valley this sequence of color is as inflexible as the tidal timeclock of the sea. In spite of the problems posed by such pronounced seasonal changes, the white man recognized the promise of the grasslands. The original prairie, which has now all but disappeared, contributed an indisputedly important chapter to the story of the state's agricultural growth.

The title chosen for this chapter implies a comparison of

California prairies with those of the Great Plains. There are resemblances and differences. Both regions were originally somewhat alike in appearance and in floristic composition, and they owe their grasslands to low and often undependable rainfall. The regions are dissimilar in cold season temperature averages and the time and length of the growing season. The Great Plains experience far more severe winters than does the Central Valley. Blizzards and freezes characterize their cold months; whereas lowland California rarely has a temperature drop lower than 25° F., and such a period of chill does not last for any length of time. The midcontinental states enjoy summer rainfall, however, and California seldom does, except for a very occasional thunderstorm. Such conditions mean that the period of dormancy—when the plants die, leaving seeds, nascent shoots, or underground root masses—is almost reversed. Late spring and summer is the growing season for Kansas, late winter to mid spring for California. Dissimilarities of growth habit are also apparent. The Central Valley has a number of indigenous annuals in contrast to the paucity of such types in the Great Plains, but it lacks the abundance of sod-forming species so typical of the latter region. Instead, the Valley's perennial grasses are bunchgrasses. The shoots begin at the basal nodes and extend up within the hollow sheaths of old dried stems. Sod formers have underground rhizomes—modified shoots from which both roots and leafy stems develop. Both regions relax in fall, one in preparation for a winter of bitter cold, the other for the first warm days after the onslaught of the autumnal rains. The perennial grasses are ready to spring into action and take advantage of favorable temperatures and available moisture, sparse though it might be.

The climatic and edaphic features that regulated the Valley prairies also controlled almost all the rangelands in California. Even today, the oak-pine woodlands with their carpeting understory of grass, the balds and potreros of the Coast Ranges, as well as what remains of the range in the Great Valley must bow to the commands of sun and rain, soil and slope face. The rules have not changed though foothill and valley grasslands have undergone profound alterations since white men entered the region. Not only have thousands of acres been turned over to agricultural pursuits, it is no exaggeration to say also that most original native grasses of low altitude California have been replaced by immigrant species. This successful invasion is one of the most striking examples of its kind to be found anywhere. Aside from the deliberate introduction of agricultural and urban development, no other plant community in western North America has changed so much, over such large areas, and in so short a period of time. Forests and brushlands, after fire or commercial removal, tend to return to their former composition, if left alone. But California's grasslands will probably never again look as they did before the great "catastrophe" of civilization's arrival. Too many aggressive newcomer plants have settled down and are doing very well in their adopted land. Though many of the alien grasses were deliberately introduced from Europe and elsewhere, most appeared accidentally. Mixed with crop seed or caught in the wool or hair of imported livestock, their seeds found a fertile land and a familiar climate.

How did the invading species achieve their spectacular victory? Many factors contributed to the ease of the rout. The native perennial bunchgrasses do not cover the ground completely, but they leave small patches of bare soil between their clumps which are open to invasion. Besides needing dependable soil moisture for optimum growth, they do not recover well from heavy grazing. This is especially true if springtime foliage is removed before it has time to manufacture enough food to replace reserves used in making the season's new tissue. When these grasses are cropped and crippled, water and nutriment demands are much reduced. Invading herbaceous species benefit from the increased supply of these essentials. Perennials also grow more slowly than do the vigorous annual species.

Curiously enough, the first grasses to benefit from the impact of the white man's coming were California's own annuals. They took advantage of the plight of the perennials, now heavily besieged. Through remote eras of time, the bunch grasses had provided fodder and feed for the many herbivorous animals—ruminants such as elk and antelope, rodents, lagomorphs, and even insects—but they had never been subjected to the trampling and concentrated grazing of large herds of domestic livestock. Most animals prefer the more palatable perennials over the less nutritious annuals. In a few short years, such unrelenting attack during the rancho period of California history thinned the ranks of the bunchgrasses, enlarging the bare spaces that were already present because of the growth habit of these species. Ready for invasion into the disturbed areas were the native annuals—six-weeks fescue, three awns, and lovegrass—whose ranges, until then, had been restricted by the flourishing perennials.

Carried along by the wave of the first successful sortie, immigrant species began to take hold. The weedier types—wild oats, soft chess, ripgut, goatgrasses, and such forbs as mustard and filaree, together with the indigenous tar weed, turkey mullein and the like—marched into abandoned wheat fields, overburdened pasturage, and the periodically drought-stricken rangeland. Annual grasses have much that contributes to their pioneering and opportunistic qualities. They react immediately to reviving rains and produce numerous seeds even under adverse circumstances. Many of them, such as goatgrass and mouse barley, are poor forage as they dry out quickly, are rough in texture, and have barbs or other objectionable fea-

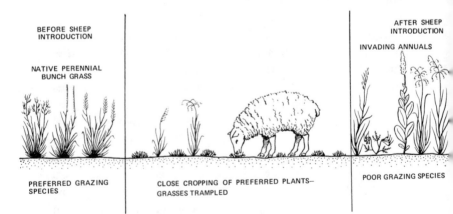

Figure 16. History of alien grass invasion in interior prairie

tures harmful to stock. The less desirable species escape the pressure to which the preferred types are subjected, allowing the former to spread to new terrain. Grazing, incidentally, is by no means always damaging. Light use actually stimulates the plants and during drought may prove of value. When they are kept small by casual cropping they need less water which, however, is then available to tar and other undesirable weeds. Even moderate use, however, at the wrong time may destroy reproductive tissue before the seeds are set and thus slow the annual recovery rate.

The needlegrasses, melicgrass, wild ryes, bluegrasses, deergrass, and perennial bromes with their long graceful stems growing from roots and the compact mats of vegetative material from previous years have retreated from the fields of the Great Valley. With them went many of the animals and other plants which, in adjusting to each other by the laws of communal living, had succeeded in creating an extensive and flourishing community. Though it appeared to be stable, and its species were those well adapted to conditions of soil and climate, the inherent weaknesses of its dominant plants and white man's fatal advent compounded its doom. What lowland prairie remains in the vast tracts of peach groves, grape vineyards, alfalfa, and sugar beets is a poor kind of thing—too small in size, or too alkaline for other than a few specially adapted species, or bristling with sock-infesting foxtails.

Such tenacious barbs on the seeds of many of the invading grasses proved of no uncertain value in the spreading of their populations. Some of the attributes of weedy plants are unique types of seed dispersal. The early settlers did not plow the range and sow it to filaree. All they did was to bring it here, and the spirally twisted hairs at the ends of its seeds saw to its distribution. These awns, as they are called, curl and uncurl with changes in air moisture. Such motion propels the seeds along the ground until suitable germination sites are encountered. Seeds with barbs or hooks are dispersed by the animals to which they become attached. Tumbleweed, another obnoxious import from Europe, rolls with any breeze, scattering its seeds as it literally sails along. No doubt dandelion is prevalent in gardens and lawns because of the tiny parasols of its seeds which are wind wafted for considerable distances. There are so many devices to ensure ease of dispersion that one would think that species without such special adaptations of this sort would never get a chance to replace themselves. But fortunately for the less adventurous plants, other features of the environment have their influences as well; and in the end, it is those types which best balance their tolerances and their needs that remain members of the community.

There were three variations from the monotony of the seemingly endless rangeland, two seasonal and one edaphic. Winter rain and springtime warmth not only awakened the grasses, but encouraged in many places a rich floral display. The rosy owl's clover, pale yellow cream cup, bird's-eye gilia, popcorn flower, lavender thistle sage, blue lupine, and sunlit poppy were first to bloom, followed by such bulbs as blue dicks, blue-eyed-grass, harvest *Brodiaea*, and mariposa lilies. To this day, where rangeland still rises above the crops of the Valley floor, wild flower fields are visited by thousands of enthusiasts in nostalgic search for the remnants of what must have been a Persian rug of color.

Certain curious patterns of wildflowers in what are called "hog wallows" have attracted much botanical attention. These small hard-pan floored depressions create a type of semirolling landscape with little knolls overlooking the wallows. Winter rainwater is captured in the depressions; and as it slowly evaporates, concentric rings, each of one particular plant species, bloom and die in a fascinating pattern of temporary succession. It begins when the pool is at its largest size and ends when it is completely dry, and the basin center is black with dried algae and sedge stems. To come unexpectedly upon one of these vernal or springtime pools is an enchanting experience. One sees it only from one point in time and must guess what was there before and what will come after. A typical set of pools, near Pixley, in the southern San Joaquin Valley, has been declared a research reserve by The Nature Conservancy. During a certain portion of the spring, several kidney-shaped pools are surrounded by rings: cream-colored valley tassels almost gone on the outer edge, a bright yellow band of gold-fields closer in, and the beginnings of ponds of blue *Downingia* —of the lobelia group—at water level. The entire reserve at this time is reticulated with little trails of yellow-flowered plants, sponsored by animal activity. The vegetation growing in the labyrinthian network is different from that on the hillocks, which are usually covered with grass, and from the pool-encircling rings. Owing to animal traffic, the soil of these trails is compacted. The surrounding grasses find it difficult to invade the bare paths, and more weedy species move in instead.

Where the substrate is heavy with salts and other solutes to which is given the name "alkali," only certain plants will grow. They must be able to compensate for a potential reversal of osmosis or fatal wilting will take place. Two native perennial grasses, alkali sacaton and salt grass, still thrive in these sinks. Apparently, few newcomers could successfully compete under such ecologically severe conditions. Other alkali tolerant plants are also present—various saltbushes, pickleweeds, and other goosefoots, particularly in the southern end of the Central Valley.

The nutritious grasslands of the world are the homes of most of the great herds of herbivores. This is certainly true in Africa where zebra and antelope such as wildebeest congregate so impressively. It was equally true in the Great Plains, though the buffalo was the only large grazer of any appreciable numbers remaining when the white man entered its domain. Two grazing ruminants took advantage of the Valley prairie, tule elk and pronghorn antelope. The former, the smallest type of its genus in the New World, is exclusively Californian. The only other elk native to the state is the Roosevelt, and it is the same as the Olympic elk of the Pacific Northwest. Members of the deer family, all North American elk belong to the genus *Cervus*, which includes the red "deer" of Europe. Only the western hemisphere has what we refer to as deer, or *Odocoileus*. The rest of the world's "deer" are other genera, though in all fairness, the Old World could say that it has the true deer, since it named them such first, and the western hemisphere has something else. Be that as it may, the tule elk suffered greatly during the conversion to agriculture and the consequent disappearance of the Valley grassland. Legend has it that the subspecies was reduced to two individuals, a kind of Noah's Ark predicament. Through the efforts of conservationists, however, the animal has increased numerically. Several dozen are kept in a small state reserve near Buttonwillow, in the southern San Joaquin Valley, some are scattered about in zoos, and another 300 roam in the Owens Valley, subject to controlled hunting.

The story of the pronghorn is much different. It has largely disappeared from California except for a restricted range in the northeastern part of the state. It occurs, however, in many places in the rangeland West and does not seem to be threatened with extinction, as is the tule elk. Not a member of the deer group at all, it is the only remaining species of its family. Nor does it have much connection with the Old World antelopes, though its pretty markings bear some resemblance to those of the graceful wanderers of the African plains. A major difference is in the horns. Pronghorn antelope have a permanent bony core which is not discarded though the outer covering is lost once a year. African antelopes never lose any part of their horns, but keep them for life.

There were and still are numerous grazers among the smaller animals of the Valley plains. Many rodents share a liking for grass and other prairie plants, this species preferring one part or type, that species other plant materials. The San Joaquin kangaroo rat feeds largely on the seeds of wild oats and bromes. Meadow mice rely on herbaceous shoots, leaves, and roots, but also include seeds and even bark. The nocturnal harvest and pocket mice are primarily seed eaters, sharing their bounty with the seed-harvesting birds—goldfinches, linnets, sparrows, and the like. Gophers eat juicy stems, roots, and foliage, pulling them down into their burrows and runways.

Evidently there has been an upsurge of gophers since the great change in grassland composition. Lloyd G. Ingles, in *Mammals of the Pacific States* (Stanford University Press, 1965), estimates that up to thirty individuals of this species can be found in just one acre of Valley grazing land. Though its numbers appear to be on the increase, owing to the elimination of many of its predators through government control, poisoning campaigns are causing many other rodent populations to diminish rapidly.

Jackrabbits, or black-tailed hares, technically not rodents but lagomorphs, are unparticular about their menu; and they browse and graze through brushy patches, and in grassland and crop field alike. California ground squirrels are the short-tailed, heavy-bodied little fellows one sees sunning themselves by the entryways to their burrows or darting back and forth on the dirt shoulders of Valley and foothill roads. Like the jacks they have a wide range of food interest, and readily raid farmlands for nuts, fruit, and greenstuffs, as well as making use of what native vegetation is provided. They, too, have been the victims of an extermination campaign, not only because of the crop damage they inflict, but because they have been proven to be carriers of fleas responsible for outbreaks of bubonic plague.

Grasshopper mice, as their name implies, rely heavily on insects, a rather unusual departure from the feeding habits of most of their relatives. Their stomachs are specially equipped to digest the chiton-covered fare. Deer mice also take insects, relying on them in the spring and reverting to seeds in the fall. These last two species could be said to be useful to the farmer in helping him get rid of such pests, in contrast to the rodents whose feeding activities are harmful. Many types of rodent behavior are beneficial, however. Their burrowing breaks up and aerates the soil. Nor should one ignore the value of their nitrogenous wastes.

In areas where there is such pronounced seasonality as in the California grasslands, its creatures must adapt to these great annual rhythms, particularly in regard to available diet. When green feed is present in spring, those who prefer it feast on it. After the summer drought has cured the grassy cover to hay, which still retains some nutritious material, many forbs remain juicy for a longer period of time. Soon, however, they succumb to the relentless heat of the Valley summer. Then the seeds, now mature, are wonderful sources of food owing to their concentrated nutrients. Other nourishing plant sources are harvested. On investigation, the tightly rolled leaves of the bunchgrass in one of the few patches of original prairie still remaining proved to contain some green material, even in mid-August, as the curling decreased the amount of evaporative surface and retarded dry out. Since the coming of agriculture, most of the herbivorous dwellers of the grasslands have not neglected to take advantage of the succulent results of irrigation and farming, though, as we have already noted, such supplementation of the natural summer diet has lead to the endangerment of some of the species.

The role of insects in grassland is not to be underestimated. They take their toll of vegetation, and it has been proved that ants, crickets, and grasshoppers are responsible for the destruction of much herbaceous material. Harvester ants are common in range areas. Their mounds are often in the centers of bare patches as large as fifteen feet across. Not only do they consume the vegetation cleared in such circles, but they also transport seeds from the nearby forbs and grasses into their underground homes.

As in all natural communities, there are checks and balances operating in the prairie to prevent the unrestrained growth of any one of its populations. When the herbivores multiply to the point of threatening the food supply, carnivores help control the burgeoning numbers. Burrowing owls, sparrow and red-tailed hawks, and shrikes victimize plentiful rodents, while nighthawks, kingbirds, meadowlarks, and horned larks take advantage of insect increase. Coyotes, badgers, and kit foxes are on the prowl along the numerous trails cutting through the grassy plain for plump mice and ground squirrels. Coach-whips, long-nosed snakes, kingsnakes, and gopher snakes wind through the sparser cover and along the little grass-walled trails, as ready as the predatory birds and mammals for a chance encountered meal.

To escape both the summer heat and their enemies, many rodents—kangaroo rats and deer mice, for example—conceal themselves in underground burrows and confine their foraging activities to the friendlier hours of darkness. Deprived of the shelter of shrubby thickets, some animals, jackrabbits among them, make use of the matted grass stems. They hollow out forms where they crouch quietly away from the pitilessly bright sun of the open country.

Midsummer was the beginning of hard times for the original California prairie. A few bees stirred over the straw-stiff grass. Rodent activity slowed down, as the babies were now grown and able to fend for themselves. On the floors of the vernal pools the last of the hardier flowers were bright against the black of dried, decayed vegetation; and the spadefoot and western toads had already escaped the desiccating drought by estivating—that is, they burrowed underground and entered a state of torpor, or deep sleep of a low metabolic rate, to conserve energy, moisture, and body weight during this time of scarce food and drying heat. Some of the predators left to look for better hunting grounds up in the foothills.

September was the month when the true carrying capacity of the range could be judged. This is the amount of wildlife the prairie could support during its most critical season. Then the biomass, which is the totality of all the organisms living within the community, still present during the lean days of early fall indicated the tremendous productivity of the prairie. Though many of its ordinarily day-active creatures spent longer periods of time within their underground passageways than they did in spring, they ventured out in the cooler hours to look for unclaimed seeds or an overlooked juicy stem, or to find the nearest water. Hawks soared in the pale blue sky, watching for a stray ground squirrel. Vultures gathered for the inevitable toll of drought upon April's crop of offspring. But much of it was waiting. Toads slept deep in their cozy pockets; and seed and shoot rested in readiness for the first gray clouds to linger over the parched distances.

Foothills of the Sierra Nevada, near Jackson

# 11. Where the Diggings Were

The Indians of the Sierran foothills had no notion that they were literally sitting on a gold mine. If they did note the stray shiny specks in creek beds and in the gravelly rubble of canyon floors, they most probably dismissed them as useless. In the simple routines involved in living at subsistence level, only the patently useful objects and materials were of significance—obsidian for arrowheads, willow bark for baskets, acorns for food, and deer hides for clothing. On the other hand, ornaments such as beads and certain shells were much prized. It runs as a universal thread through man's diverse

culture patterns that some objects, intrinsically of merely orna-
mental or decorative worth, become symbols of wealth and
hence valued media of exchange. Among the many types of
small shells so plentiful on the California coast, the pale purple olivellas would seem to be usable for adornment but not
much else. If, however, a tribe had fostered a tradition that a
kind of small purple shell was exchangeable on a rough unit
basis for useful or otherwise desirable objects, olivellas were
wealth.

Gold is nothing more than olivella value on a huge scale, and
the Indians of 1849 must have quickly realized why their
ancient homelands were being overrun by hordes of frantic
gold seekers. It must have been harder for these gentle people
to understand the violence, greed, outlawry, and chaos of the
camps which were scattered like proliferating cells over the
foothills of the Mother Lode.

There is no denying that a miner's life was hard. Not only
were the diggings on recently established frontier and every
necessity or convenience in limited supply, mining itself was
grinding physical labor. For many of those who came to find
gold, however, the task of getting to California was the worst
part of the whole experience. The long arduous journey over-
land or the even longer and more difficult passages over the
Isthmus of Panama, through the Straits of Magellan, or around
the Horn were harrowing to the point of causing modern readers of history to wonder how the lure of gold could have been
strong enough to induce thousands of men to undertake such
perilous adventures. Though many of the forty-niners would
have vigorously denied it, the Mother Lode was not the worst
place in the world for mining gold. Alaska and the high Rockies
were far less friendly to their exploiters. Indeed, the foothills,
rough and canyon cut though they often are, must have appeared to be hospitable and friendly country to many who had
struggled over the barren alkali flats of the sagebrush country
or faced the formidable dangers of a High Sierra winter. The
summers may be warm at these low elevations, two hundred
to three thousand feet, but the winters are comparatively mild.
Snow rarely troubled the men of the diggings, and when it did

it quickly melted off. Wood and water were plentiful for domestic use and for mining equipment and procedures. Civilization, if one can call it that, was not far away, and roads soon connected the main mining centers with Sacramento and San Francisco. Food, though expensive, was available from the ranches and farms of the Great Valley. The monotonous meals of salt pork and beans were supplemented by game of many kinds. Hunting was a common pastime between the chores of minding sluice boxes and blasting out ore.

As they clambered up the ravines looking for telltale veins and placer deposits or rode into Hangtown and Volcano over links in the chain of dusty tracks that connected the camps, were most men aware of the beauty of the hills that had so long held in trust their treasure? Did they come to love the richly cascading rivers and streams that not only could be harnessed into ditches and flumes to wash through rockers and long toms, but could rinse out a man's laundry and quiet the thirst of a hangover? Did they note the effects of the seasons on the landscape, the wealth of young grass and wildflowers in May which become a special kind of gold in August?

No doubt many did, and perhaps even remarked to the more understanding of their pick-ax wielding companions their admiration of a land so blessed with beauty. It is safe to surmise that much speculation took place on how nature formed the precious metal they had come so far to find. Much of it was just that, unfortunately—speculation. Accurate geological knowledge of the Sierra Nevada, missing in Gold Rush days, has been painstakingly gathered for many years by survey teams and other experts, first on foot and horseback and later by motor vehicle. Though these efforts have helped uncover many clues to the story of this great mountain range, some puzzles are still unsolved. It appears that we do not yet know just how the lode came into existence.

Geologic evidence points to a series of events that began a hundred million years ago in the middle of the Mesozoic era. Marine sediments and volcanic material had been deposited in the general region of what we know as the Sierra Nevada for countless ages prior to this time. During the Upper Jurassic, while the dinosaurs still roamed the earth, these beds began to rise from the basin of an inland sea. Folding, faulting, and crushing took place as well as the intrusion of massive quantities of magma that cooled to become the white granite so characteristic of the range. The beds adjacent to the hot body of molten material were changed by heat and pressure to become slightly different types of rock (a process called *metamorphism*), and they were fractured. The outer edges of the granitic mass itself eventually cooled, and fractures occurred in them as well. Solutions from the magma filled the cracks and formed veins of quartz containing gold and other minerals.

Through the succeeding eons an overburden of rock, two miles thick, was deposited on the gold-bearing veins. By the end of the Mesozoic era this had been removed by erosion. Now the ore bodies were exposed to weathering and decay. The climate became more humid, and the temperature and rainfall patterns resembled those of the present-day Deep South.

The weathered, eroding veins lost much of their precious metal to the streams of that period. If there had been any miners grubstaking during the Eocene, they could have found the shiny nuggets easily, for the streams of that era were tapping the original ore-bearing veins as they flowed down the hills ancestral to the Sierra. Time and the great orogenic upheavals that fashion the foundations of the earth's landscapes conspired to hide California's treasure once again. Volcanic activity covered the hills with layers of ash, mud, tuff, and lava. At last a series of uplifts, in fairly recent (Pleistocene) times, thrust up the granite of the ancient batholith. A system of faults, four hundred miles long, created a huge block, tilted so that the western slope is gradual and the eastern scarp face is steeply abrupt. Now, erosion once more could attack the concealing layers. The streams flowing down the long slope from the crest went to work, exposing the ancient Eocene stream beds with their placer deposits, washing the rubble into new drainage patterns, and cutting into the veins themselves—the real Mother Lode.

No doubt, most forty-niners were aware of the more noticeable natural features of what they considered their temporary home. They knew of higher ridges and peaks to the east. They realized that their creeks and rivers were the offspring of snow fields in the rugged back country. They were aware that certain trees had certain uses. The soft wood of conifers was more easily worked, but some of the broad-leaved species—oaks, for instance—had harder, more durable wood. They may have heard rumors about huge trees a hundred feet around at the base. They discovered wild berries, and some probably learned that wild onions added flavor to back-of-the-stove stews. They relished the vension from deer browsing through the open glades and certainly heard many a tale of harrowing escapes from grizzly bears that lived in the thickets of the lower Sierra before their extinction around 1920. A few lonely souls probably made pets of white-footed mice, coons, or ringtails (these normally shy nocturnal carnivores were so useful in keeping rodents in check that they earned the nickname "miners' cats"). If so, they joined the ranks of those to whom the companionship of wild creatures is a rare and wonderful thing. Yet how astonished they would have been if they could have known that in a short century, there would be more people seeking recreation and outdoor experiences on the Sierran slope than there were living in California in 1849.

Like geologic investigations, those of the natural history of the state meant years of slow accumulation. Early research was mostly systematic in character, describing and naming the various types of flora and fauna. It was not until C. Hart Merriam, Joseph Grinnell, and others worked out concepts known as life zones that biologists took a somewhat different look at natural environments. They began to see that these occurred consistently under certain climatic conditions. The life-zone concept proved most useful in that it stressed the correlation between latitude, elevation, and life associations and provided a simple means of establishing a common understanding of the major biotic regions of the West. Six major zones were identified, and they were named in accordance with the geographical areas in which corresponding plant-animal groupings were most characteristic. Since desert and scrub plants of North

America are well represented in what is known as the Sonoran Desert, which includes the Colorado Desert, the two lower zones are called Lower Sonoran and Upper Sonoran. A Transition zone, identified by the occurrence of such trees as yellow pine, is usually found between the arid lowlands and the Canadian zone whose lodgepole pines and red firs are reminiscent of the great tracts of conifers in southern Canada. The Hudsonian zone occurs higher on mountain ranges, close to timberline, where conditions are like those met in the taiga around Hudson Bay. The highest of all is the Arctic-Alpine zone, and here life must adjust to as rigorous an environment as that of the Arctic tundra. In the Sierra the zones are plotted by the ranges of altitude (shown in figure 17, p. 174).

Though we see references to these zones and current modifications in recent publications, for the most part the system has been found to be far too general and not definitive enough, particularly where there are so many exceptions as in the mountainous and climatically inconsistent West. A much more precise organization of habitat and life form is possible using the concept of natural communities. It is now standard to refer to a classification developed for California by two eminent botanists, Philip A. Munz and David D. Keck, based on dominant plant species. This community approach has been extremely useful for all ecological work, as it can be enlarged to include typical faunal representatives. Variations of the original Munz and Keck list have evolved, and this book, though it adheres quite closely to the basic twenty-nine as defined by their developers, has taken a few liberties with a view toward simplification.

In the Sierran foothills we return to four communities which have already been introduced—foothill pine woodland, broadleaf evergreen forest, chaparral, and riparian. For the most part, they show but little change from their counterparts to the west. One must travel higher on the range before new communities and new plants appear.

As would be expected, rainfall begins to increase a few hundred feet above the floor of the Central Valley, and the Sierran side enjoys a larger amount of precipitation in contrast to the lower rainfall at the same elevations in the inner coastal hills. There are many more permanent streams and rivers draining the Sierra than flow either east or west from the central Coast Ranges. Distance from the ameliorating influences of the sea has resulted in a climate more characteristically continental than maritime, and the winters are colders and the summers warmer than in coastal regions of comparable latitude and elevation.

These differences notwithstanding, one can wander through an oak-shaded meadow or drive by a patch of chaparral and find it difficult to tell from vegetation alone whether one was closer to the Golden Gate or to Yosemite Valley. The Sierra foothills have the same natural mosaics, the same mixed bag of brush, prairie, and woodland as the Coast Ranges around San Francisco Bay, but on a somewhat larger scale and, by and large, less interrupted by urbanization and intensive farming. This is ranching country still; and though livestock raising, recreation, logging, fire, and gold mining have left their distinctive traces, much of the land, particularly south of Yosemite, looks more serene, undisturbed and less harassed than its coastal counterpart.

Only in the lower foothills is the terrain gentle and unassuming. Grass-covered hills succeed each other, gradually increasing in elevation and ruggedness, until steep V-bottomed gullies and canyons begin to predominate. The miners knew these gulches and probably cursed their plunging and unstable slopes as they worked them over for their precious contents.

The open savannas of the Great Valley—or what is left of them—are spattered with dark dollops of shade as the valley oaks are joined by their foothill cousins, interior live oaks and blue oaks. Before man's influence, it is estimated that most of these rolling landscapes were thick with brush or trees, particularly on shaded or north-facing slopes. Where more mesic wooded areas remain, humus-rich, moist soils encourage many shade-tolerant, thin-leaved herbs and winter-deciduous shrubs. Similar in behavior to riparian trees, such shrubs as redbud and snowberry can experience leaf loss and bear the strain of complete spring refoliation if their substrates retain some moisture throughout the warm season. Digger pines join the blue oaks or straggle up through the chaparral. Some infertile rocky areas are occupied by the hardy knobcone pines. Clusters of buckeye seem indiscriminate in their need for moisture, thriving on dry and moist terrain alike. Golden oaks billow out from their canyon walls like small brown-green clouds.

One plant often encountered in shady nooks of ravines or using other vegetation as support is pipe vine, a California member of a family whose usual habitat is tropical. It is a woody-stemmed vine that hangs like a loosely woven coverlet over rock or shrub, behaving like other common foothill vines —wild grape and wild cucumber. The maroon flower is similar in shape to a curve-stemmed pipe. The upturned end of the tubular flower is constricted. Insects—small flies and the like —attracted to it by odor, and possibly for other reasons, can easily enter the opening; but tiny hairs, pointing downward, make escape almost impossible. They must wait until the hairs relax before they are released. Then they fly to another flower and, retrapped, pollinate it by means of the tiny grains adhering to them after contact with the stamens of the previously visited flower. Because of the structure of the flower and nature of its reproductive parts, the plant must be pollinated by insects. Though the flies are temporarily imprisoned, they flourish on a diet of nutritious pollen. Such interaction is another example of mutualism in the foothill world.

As in the Coast Ranges, open spaces between the scattered oaks hoard a springtime wealth, wildflowers flourishing with bright prodigality. In March and April, when valley and blue oaks are first leafing out, buttercups, yellow violets, and baby-blue-eyes are embroidered on the green of the awakening slopes. Fiddleneck, poppies, lupine, popcorn flower, owl's clover, and cream cup begin to spread blankets of color much as they do on the lower prairies of the Central Valley. May and early June are the best months for breathtaking displays in the higher foothills, well back on the Sierran slope. One soon learns to recognize the habitats which certain favorites prefer. Out in the grass of open, drier terraces and hillsides, look for mariposas, harvest *Brodiaea* with its clusters of indigo trumpets, and its distant relative, golden star. Some of the most charming of the mariposa group are the nodding fairy lanterns. One is creamy white; another has three petals of pink satin curving together under sepals of maroon. They grow seemingly as well in the dry soils of roadside cliff edges as they do in the shade of taller brush and woodland. The latter environment is a good place to see Chinese houses, already described in chapter 4, the red starbursts 'of California *Silene* or pink, and the coral circlets of wind poppy. Here, too, pale violet grass nut or Ithuriel's spear, another species of *Brodiaea*, is much at home. Farewell-to-spring masses pink and magenta on the shallow soils of rocky cliffs, and various daisies and asters are common along the road and in the field.

Though most perennial grasses such as needlegrasses, bluegrasses, and melicgrasses have retreated under the advance of the annuals, some pockets of the former remain here and there in the foothills. We have already discussed the disastrous results of preferential grazing on the perennial grasses of California (see p. 149 above). Here, as in the Great Valley, the annuals are now in almost complete control. Some, like foxtail fescue which thrives on shallow soils, are native. Others are introduced: soft chess, red and ripgut brome, slender oats, European fescue, and mouse barley.

In summer the hills rise through the haze with such understatement that one often questions their presence. It is only when the road encounters the profile of a canyon or curves around an outcrop that the shimmering swells begin to have validity. The brush and arboreal communities of the foothills help sharpen the definition. Patches of chaparral lie about like discarded fur coats, moth-eaten in places where rock slides and other inhospitable soil conditions interrupt the cover. In spring pink sprays of redbud and the little yellow parasols along the branches of *Fremontia* are as colorful as the flowers of their herbaceous neighbors. Canyon floors can usually boast of permanent water, surface or underground; and once again we meet sycamore, alder, big-leaf maple, creek dogwood, ash, willows, cottonwood, live oaks, laurel, and the first of the yellow pines, Douglas-firs, and incense cedars that have crept down from the great green wall of Sierra conifers.

The same influences responsible for the coastal mosaic operate here. Prairie spreads its wind-quickened grasses over the more gentle slopes and valley floors interrupted by oaks, digger pine, buckeye, and shrubs in light or heavy stands depending on edaphic conditions. North-facing hillsides and canyon bottoms support broadleaf deciduous or evergreen trees, mesophytic shrubs such as chokecherry, and adventurous conifers more characteristic of higher elevations. Thin-soiled and rocky ridges back in the foothills are often covered with chamise, manzanita, and other species typical of the dry chaparral. Serpentine sites, of which there are many in the metamorphosed substrates of the western Sierra, have their own characteristically adapted plant life. Where these outcrops occur, lush woodlands halt, and other abrupt changes in the vegetation pattern are not uncommon. In a region where thin soils frequently mantle hillsides and ridges, many serpentine soils are exceptionally shallow and look as though the bedrock was sprinkled with a few handfuls of gravel and left to itself. Here even brush, typical of many serpentine areas, thins out; and stunted annuals, many endemic to these pockets, grow sparsely. Digger pines make occasional appearances.

Much of the foothill belt has a soil mantle startlingly red in color, particularly when damp. In early spring the brilliant green of grass overlaying the vermillion of roadcut is a splendid contrast of color. These soils, often called lateritic because they resemble, in color and other ways, the tropical laterites, were derived from basic igneous rock such as andesite and basalt, and their sedimentary and metamorphic derivatives. Many specialists feel they are the result of long weathering. During this time, hundreds of thousands of years, many minerals were leached out, leaving high concentrations of iron oxide which account for their bright color. At low elevations on the Sierran slope where the precipitation is only moderate, even low, these soils are neutral to alkaline; when rainfall increases beyond a critical amount, they become acid. Characterized by a deficiency in phosphate, some plants cannot grow in them at all, but most of the trees and grasses of the woodland tolerate this condition. The brighter soils are usually less fertile than those on the brownish side. Brush is the typical cover of the more sterile sites. Other edaphic varients control the vegetative cover. Highly acid sediments near the town of Ione, in Amador County, have resulted in very infertile substrates. Shallow soils of low water-retaining ability mantling certain types of volcanic rock, such as andesite and tuff, are hostile to mesophytic growth and usually support grass with sparsely scattered oaks or brush. Limestone areas are scattered in a number of places on the Sierran slope. Soils derived from them are relatively infertile and unable to hold much water.

The enigmatic arbiter of California landscapes, fire, once again proves to be of great importance. J. R. Sweeney in an informative booklet, *The Responses of Vegetation to Fire* (Berkeley and Los Angeles, 1956), makes several interesting points. On the foothill areas he studied, grasses seem to be slow starters. They do not become dominant until three or more years after a fire. Forbs are the typical plants during the first and second years. He maintains that the seeds which germinate the first season after the burn are already present and on the site during the blaze. How do seeds survive such an experience? Many plants germinate only after the seed coats have been heat treated or scarified. Lying dormant through the intervening years, they are the offspring of plants that last sprang up the first year after the previous fire. These fire types rarely appear the second year, as their seeds must wait for the same process that released their parent plants. Some remain secure under the effective insulation of soil. Just an inch or two will protect the more vulnerable seeds from destruction. Other species can sprout only when the duff is removed from the topsoil. They need bare mineral earth to begin growth. According to Sweeney, this may be involved with the larger amount of oxygen present in such exposed soils. Increased fertility resulting from ash deposit is an additional factor, for fire releases nutrients captured in both debris and living tissue. Many brush seedlings take advantage of all these improved conditions, particularly those whose seeds require heat treatment; but quite a number die during the first year. Not only does competition from the light-requiring, pioneering herbaceous or subshrub intruders threaten them, but some have a hard time enduring summer drought when the exposed soils of the new burn are open to increased evaporation.

Fire plays a great role in determining the vegetation patterns of the coastal hills. Equally important in the western Sierra, here also it has established a partnership with topography and soil factors. Though chance and wind direction often determine a fire's path, observers have noted that rolling terrain burns less patchily than broken country, and southward-facing slopes are more fire prone than moister north exposures.

It is often taken for granted that a fire holocaust means total disaster to the animal residents of a fire hit community. This is not quite true though some animals do die. A fire does not mean total destruction; there are always islands of unburned vegetation and cooler sites, such as north-facing exposures and riparian bottomlands, which may escape complete ravagement though the fire is raging around them. No doubt some animals simply leave; a whiff of smoke and they are off. Many birds fly away immediately. Burrow-dwelling creatures are protected under as little as five inches of soil. Animals hidden in deeper crannies and on rock outcrops have a good chance of survival. Hollow logs and gnarled and hole-ridden trunks also provide shelter. Grass fires, in particular, are relatively cool and quickly over. Temporary refuges, possibly inadequate during hotter fires, safely harbor many animals making use of them.

Though many animal populations decrease immediately after a blaze, some may even experience growth surges, especially seed eaters and grazers as the herbs take over. It has been long known to biologists that catastrophe often results in an increase in the number of offspring, and this feature alone helps to repopulate the burn. There are other positive features of fire. The newly opened brushlands provide more grazing and browsing opportunity. If islands of mesophytic vegetation are left, they attract animals from less sheltered neighboring areas. Predators are drawn by the newly opened hunting grounds and by possible increase in prey populations.

Of these last there is usually a goodly number in an environment that furnishes grass and other seed-rich plants. In a bulletin published by the University of California College of Agriculture (No. 663, April 1942), thirteen rodents and one rabbit are listed as being resident on the San Joaquin experimental range administered by the college. Their food and nesting-site preferences are examples of a well-developed ecological niche structure:

> The Merriam chipmunk is scarce and usually found in brushy ravines, where it depends largely on shrubby plants for food. The gray squirrel is likewise scarce. It usually stays in or near digger pines and lives on the pine seeds. The San Joaquin pocket mouse, present in a population of at least one to the acre in 1939, is a small species which subsists mainly on minute seeds. The California pocket mouse is rare. The harvest mouse is even less numerous, and is restricted to the larger swales which retain moisture through the dry season. The white-footed mouse is one of the commoner rodents, and was present in a population of at least one to the acre in the summer of 1939; it occurs mainly in open grassland. The brush mouse and the rock mouse are both common where there are rocks and brush thickets; populations were computed at several to the acre for both in the summer of 1939. The wood rat is partial to situations where there are large outcrops, brush thickets, or live oaks, where it may occur in a population of several to the acre, but it tends to avoid open grassland. Because it feeds mainly on leaves of shrubs and inner bark of twigs from oak and chaparral, it is unimportant as a forage destroyer but may compete with livestock for browse. The meadow mouse is scarce and confined to a small portion of the range, the large swale bottoms with permanent covering of thick vegetation, where the ground remains moist through the summer. The jack rabbit is rare on the range.

All these smaller animals compete with the larger wild herbivores and range livestock for the vegetation of the foothills and, as a result, are resented by ranchers and game management personnel. Not only do they compete for more palatable forage, they may damage extensive areas of rangeland by burrow networks. There is reason to suppose that they were partially responsible for less desirable weed species invading the prairies and savannas as they helped keep the vegetation thin and open to interlopers. These habits alone indicate that the presence of controlling predators such as hawks, owls, and coyotes is highly desirable.

Green and gold and green again, nature's great brush washes color on color as the seasons come and go. At a casual glance, the hills of the lower Sierra appear almost as untroubled as they were before the forty-niners claimed their treasure, but this serenity is often rudely broken along the Mother Lode and major traffic routes. Man has done more than create unsightly piles of gravel residue from dredging operations and more than scarring the land with quarries and artificial badlands from hydraulic methods of placer mining. He is busy carving these gracious hills into vacation and retirement developments and is too often totally unconcerned about the mushrooming of shoddy business construction, out-of-place and in poor taste. He has ruthlessly thrust superhighways through tranquil little towns rich in Gold Rush history and scenic charm.

Lovely though these hills still are, they show in many ways that their beauty is fragile. They will remain lovely only if man allows them to, only if intelligent appreciation rather than destruction guides their destiny.

Yellow pines and black oak, Yosemite Valley

# 12. The Great Green Wall

No unbreachable rampart such as that which often lines a tropical river, the coniferous forests of the Sierra Nevada—its Great Green Wall—are usually open and readily entered. There are exceptions. Close thickets of saplings are decided hindrances. Patches of manzanita or chinquapin can be difficult to negotiate, and mazes of fallen timber impede or stop progress entirely. On a sunny day the forest is cheerful and welcoming. Atomized by numberless yellow-green needles, sunlight spatters in golden sprays through the fanlike branches of firs or falls in heavier showers where the cover is broken. Screened in by the coniferous foliage, this zone of the Sierra has few vistas. The delights of trail and road at these elevations are immediate—a meadow bright with wildflowers, a blossoming dogwood, a stream cascading into pools of green champagne. Only on occasion does the forest give way to a wider sky, where domes and peaks, waterfalls and gorges disclose the granitic foundation.

Though the life-zone names for the vegetation belts of the Sierra are rarely used today, the obvious altitudinal zonation of its plant life has led to several similar systems but with more appropriate designations, many of them based on currently used names of natural communities. Storer and Usinger in *Sierra Nevada Natural History* (Berkeley and Los Angeles, 1963; highly recommended as a guidebook) list Central Valley, foothill belt, yellow pine belt, lodgepole pine–red fir belt, subalpine belt, and alpine belt on the west slope and designate a Jeffrey pine belt, a sagebrush belt, and a southeast desert region on the east side of the range. Another classification separates western mountains into the grasslands of lower elevations, then foothill forest, montane forest, subalpine forest, and above timberline alpine tundra. The lower portion of the Great Green Wall is called the yellow pine belt or montane forest, depending on which system of nomenclature is pre-

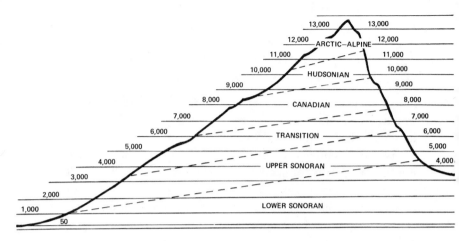

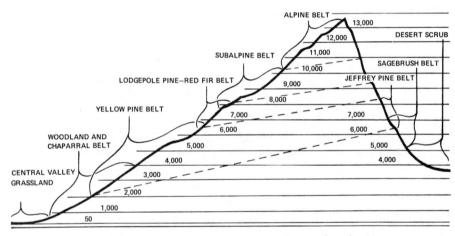

Figure 17. Comparison of two types of zone identification

ferred. It corresponds to Munz and Keck's yellow pine forest community, found roughly at elevations of 2,000 to 7,000 feet in the Sierra Nevada, and is named for one of its dominant species.

After the heat-burdened foothills, the first ranks of the conifers seem almost exuberant with growth. Their abundance, rich variety, and differences in texture and color make traveling through these living canyons a most rewarding experience.

One rightly surmises that such a community indicates an abundance of water, and in fact rainfall often exceeds 60 inches a year. Progressing upward from the floor of the Great Valley, there is an average increase of 8 to 10 inches of rain per thousand feet. This continues to a midelevation maximum and then slacks off. For white firs to be as tall as 200 feet and giant sequoias over 300 feet, not only must there be sufficient moisture, but the growing season must be fairly long and dependable enough so that life processes can continue unhindered for a good portion of the year. It averages from four to seven months depending on elevation, local conditions of relief, and degree of exposure. Growth periods of these durations are considerably shorter than any encountered so far, and they are further constricted by summer drought. Thundershowers notwithstanding, Sierran seasons reflect the general rainfall pattern of the state. Such dry conditions during the growth period plus cold winters that are by no means short have challenged native plants. Here again, evergreenness proves to have survival value; less energy is needed to activate already existing foliage during the first warm days of spring than to grow a whole new crop of leafy tissue.

Sierran forests are not without other defenses: snow and the character of the forest itself. If all the moisture fell as rain it would be far less beneficial to plant life. Snow functions as a reservoir, slowly releasing its meltwater, allowing it to sink into the soil. The fact that streams run far into the summer and some are permanent testifies to the reserves of moisture locked into snow banks. Moving up into the Great Green Wall, one enters country that expects winter snow. For the first time in our trek across California snow is important, something with which to reckon, not only because of its runoff potential and involvement with highway maintenance and winter sports. Snow acts like a blanket, for air trapped in tiny pockets between flakes is excellent insulation. Snow-covered plants are protected by this naturally fluffed quilt from wind and freezing temperatures of damaging degree.

It has been often said that forests make their own climates, which is surprisingly true. Though the overall climate pattern is the main determining factor, the forest itself contributes to its mesic environment. Shade and the presence of litter and humus decrease evaporation in upper soil levels. Wind is considerably less, and temperatures tend to be slightly cooler in summer and warmer in winter than in open fields. Not only shade but the daily evaporation of hundreds of gallons of water from the leaves of constituent trees increases the humidity.

Shading, the interception of direct sunlight, has profound influences on vegetation. In all but the densest forests, there is usually enough light for some photosynthesis, even at ground level. Leaves and boughs are twisted and swung by the wind, scattering sunflecks down through canopy and understory onto the lower layers. Light is diffused and reflected by shiny leaf surfaces, boulders, and the like. Nevertheless, reduced light is a feature of the forest floor and has a large role in a complex survival problem. Plants contending with low light intensities frequently have poorly developed root systems. It appears that young trees with meager roots find it difficult to compete successfully for soil moisture and nutrients with well-established trees possessing large vigorous roots. Thus many seedlings under a closed canopy die, not because of any inability to make sufficient food but because of their poor showing in the competitive struggle for water and nutrients.

In adjusting to the great range of light conditions in most natural communities, a number of adaptations to both sun and shade have evolved. Many plants are able to grow two types of leaves, depending on available illumination. Shade leaves are usually thinner and spongier, have thinner cuticle and fewer palisade cells, are larger in area, and have more openings or stomata, through which gas exchange takes place. Light can enter the food-making cells with greater ease; food production can be carried on more efficiently; and there is a larger amount of photosynthetic material to make use of the available light. Such leaves, however, may wilt under strong sun and even die. Sun leaves, on the other hand, are smaller, more heavily cutinized, and have fewer openings. Very shade-tolerant plants, adapted to life on the forest floor, usually grow only shade leaves. Those requiring full sun normally produce only sun leaves. A number of species grow sun leaves when the site is open to the full sun and shade leaves when the conditions are in reverse. Many California conifers have the ability to inch along in the dim light as saplings, sprouting twigs wth tufts of outsize or "shade-leaf" needles in what is termed a suppressed condition until released by the opening of the canopy because of tree fall or some other circumstance. Then they respond with great vigor to the increased sunlight. Tapered shape is also useful, allowing the longer branches of lower levels to receive a share of the light.

People developing an ecological point of view soon become aware of the structure of this magnificent plant community. The canopy, or overstory, is composed of dark pyramidal masses of needle leaves breaking into silver-green where new growth tips out. They are supported by trunks that hardly seem to taper and which are often girdled by tufted rows of brilliantly chartreuse staghorn lichen. The understory is mainly composed of young conifers and brush, heavy in some places, light in others. Where streams work down gully floors, dogwood, box elder, alder, black cottonwood, big-leaf maples, and other moisture-requiring species encroach upon the coniferous ranks. In the canyon country of the lower Sierra vegetation is frequently missing from riverine areas where one would expect luxuriant growth. Periodic floods, with their pounding boulders and uprooted debris, sweep away any riparian plant life. Some of the most strikingly handsome rivers of the range, such as the Merced and Kings, boil down steep walled canyons whose beds never support a large number of trees during portions of their journey. They are too narrow and boulder choked, and have too little soil and too many floods.

Five broad-leaved trees soften the conifer spired overstory. Tankoak, bay and madroño, familiar from the coastal forests, are residents in the yellow pine belt. Canyon oaks sometimes cluster in thickets along with California bay on dry ridges and on the steep rocky walls and talus slopes of valleys, but they are often found in isolated perches, as lonely as eagle nests. Black oaks are among the loveliest of deciduous trees. Their dark trunks and spreading masses of large glossy leaves are remindful of eastern hardwood forests with their wealth of oaks. When it first leafs out, no tree is a more charming introduction to spring; the velvety new growth is the color of a ripening peach. Though it is scattered throughout the yellow pine belt, occasionally one sees impressive stands of this species. There are several noteworthy groves on the floor of Yosemite Valley.

Each major level in the forest has its typical animal inhabitants. Some seldom shift from one to the other; whereas others move about freely while feeding, though they may prefer certain foliage and branch strata for nesting and shelter. Few mammals spend much of their time in the canopy layer. Chickarees, or pine squirrels, and flying squirrels are the exceptions. Several birds confine most of their food-searching activities to the treetops. Olive-sided flycatchers dart out for insect prey from observation posts high on topmost snags or dead branches, pausing to whistle the "hick, *three* beers" so typical of the Sierra forests. Two nuthatches, red-breasted and pygmy, hunt through the higher portions of coniferous trees. The first keeps close to the top levels of trunk and main branch, while the second forages in the needle tufts at the tips of coniferous branches. A related species, the white-breasted nuthatch, is content to remain in lower levels.

Midheights have their characteristic flycatchers. The wood pewee is joined by the western flycatcher, one of five little gray fellows so indistinguishable individually, each is often referred to simply as an empidonax, the generic name for the group. Another bird of occasional flycatching habit, though of different family, is the Townsend's solitare. Active in the middle layers of foliage growth, it may consort with ruby-crowned kinglets, solitary vireos, and Nashville, Audubon's, and hermit warblers. Males of the last three species have bright yellow patches of color in contrast to gray, white, and black plumage elsewhere on their bodies. These small birds are gleaners, busily assessing twigs for insects, though many go after flies on occasion.

Two larger birds are occasionally seen at these elevations—band-tailed pigeons and Sierra (or sooty) grouse. The first species flocks in groups of a dozen or more and is the only native member of the dove group nesting regularly at such altitudes.

Understory occupants have two features of the environment to their advantage. The canopy overhead affords them protection from exposure to the elements as well as aerial predation. Their habitual distance above the ground keeps them well away from most four-footed enemies.

The amount and extent of shrub growth vary within the Great Green Wall. Several important groups such as manzanita, *Ribes*, and ceanothus are represented in practically all of the zones of the Sierran slope. In general there are three major brush zones: foothill chaparral, mid-altitude shrub growth, and montane or mountain chaparral of the lodgepole pine–red fir community. Though some tree species of the yellow pine zone forest maintain forward positions down in the foothills, only a few of the brush species of the lower elevations penetrate the coniferous tracts above, one being silk tassel. Chamise, white-leaf manzanita, a number of ceanothus types, flannel bush (*Fremontia*), scrub oak, toyon, and their companions buffer the hills between the rolling oak savannas of the piedmont and the forests of the Great Green Wall.

Within the yellow pine belt, shrub cover varies. Where soils are very poor or shallow, as on many steep and rocky hillsides, or where the forest has been removed by fire, disease or logging, service berry, bitter cherry, birch-leaf mountain mahogany, and several types of manzanita, ceanothus, and *Ribes* form ragged tracts. In time, most plants pioneering after a disturbance will be shaded out by the reestablished trees, though patches of common brush species appear sporadically under mature cover if it is not too dense. Bracken is another fire opportunist, but great expanses of it also occur under trees or in meadows, particularly on highly acid soils. Two species grow in extensive covers under uncrowded forests or on open slopes. One is a low-growing, spicy-odored shrub with featherlike leaves, known by the uncomplimentary name of mountain misery. The other, less common, is squaw mat, a dwarf ceanothus. Aside from the last three plants, shrubby growth under the conifers is irregular. Under heavy stands of yellow pine and white fir it may be completely absent, primarily because of shade. Some species flourish under moderate shade—thimbleberry, wild rose, mock orange, chokecherry, mountain snowberry, and spirea. Others apparently need even more mesic sites such as stream banks—western azalea, willow of many types, hazelnut, creek dogwood, twinberry, and spice bush with its turkey red chrysanthemum-type flowers—though some of these species have quite wide amplitudes of tolerance. Like bitter cherry, they can be seen growing with seeming lack of stress exposed at roadside or clearing edge.

Montane chaparral consists primarily of huckleberry oak, pinemat manzanita, and chinquapin, a near kin of the oak group. It is characteristic under yellow and Jeffrey pines or firs and scattered about on granite slabs where soil patches alternate with expanses of bare rock. These three shrubs congregate in small, prostrate thickets, or hang on to solitary footholds in cracks or fissures. Pinemat manzanita, like squaw mat, sprawls in carpets as well. Both also occupy occasional sites within less dense lodgepole pine and fir forests. Some shrubs like tobacco brush—a large-leaved ceanothus—bitter cherry, and various currants creep up to relatively high altitudes.

Many birds preferring riparian growth feeding niches are bright specks as they flash through the willows—Wilson's and yellow warblers, downy woodpeckers, and black-headed grosbeaks. Plainer birds such as warbling vireos, Traill's flycatchers, and the russet-backed thrush—a ground dweller—make use of the insect wealth of streamside environments. Out on the sunnier chaparral-covered slopes, fox sparrows and mountain quail comb through the brush. Dusky flycatchers "hawk" for insects in the air over open hillsides. Where the shrub and herbaceous layers are shaded by a forest canopy overhead, winter wrens dart through the tangles of twig and stem, pausing on the roots of upturned trees to twitch their tails or sing surprisingly noisy songs. MacGillivray's (Tolmie) warblers also frequent thickets where cover and a variety of nest sites and food are available. The shrubs provide flowers, fruit, bark, and foliage for various appetites and attract insects which in turn bring those birds feeding on them.

Herbs are certainly not in short supply in the forest community. Like all their plant and animal neighbors they have their habitat preferences. Many pentstemons, like the magenta Sierra pride, claim cracks in exposed bedrock holding but a thimbleful of soil. Stonecrops and even some drought-resistant ferns share such unlikely seeming homes. Other pentstemons—the spectacular scarlet bugler and equally colorful species that are lavender, pink, and electric blue—join scarlet gilia, the satin-petaled blazing stars, Sierra iris, sometimes the color of weak tea, paintbrush, orange or yellow wallflowers, locoweeds, vetches, and lupines in hill and roadside gardens flourishing in July and early August. A handsome lupine is appropriately named the harlequin because of its bright pink and yellow blossoms. Where moisture lingers, near a spring or on a creek bank, one of California's few native orchids, rein orchid, thrusts up stalks along which tiny, delicately scented white flowers are arranged in tidy vertical rows. These are towered over by the elongated stems of monkshood, bleeding heart, red columbine, the spreading panicles of flowers of the carrot family such as swamp whitehead, wild onions with their ball-shaped blooms of delicate rose, and the brilliant scarlet monkeyflower.

Shaded woods are not without their herbs. Even though one knows they are to be expected, a clump of bright red snow plants, saprophytic members of the heather family, blazing up from the needle-littered floor is a delightful shock. Here, too, are the slender stalks of wintergreen and coralroot, a saprophytic (that is, it obtains food from decaying organic material) orchid. In more open forest, where the humus is less thick, yellow-throated gilia, often called mustang-clover, spreads like a blanket of foothill flowers transplanted to these altitudes. In the deeper shade and on moister slopes, one may find miterwort, with its tiny circles cut from fragile green lace, and a small white-flowered relative, woodland star. Nor are grasses missing. Species of wild rye, needlegrass, squirreltail, bluegrass, fescue, brome, melicgrass, hairgrass, wheatgrass, and reedgrass grow in glades as well as in clearings and around the edges of wet meadows.

Scurrying about over the roots and between the stems of the plants of the forest community are avian ground dwellers— robins, Oregon juncoes, and chipping sparrows—usually going about the business of food hunting on the shady floor. One such bird is relatively shy and, brown backed with a spotted cream-colored breast and reddish tail, would probably escape attention but for its song. This is the ethereal fluting of the hermit thrush which rises to meet the first stars in a series of spaced, ascending phrases. It has a quality shared by few other sounds in nature, and it makes little difference to the listener that the singer may be merely reestablishing his territorial boundaries or is communicating with his mate. His song is of firs and pines darkening against the sundown sky.

Insects, earthworms, and other soil dwellers claiming the attention of robins and thrushes are also eagerly sought by shrews and moles. Seeds dropped from the foliage layers overhead are harvested by a host of small herbivorous mammals— chipmunks which take to shrub branches on occasion, golden-mantled ground squirrels, and brush and deer mice. Wood rats and gophers make use of the green vegetation usually found somewhere within foraging reach all summer long. The largest herbivorous mammal is the mule deer. Visitors often see one or more of these graceful animals in open glades or out in meadows, browsing or filing along wildlife trails. Many larger predators are more omnivorous than strictly carnivorous and rely upon plant augmentation of their diet in season, almost as much as they depend on animal prey. Coyotes, gray foxes, and those engaging pests, the black bears, scout for anything appealing to their appetites. The same is true for some of the smaller meat eaters—spotted and striped skunks, raccoons, and ringtails. Only weasels, martens, bobcats, and the few remaining mountain lions on the Sierran slope are strictly carnivorous.

If one is fortunate, one can get a glimpse of California's most beautiful snake, the mountain king, as it winds through the duff of the forest floor. Though many people, particularly those from the East, react strongly in the negative to the striking combination of red, black, and cream because of its superficial resemblance to the poisonous coral snake, this handsome montane species is thoroughly harmless. Rattlesnakes, however, are a different story. One species, western rattlesnake, occurs throughout the Sierra, except in the higher elevations. The rubber boa is a reptile that looks much like a long, shiny, light-brown worm with its blunt tail and small size; it is one of the most gentle creatures in the world. Garter and gopher snakes are as frequent here as they are in other natural communities of California. Three types of lizards are common—fence, skink, and alligator. The last two apparently need more shaded and protected habitats than the first, which can often be seen sunning itself on rocks and stumps.

Many animals range widely through the forest. Owls and hawks soar over the canopy and keep watchful eyes for game below. They often perch on snags or rest in the upper branches for the same purpose. The spotted owl is partial to golden oak thickets. Bats seldom rest away from their accustomed roosting places but make use of the open foraging space, above the overstory and between the trees. Traveling up and down, either by flight or by working their way over trunks and branches, many birds utilize almost the entire length of the trees. Brown creepers and several woodpeckers—pileated, hairy, and white-headed—constantly check the bark of trees in their feeding rounds. Yellow-bellied sapsuckers, specialized woodpeckers, add nutritious sap to their insect diet.

The noisiest flitter is the crested jay. Though often encountered on the ground, it works up the trunk by hopping from branch to branch as if going up stairs. It is one of the most obvious birds of the Sierran slope, and one cannot spend a day in the white firs without making its blue-and-black acquaintance. Chickadees frequent many levels while inspecting foliage buds and needle clusters. The most colorful bird in California, the western tanager with its red head and yellow, black, and white body, often behaves in the same way as a flycatcher. It perches on snags and branch tips, swinging out like a little burst of flame to snatch insects while in flight. Two mammals have arboreal habits in these lofty forests. Gray squirrels, residents as well of the yellow pine forest, scamper across the duff, run up on boulders, and disappear into the lower limbs almost faster than the eye can follow their quick movements. Telltale patches of raw and bleeding sapwood where the bark has been gnawed away indicate porcupine damage. These slow-moving, formidable-appearing rodents account for the destruction and injury of thousands of trees yearly. Their sluggishness on the ground gives very little hint of their agility in climbing, particularly saplings or young trees whose lower branches are close to the forest floor.

Though most trees of the Great Green Wall are common to other parts of the West, one species is a famed native of California. This is the big tree or giant sequoia (now named *Sequoiadendron giganteum*) scattered in isolated groves throughout the middle elevations of the central Sierra, commonly on slopes between valleys glaciated in the Ice Age. Like its coastal relative, the redwood, it is remarkably resistant to fire and contains so much tannin it is unpalatable to insects. The absence of pitch is an additional fireproof asset. Though no longer considered the oldest living things, as the bristlecone pines of eastern California surpass them in age, big trees have enviable longevity records, and their 3,000 or so years are to be respected. They can claim title to being the largest plants on earth. They are not the tallest, for the coastal redwoods top them by several dozen feet; but their girth and board footage elect them over their relatives for sheer size. Many individuals would be tall enough to rival their coastal cousins except that lightning has blasted away their tops. Even so, their fire scars heal over, and they maintain incredible vigor in spite of thousands of years of storm and wind. They are not easily destroyed, but their shallow spreading root mats give way when exposed by erosion. Then the giants topple to lie undecayed for centuries. Seedlings rarely begin life on rich humus soil; like the redwoods, they do best in disturbed sites where mineral soils have been exposed by fire, road building, tree uprooting, or other circumstances. They need sunlight in the sapling stage; and though they will remain in suppressed condition for a number of years, growing slowly and adding small annual increments of woody tissue, when fire or tree fall opens them to light, they respond with renewed vitality and soon dominate the canopy.

The other members of this coniferous royal court are no mean princelings. Each is a monarch in its own right in certain advantageous environments. Four species—white fir, sugar pine, yellow pine, and Douglas-fir—have individuals whose heights tower close to or over two hundred feet. In the face of such an impressive community, it seems difficult to accept the view that conifers, in general, have retreated in the advance of the recently evolved broadleaf trees. Though both the Sierran yellow pine belt and the coastal slopes of the Pacific Northwest have easygoing climates, elsewhere coniferous forests have been pushed to sites of adversity—dry highlands, subarctic muskeg, sandy lowlands, and infertile pockets. Conebearing trees have features that enable them to cope with numerous hardships. Some thrive in highly acid soils, intolerable to many plants, which are characteristic of cool, moist climates where humus accumulations decompose slowly in cold, poorly aerated soils, producing varied amounts of acid. Nutrients and fine particles, important in plant growth, are leached or washed down to lower levels along with basic salts, which, if remaining in the topsoil, would have neutralized its acidity. Certain heaths and conifers have adapted remarkably to such hostile circumstances and may even benefit from the reduced competition. The ability of the latter to live in very acid soils where other plants cannot compete may be a major factor contributing to their continued survival in the face of the aggressive broadleaf trees. Since their decaying needles contain acid which further aggrevates the soil condition, the coniferous group must have been in danger of destroying itself. Becoming tolerant to soils high in acid, in which a partnership with root fungi plays no small part, was superb strategy on the part of a versatile, tenacious group of trees.

The pines are even sturdier members of a robust tribe. Many

species of this hardy and flexible genus have taken on extremely rigorous environments. Some, like the closed-cone pines, flourish in regions subjected to frequent burns, germinating best in bare mineral soils and fire adapting to the extent of producing offspring only when the cones have been exposed to heat or possibly other stimulating circumstances. Many pines thrive in thin or coarse dry soils. In California, pines of the forest must live through the dry summers in an environment where the shade-limited root systems of young trees prevent them from competing successfully with older or better established neighbors for the scant soil moisture. How have the pines met these adversities? Head on, as it were, with a vitality apparently able to overcome all but the most rigorous conditions.

As a group they have long roots, are xerophytic with many drought-resistant leaf features, and are high photosynthesizers, efficient in producing food. Being only moderately shade tolerant, though there is much variation throughout the genus, they seldom close in dense ranks. One local exception, lodgepole pine, is discussed in the next chapter.

To return to the important cone bearers of the Great Green Wall, we first take note of the tree giving its name to this vegetation zone, western yellow pine. This important lumber tree shares some of the characteristics of both redwood species and Douglas-fir. It pioneers after fires and appears to germinate best in fresh soils. It does not stump sprout, however, and is relatively light requiring. Most stands of yellow pine are open and easily penetrated. The trees seldom crowd in on one another. Thick as incense, the pungently resinous pine-woods odor is best on a summer afternoon when warm winds sweep upslope and sing in the needles overhead.

Though great tracts of these pines are common throughout mid and higher elevations in the West—notably near Flagstaff, Arizona—in much of the Sierra they are scattered here and there. They move into openings in the forest where tree fall gives them light, and they often cover larger areas that have been cleared by fire or that are exposed or relatively dry and unattractive to more mesophytic species. Strong, deep roots help the western yellow pine live in areas of comparatively low rainfall where one would expect more xerophytic growth. Quite often it is the harbinger of the great coniferous tracts of the Sierran slope, straggling along a foothill streamcourse or standing over the clustered oaks of a north-facing hillside. Where it keeps to itself in groves on upland flats, underbrush is usually scarce, and the litter is a springy layer of golden-brown needles broken by occasional carpets of mountain misery, squaw mat, bracken, grasses, and flowering forbs.

Jeffrey pine, its close relative, is usually distinguished by the vanilla odor of its bark and larger cone size. It has been pushed to even more extreme positions, the real outposts of the western ranges. It occurs on serpentines, at higher elevations where the winters are colder and longer, on dry eastern slopes, on exposed ridges and less favorable sites. It is relatively uncommon in the yellow pine belt proper.

Sugar pines are moderately shade tolerant, and young trees do fairly well in the understory; but unless released in later life, they seldom grow large enough to dominate old-growth canopies. At full size their height is balanced by long slim branches held out like stiff straight arms at right angles to the trunk. Their tips are often pulled down by cones measuring up to two feet in length, the longest of any conifer in the world. This species is less xerophytic than ponderosa or Jeffrey pine. Best growth occurs where precipitation rates range from 40 to 50 inches. Besides the pines we have just discussed, the yellow pine belt has other outstanding cone bearers.

Though very common in much of the mountainous West, the Douglas-fir is somewhat of an enigma; it does not seem to fit easily into any coniferous family. One of its Latin names, *Psuedotsuga taxifolia*, means "false hemlock with the leaves of a yew." It has been called Oregon pine and Douglas spruce as well as Douglas-fir. The last two common names refer to David Douglas, enthusiastic collector of botanical specimens in the palmy days of western exploration. It is unique, however, and has no close relationship to these other species except that it is a conifer with some characteristics very much its own. Unlike true firs, the cones hang down with bracts that are whimsical miniatures of mouse hindquarters, tails and all, tucked in between the scales. The needles are soft and two ranked, spread like those of the coastal redwoods or drooped to give the pliant twig a weeping aspect. Apparently it needs more light than many other cone bearers, although seedlings seem to do best in some shade at first. Being only midtolerant of shade when older, other species that are more so, such as white fir and incense cedar, can crowd it out when it is weakened by too long a sojourn in the understory. Because it survives best in exposed soils and thrives in the light shade of temporary cover, it is a fire or disaster pioneer. Pure stands of Douglas-fir can usually be attributed to some such opening of the forest, particularly on mesic sites such as moist north-facing slopes where it is most at home in the drier parts of its range.

To many people, incense cedar looks like a small cousin of the big tree, with reddish bark and scalelike leaves. It has a much wider range and occurs in the northern Coast Ranges, the Klamath Mountains, the Sierra, and the mountains of southern Oregon, as well as in southern California. No near relation to the other western cedars—various cypresses, junipers, and other cone bearers given the common name of cedar—it is, like the Douglas-fir, a member of a small but widespread genus. More shade tolerant than Douglas-fir, it suppresses very well and can live for years waiting release to the sun.

One of the true firs, white fir (the genus *Abies*) is a close relative of its higher dwelling cousin, red fir. Both cones and needles, particularly those on the higher branches, thrust up from the branchlets with a jauntiness not found in most conifers. While it fares well under conditions of moderate light, its flourishing saplings account for the firm, almost solid compaction of young forest along road shoulders and at meadow edge. In spite of its shade tolerance, this hedgerow behavior testifies to aggressiveness in most light conditions. Moisture is a requirement, however, and white fir does well only where there is a plentiful supply. Those traveling up the Sierran slope usually first encounter it after the other conifers of this zone have appeared. Where it occurs in pure stands, it is quite dense and there is little or no underbrush.

All these species seem to be replacing themselves readily when circumstances permit and to be companionable to a remarkable degree. Two others, California nutmeg and yew, occur here, though not in great numbers, and we find them scattered about much as they are in coastal forests.

Life in a forest is no simple enterprise. For plants, five important factors help control distribution: soil type, moisture, temperature, wind, and light. Sandy soil, five inches of rain, warm climate, gusty winds, and 360 days of bright sun create deserts. Deep loams, 50 inches of rain, temperate climate, moderate winds, and 200 days of bright sun result in forests. Soils must not be neglected in any discussion of natural areas and their causative features. Their influence in determining the communities found on serpentines, in salt marshes, and on thin-soiled steep hillsides has already been discussed. It is time to consider the soil as such, and be introduced to its various properties. Without it and the moisture and minerals it holds we have a moon, a lifeless, ungenerous, sterile floor. With it, we enjoy the richness and diversification of the living world, dependent as it is on the often ignored vital cover beneath our feet.

Stated simply, soil is a mixture of air, water, and its solutes, mineral particles from the parent bedrock, decaying organic matter, and organisms responsible for this decay. Nutrients may be present in cereal-dry or frozen soils, but they are unavailable to plants in these circumstances. To be at their best, soils should contain much organic matter decomposing under warm, moist, and aerated conditions. Then the organisms responsible for decay can easily break down the litter and reduce it to water-soluble elements and compounds which only then are readily assimilable by the living plants needing these chemicals for growth.

Soil specialists speak of this living "skin" in terms of horizons. The O horizons include fresh leaf drop and partially to completely decomposed matter. They rest on the A horizon, sometimes divided into an upper A1 where decaying debris is mixed with mineral material, and a lower A2. This last is rather depleted because it is the zone of leaching. Water, pulled down by gravity, carries with it much of the organically derived nutrients from the upper layers and deposits them, with fine rock particles, in the *B* horizon lying below. Hardpans and claypans, impervious layers through which water cannot percolate, may consolidate here under grassland and other types of community. The *C* horizon, lower still, consists, for the most part, of partially weathered rock fragments, close to the bedrock from which the mineral particles are derived. Little organic matter is trapped here, and the soil profile passes into the *D* horizon. This is primarily bedrock and, generally, is uninvolved with the organic breakdown occurring above. Horizons may be missing or thin, depending on local circumstances.

The typical soils of the Sierran coniferous forests, at their best, are deep and hold water well. But they may be podzolic, that is, moderately to highly acid and unkindly to species not adapted to this chemical condition. Summer drought also complicates matters. Needles, twigs, and other organic material continue to accumulate, but dry soils, though warm in the summer months, further retard the decomposition of decay-resisting, acid humus. Thus the major agents of soil fertility, the living organisms responsible for soil enrichment—bacteria, earthworms, insects, and the like—are hampered by acidity, drought, and the nature of the plant litter itself. Needles contain large amounts of lignin, woody material that is slow to break down. Nevertheless, soil production continues, though at less than optimum pace. Snow meltwater reserves and occasional thunder showers contribute moisture, and nature has other devices as well. Bacteria, living commensally with roots of certain plants, notably the legumes, fix atmospheric nitrogen into compounds available to plants. Since this necessary substance is scarce, leachable, and often destroyed by fire and other disruptions of the natural community, agents able to transfer free nitrogen into water-soluble and easily absorbed soil substances are of tremendous value to neighboring plants. Vetches, lupine, and other wild legumes of the Sierra are very useful in this respect. More acid tolerant than bacteria, fungi, discussed more fully below, have a very important role in the decay processes of coniferous forests and are responsible for decomposing large amounts of organic litter.

In spite of the efforts of these organisms, evergreen forests often have relatively poor soils. One has but to think of the nitrogenous reserves locked up in the great boles and foliage masses of coniferous forests to realize that not much nutriment is being returned to the soil. Local conditions vary. Decay and the replenishment of nitrogen are slower in the Great Green Wall than they are in the always warm, moist climate of the Amazonian rainforest with its broadleaf trees, but the process is faster on the western slopes of the Sierra than in the arid pinyon woodlands to the east. Throughout the summer-drought regions, nevertheless, what needle litter falls is not only resistant to decay but is protected from decomposition by the nature of both the climate and soils found in the habitat.

Fungi are key links in the chain of decay and soil buildup, and they play an immeasurably important part in the continuation of cone-bearing forests. Hyphae—microscopic filaments from such simple plants as mushrooms, toadstools, bracket fungi, and the like—are woven through the soil in an incredible fabric. Thousands of miles of these threadlike structures are estimated to live in each acre of forest soil. They digest the organic debris by the excretion of enzymes, freeing the elements and compounds so necessary for continued plant growth. Some fungi engage in mutually helpful symbiotic relationships with certain trees. The hyphae either surround the rootlets or enter them, in both cases making nitrogen compounds available to the partner plant. It is quite possible that the fungi prefer acid soils and condemn the trees to live in these unfriendly substrates. If so, they have certainly compensated for their choice of homesite by aiding in the liberation of vitally needed elements.

The same organisms responsible for soil fertility are active in the disintegration of woody tissue. Fallen logs are reduced in time to the basic elements which were needed for their growth in the first place. Each is a small ecosystem, literally crawling with a life of its own. If you examine such a decaying log, you are likely to find centipedes and pill bugs curled in the dirt, perhaps startled by the unexpected light. There might be holes where carpenter bees have entered, and by lifting a portion of the loose bark, you can see where bark beetles have excavated their wandering, apparently aimless channels between sap-wood and bark. Termites may have penetrated into the heart, and carpenter ants may have begun long galleries as circuitous as those of medieval castles. Probably part of the heartwood will be pithy and punklike because of fungi, those insatiate digesters which bind not only soil but fresh fallen wood with mats of mycelia that exude juices into the dead tissues. Where the wood is really rotten you can rub it to dust between your fingers. Here, skulking in tunnels, are the larvae of wood-boring beetles and flat bugs feeding on the fungus-riddled wood.

One type of decomposer succeeds another as the breakdown continues. While dead or discarded animal debris and wastes are being worked over by ants, carrion beetles, and flies, springtails and silverfish are ingesting dropped leaves and other dead herbaceous material. At the same time, bacteria and fungi are exploring these new additions to the litter of the for-est floor. Softened by initial attacks, the humus attracts pill and

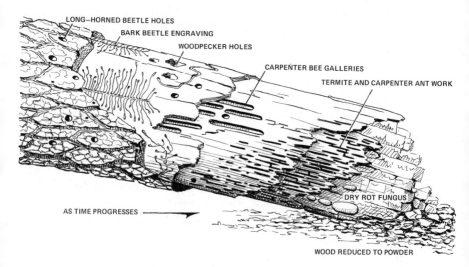

Figure 18. Reduction of fallen log to soil

sow bugs, earthworms, and millipedes. The droppings of the decomposing insects and other small invertebrates are worked on in turn by still smaller organisms. The litter is constantly being reduced to particles that decrease in size as the process continues. Each stage results in the release of additional enriching substances. Finally everything has been removed from the picnic table. All that is left is inorganic matter. It remains in the soil, ready for use by another generation of plants and the succeeding consumers of the forest food web.

In time, even the stricken giants of the big trees, lying here so long without noticeable decay, will succumb to the forces of weather and decomposition. Nothing, once alive, can fully protect itself from eventually returning to the soil from which it came originally. Elements circle and recircle, occasionally caught in the life histories of various living things. It is entirely possible that each of us carries an atom of potassium or carbon once in the tissues of a tree fern of the Dinosaur Age or an ancient trilobite. Tens of thousands of years from now, other organisms will reuse the same basic materials life on earth has found indispensable for its growth and evolution.

Lower State Lake, Kings Canyon National Park

# 13. Mountain Meadow

Mid-October is a good time to discover the responses of the high country—that above 7,000 feet—to approaching winter. The experience will be all the more delightful if you start your trip in the lowlands of the Great Valley, in Sacramento, for instance, as the temperature there will probably be in the seventies or eighties, and the watered lawns still green. The road up Carson Pass is an easy and excellent introduction to the Sierra Nevada. You will be spared the trucks of Highways 80 and 50 to the north and the speed of newly straightened roads in Yosemite further south.

At the outset, try to ignore the conifers or, at least, don't let their impressive ranks keep you from watching for the sometimes elusive deciduous trees and bushes. These are the color bearers, the rich bunting that decorates the solemn groves of needle-leaf trees. In the yellow pine zone, dogwood leaves slowly shift from deep green to reddish purple. At the beginning of the cold season, while the days are still warm, the transformation is barely noticeable. The centers of the large oval leaves first become tinted with magenta which finally spreads throughout the entire leaf. Branch follows branch in catching fire as frosty nights succeed each other. Then the foliage lightens in color to a rose-gold before dropping off entirely. Another colorful tree of mesic sites is big-leaf maple whose leaves burn with clear yellow or orange flame. Black oaks vary from golden-brown to topaz, when backlighted by a sun now firmly in the southern sky. The elegance of their sharply scalloped leaves compensates for any lack of brilliance of hue. Of the many deciduous shrubs and woody vines in the foothills and lower slopes, poison oak and wild grape have the handsomest fall foliage. Both begin to flush rose-pink soon after Labor Day without waiting for temperatures to drop to freezing.

Ascending the Sierran slope, one sees but flares of color here and there—in a canyon, out on a brush-covered slope. Where are the masses of brilliance, the would-be rivals of the eastern hardwoods? Persist on to higher altitudes; and if you are fortunate in your timing, you will be properly overwhelmed. As the yellow pine community gives way to the lodgepole pine–red fir zone, the long, conifered ramps of the range begin their break into the granite heartland, the basins and ridges of the High Sierra. The first true mountain meadows open into surrounding groves of pine and fir. Here, the quiet pools of autumn's shallow creeks reflect the slim fingers of willow leaves, the color of buttercups. Around the meadow edges, away from the marshy center, mountain blueberry spreads low growing clumps of burgundy and cerise.

The meadow floors themselves are wondrous autumnal tapestries. Corn lilies, tall monocots that seem to have escaped from farms in Iowa, stand in golden shocks. Sedges and rushes run in streaks of russet through shining grass. But the glory of these meadows, the rocky benches around shores of alpine lakes, and wide upland slopes is the groves of aspen—the West's answer to New England's fall. Framed by peaks silvered with the year's first snow, reflected in lakes of gentian blue, flickering in a wind fresh out of a sky the color of the lakes, these tall, white-barked torches of orange-gold flame for a brief week or so of incandescence before dying out in the chill air of coming winter. They are at their best when they mingle with a few conifers. The contrast of smoldering silk and somber plush is startling and effective. For the most part, their neighbors are the pines and firs of this upper midzone—red fir and Jeffrey, lodgepole, and silver pines, the last a relative of the sugar pine of lower altitudes.

These high mountain meadows, with their handsome stands of aspen, have been called the jewels of the Sierra by that greatest of all mountaineering naturalists, John Muir. Tucked in walls of dark green needles, they spread out to the alpine sky. One rarely sees them below 6,000 feet, except for such valley floors as Yosemite. Here, however, the vegetation is typically that of the yellow pine community, and it has but few species representative of higher elevations.

Why do these open swales seldom occur below the lodgepole pine–red fir zone, roughly 6,000 to 9,500 feet? The answer is found in the circumstances of their birth which forecast their death as well, for these gemlike natural gardens are doomed to disappear from the Sierra in a process as inexorable as that of ice melt in a warm room. Their origins stem from glaciers that sculptured the range during the Ice Age. After the slow rise of the western slope, which culminates in the Sierran crest, the streams draining it were forced to reorient their channels in a westerly direction except at high elevations, where many tributaries continued to flow to the south or north before joining the major rivers. These reconstructed drainage ways were used by glaciers which the Sierra supported four times during the Pleistocene. Several ice fields were formed by the pressure of accumulating snow. Glaciers spread like great tongues from these masses, moving down such valleys as the Hetch Hetchy and Yosemite.

An active glacier alters considerably the landscapes under its control. It excavates a cirque, or rounded basin, at its head. Where several glaciers grind cirques at the base of a peak, it may be carved into a pyramidal mass known as a horn. Such spectacular relief features are frequently encountered in extensively glaciated mountainous country. As an ice cap or field spills over into moving glaciers, the terrain over which they pass is considerably modified by the shattering and grinding that marks their progress. V-shaped stream courses are widened into U-shaped valleys. Jointed or cracked surface rock is plucked from place and frozen into the ice mass. This captured rubble scrapes and scours the bedrock, which when already fractured by orogenic forces, is easily quarried. Pulled away, these pieces leave vertical cliffs like those lining Yosemite Valley, which at one time was filled with ice 3,000 feet thick. Tributary channels above the main glacial body become hanging valleys, left high but not dry when waterfalls plunge from them to the canyon below, as they often do.

In time, the climate warmed and the glaciers receded, leaving behind scattered boulders called erratics, often on patches of glacial polish (rock scraped to shiny smoothness by ice flow). Moraines are piles of rock discarded by the glaciers as they melted back up their valleys. Where, in their downward journey, they encountered unresisting rock, they carved basins. The paths of many glaciers were followed by stream-connected depressions filled today with lakes or their offspring, meadows. To accurately describe what is meant by that last phrase, a little time must be spent on a major ecological concept, succession.

It was early noted in the study of ecology that disturbed sites, if left alone, would revert to a former community well adapted to the environment and capable of replacing itself indefinitely. This stability is reflected in the term "climax community." Each stage in the transition to climax is characterized by certain plants and animals adapted to the conditions of that stage. This process has already been touched upon in relation to what takes place after fires have swept through some of California's biotic communities (see pp. 74f). The first stage is usually herbaceous growth. The second may be brush, which in turn is supplanted by reinvading trees or shrubs. They shade out or, in other ways, compete successfully with temporary species.

In contrast to this secondary succession, which follows destruction of the community, there are two types of succession known as primary, ecological history beginning in a sterile area with no previous plant or animal inhabitants. These processes operate over much longer periods of time and start with open bodies of water, on one hand, and bare rock faces, on the other. Though it may take thousands of years and gradual changes of substrate and organism, both of these environments will finally support a climax community. To bring it closer to home, in the far distant future both Lake Tenaya in Yosemite National Park and the rounded surface of nearby Polly Dome will disappear under climax vegetation, whatever it might be in that period of geologic time, unless human or other circumstances interfere. The stages of transition from water to land form a hydrosere, and from rock surface to soil, a xerosere. There is a tendency on the part of both to eventually become mesic, or moderately moist.

The High Sierra has many examples of both processes. As we have hinted, every one of its mountain or alpine meadows is a stage in successional history. As the great glaciers receded, they left behind chains of basins which, collecting rain- and meltwater, quickly became lakes. They appear almost exactly as they did when deserted by their glaciers—clear, ice cold, rock bedded, and almost devoid of nutrient compounds, thus incapable of supporting much plankton or higher plant life. In places, the ice mass has so recently receded it is but yesterday, geologically speaking, that it retrenched to higher sites. There are about fifty or so small glaciers left in the High Sierra, but they are not the impressive rivers of ice we see in Alaska, on Mount Rainier, and in the Canadian Rockies.

Other features of the environment keep high country lakes in youthful stages. Succession is slowed by rigorous climatic conditions precluding much plant activity. Because of their lofty positions, little sediment drains into them from surrounding rocky heights. They tend to remain clear blue and not very hospitable to living organisms. At lower altitudes or under more favorable conditions, the transformation from lake to meadow progresses at a faster rate. Slowing their pace as they enter quiet water, streams drop loads of detritus, building deltas and distributing sediment over the lake floor. Dead plankton and the remains of higher vegetation and aquatic animals augment the deposited debris. Typical plant species of Sierra lakes include pond scums, chara, and other algae, pond weeds, water lilies with their yellow cups, arrowhead, aquatic buttercups, water starwort, and an astonishing little plant, bladderwort. The latter is one of the three carnivorous plants in California, all of which occur in areas low in nitrogen such as marshes and bogs. It grows in feather-leaved ganglions sprinkled with little beadlike bladders. These have trap doors at one end that are triggered to operate when tiny creatures such as minute crustaceans or newly hatched tadpoles swim close enough to spring them. If careless victims touch the sensitive bristles around the doors, the bladders open to suck them in, and they must surrender their nitrogen-rich little bodies for the benefit of the plant.

As the debris of dead organic material accumulates, and stream flow and runoff deposit additional sediment, the lake becomes shallower. Its edges tighten as plant life pushes out farther and farther into the shrinking pond. Sedges and rushes, several aquatic grasses, horsetails, and mosses, including sphagnum—of limited occurence in the Sierra but still present—crowd together on the rim. These plants succumb to winter, and their dead leaves and stems enrich and build the soil, raising the pond's floor little by little. Fallen trees slowly decay in the chill, poorly aerated muck, but eventually they also contribute their remains. Now other plants, many of them showy wildflowers, tolerant of wet to damp substrates begin to homestead—corn lilies, paintbrushes of varying reddish hues, white violets, shooting stars with their small pink rockets, wild hollyhock, cranesbill, the charming purple lilies known as camas, wild iris, brilliant orange and maroon Sierra lilies, a number of white umbels, monkshood, and potentillas and buttercups as yellow as turned aspen leaves. Two flowers are so interesting they deserve more than places behind commas—green gentian and elephant's head. The first, cousin to blue gentians, also meadowland neighbors, rivals corn lilies in height. Pale green flowers, whose parts all seem at right angles to each other, grow in long rows next to the stout stem. Two species of elephant's head are picturesquely named for their rosy blossoms, exact miniatures of angry elephants with flaring ears and upraised trunk. In all but the dampest places, grasses take advantage of these open sites—needlegrass, bluegrass, trisetum, hairgrass, bluejoint, fescues, and ticklegrass.

Where the meadow slopes up to enter the surrounding forest, many wildflowers and shrubs are at home. The composites are represented by cone flowers, sneezeweed, and goldenrod. Forget-me-nots and their cousins, chiming bells, open pink and blue blossoms beside clumps of willow and fireweed. Many of the shrubs have flowers as colorful as the herbs. Alpine laurel has clusters of small rosy cups. Blueberry, Labrador tea, snowberry, ceanothus, and red elderberry move onto better drained soils, as do the trees. More tolerant of poorly drained soils, lodgepole pines step in front of their red fir associates. The youngsters of both species often show snow damage. A foot or so from the ground, the trunk suddenly bends at right angles and, with another sharp turn, straightens itself again. These "knees" indicate that snow, extremely heavy in the pine-fir belts, once burdened the sapling to the point where it almost broke under the weight.

As the pond gives way to the encroaching meadow, it may become but a narrow slough, drying in late summer. If running water drains the swale, the meadow may continue, more or less, to be held at bay. Under both circumstances, however, the trees inch in, sapling by sapling, until every vestige of the old marsh has completely disappeared. Now forests of the two major climax species crowd out the herbs and shrubs and only a few of the latter remain.

Though lodgepole pine and red fir, in general, intermingle,

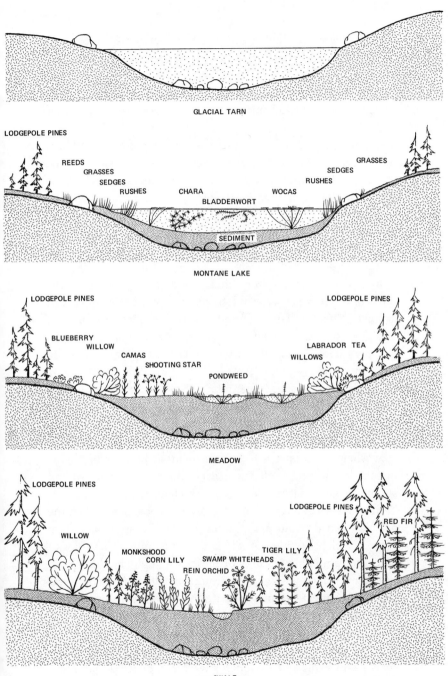

Figure 19. Stages in succession from lake to climax forest

the latter is more shade tolerant but not as moisture tolerant as the pine. It does best in deep, well-drained soils. Lodgepoles even thrive where hardpans, subsoil layers impervious to water, interfere with soil drainage, accounting for islands of this species among yellow pines and other trees requiring drier sites.

Lodgepole pine has the reputation of being a fire invader. It has serotinous-type cones and often constitutes a successional stage after fire, which is very destructive to this species because of its thin bark. Though it frequently grows in dense groves, packed together like matches in a box, the stand grows in unison, as it were, no one individual rising much higher than its peers. Self-pruning, the process whereby the lower branches of the trees die and are discarded when there is inadequate light under the canopy for efficient photosynthesis, keeps the boles of many tree species relatively free of snags. Lodgepoles, however, do not self-prune as efficiently as some other conifers. Looking into a dense stand, one is reminded of tangled lengths of heavy wire by the slim, bare branches hanging awkwardly from the trunk.

In the Rockies, shade tolerants such as subalpine fir and Engelmann spruce overtake the spindly lodgepoles and eventually cause their demise. In the Sierra, however, the pines appear to be holding their own and growing to impressive heights, except when red firs prove to be their nemesis because of blighting shade. Both these climax species crawl up to sheltered and sunny pockets that would usually be claimed by trees of timberline. Aspen is another fire species and takes over, when the field is opened, from underground suckers that remain from groves which sprang up after previous burns. Its blocky patches are notable features of meadows, high shoulders, and subalpine slopes where underground moisture is at no great depth. Like most fire pioneers, it is very shade intolerant and gives way, in time, to the dominant trees of the climax forest.

Meadows have their typical animal residents as well as visitors from the nearby forest—tangers, white-crowned sparrows, hermit and Audubon's warblers, pileated, hairy and white-headed woodpeckers, olive-sided flycatchers, wood pe-

wees, chickadees, red-breasted nuthatches, Townsend's solitaires, and fox sparrows.

Some birds are more or less confined to higher forest zones.
Ruby-crowned kinglets give way to golden crowned; Cassin's
finches replace purple; and the Williamson's sapsucker and
three-toed woodpeckers do not venture much below the lodgepole pine–red fir belt. The western bluebird of foothill fields is
supplanted by mountain bluebirds, flashes of sky blue as they
feed out in the swales. At the upper edge of the zone, Clark's
nutcrackers take the place of crested jays. They are as noisy
and cheeky but less colorful than their cousins. Several cone
openers are active, pine grosbeaks and crossbills, found in coniferous boreal communities across the continent. Evening
grosbeaks are striking with their gold, black, and white plumage. They forage either in trees or on the ground, looking for
berries and seeds or nibbling succulent buds. Two owls hunt
through forest and meadow alike—great horned and pygmy
—looking for the many rodents and small animals making use
of open, herb-covered terrain.

Snowshoe hares replace the black-tailed jacks of lower elevations. Though rarely seen, the intriguing patterns of their
paw prints, a series of little blue-shadowed dimples in the
snow, disclose their skill in negotiating deep drifts. Chickarees
are actually more common here than in lower zones. This
noisy, inquisitive arboreal squirrel leaves telltale caches of
green unopened cones, pine bough tips, and piles of descaled
cone cores throughout the woods where it is resident. Pine
marten, several weasels, mountain coyote, the rare red fox,
and black bear scout through the forest and along meadow
trails.

The drier meadows are undermined with intricate tunnels.
Belding ground squirrels are the familiar picketpins of Tuolumne and Red's meadows, favorite campgrounds for many
visitors. They are most engaging as they fold their paws on
their plump little stomachs and, with backs as straight as fence
posts, stare at their neighbors. Jumping mice and meadow mice
use the tangled vegetation of damp meadow floors; gophers
tunnel the soft, easily worked soil. Shrews often scurry through

this convenient labyrinth of passageways or forage in the grassy mat. Vegetation is affected, to lesser or greater degree, by extensive small mammal excavation. Disturbance of soil, the accumulation of nitrogenous wastes, and the transporting of seeds and vegetative shoots would tend to rearrange the distributions of plants from patterns they might otherwise have adopted. One of the gaudiest of meadow dwellers is a tiny tree-frog, strikingly marked with green, red, or yellow and but an inch or two long. At the other end of the scale in size, mule deer often browse in these open places. One should watch for them in late afternoon or early morning.

Nowhere are streams more glorious than in the high country, running through flumes of white granite, churning in natural potholes, widening into perfect trout pools. If you are patient, you will be rewarded by acquaintanceship with one of the West's most unusual birds, the water ouzel or dipper. Rather plain in appearance—robin sized and gray—he works his way along the stream, often stopping to perch on spray-wet rocks to bob up and down. He actually feeds right in the water, at times submerged, looking for the aquatic insects that form his diet.

Most high-country ponds, lakes, and streams have representatives of what may not be the most visually impressive but certainly has the potential of being the most annoyingly aggressive group of animals in the world—insects. Their numbers and representation vary with the differences between aquatic habitats. Timberline lakes in sterile bedrock or gravel-floored basins are almost lifeless. Too cold, too frozen much of the year to support much plankton or higher plant life, there is little food for the small crustaceans and herbivorous insects whose absence discourages not only predaceous insects but trout as well. Unless deliberately stocked, these lovely turquoise-hued lakes are the sources of much angling anguish as cast after cast proves fishless. Where lake-meadow succession has advanced to the stage of supporting both flourishing aquatic vegetation and well-developed shoreline growth, insect life crawls, flies, and swims into strategic positions in the local food web. Diving beetles, water pennies, water boatmen, and water striders are active predators, and the same is true for the immature forms of dragon- and damsel-flies, the larvae of Dobson- and alder-flies, and mosquitoes. Most mayfly nymphs, on the other hand, feed on algae and other types of plant material. A number of aquatic insects, stone-fly nymphs, for example, use both plant and animal material. By their eating habits they are capable of filling all kinds of intermediate positions, and their lack of dietary restriction is useful should circumstances curtail part of their food supply.

No current of water is much swifter than that of a rushing mountain stream. In many ways it is one of the most inhospitable aquatic environments, and few organisms can cope with its obstacles. Chill in temperature, often almost barren of any plant life, about the only feature in its favor is that it has a plentiful supply of oxygen. Only when it encounters restraining meadows or slows down to rest in pools or lakes can residents be complacent about its flow. To live in a swiftly flowing stream, one can either escape the relentless push by seeking shelter or develop ways to oppose the ever-present pressure. Streamlining, presenting as little resistant surface as possible to the current, is common among stream dwellers. Trout, other swift stream fish, and even some invertebrates such as certain nymphal mayflies have taken this tactic. Adult riffle beetles cling to roots with strong claws. Black fly larvae have suckers and hooks with which to anchor their bodies onto stream-swept rocks, and immature midges have hooks or suction discs for the same purpose. The adaptable caddis-flies vary both food capturing and protective devices. In swift water, several species construct nets to gather food supplies. Among those preferring not to do battle are some caddis-flies which burrow into sandy floors. Others construct little cases out of gravel, plant material, and other bits and pieces, cementing the tapered little shelter with their own secretions. The case may be weighed down with heavier pebbles. Some crustaceans hide under protecting overhangs and in crannies, but many aquatic forms simply avoid the problem entirely and never tackle the hazards of the torrential flow.

Where the streams have helped build soil by depositing rock fragments on upland valley floors or where slopes have accumulated them on foundations of talus piles or bare incline, the high world supports forests of lodgepole pine, red fir, aspen, and hemlock. Elsewhere on this rolling, swelling granitic sea, among glacial erratics and scattered boulders, there are both lone individuals and clumps of high altitude conifers wherever they can gain a foothold; and the same is true for certain shrubs—currants, dwarf juniper, pinemat manzanita, huckleberry oak, and sagebrush, which slips in over the crest from its domain to the east. In places such subalpine species as Jeffrey, whitebark, and other timberline pines and the striking, red-barked Sierra juniper appear to be growing right out of bedrock as their roots disappear into narrow cracks. Stunted lodgepole pines hang onto tiny patches of soil tucked in fissures or accumulated on the surface.

How does the process of soil manufacture start on the sterile substrate of bare rock? In other words, how does a xerosere develop? There are no cooperating streams to drop silt or gravel; seemingly, no plants add their decayed remains. There are, however, forces at work. Bare rock disintegrates into small particles by mechanical and chemical weathering. Freezing water caught in cracks or crevices expands and forces open such apertures and clefts. This action repeated over and over results in much broken and fractured rock. Heat from the powerful alpine sun performs the same task. Both work together to peel off slabs of granite in what is called exfoliation, the process that has shaped the smooth bald domes so typical of the Sierra. Gravity pulls down the cracked-off debris and piles it into talus slopes, leaving the smaller particles, gravel, and the like, in heaps scattered about on ledges, in depressions, or packed at the bottom of open fractures. Meltwater and temporary springtime rivulets carry down eroded fragments and deposit them in catchment pockets.

At the same time, biological as well as geological processes are at work. Those primitive, long-suffering plants—rock lichens—manage to persist on their heat-baked, wind-blasted, bone-dry homesites, often covering whole cliff faces with a brilliant mosaic of marmalade orange, sulphur yellow, black, and gray. Incidentally, where there are seeps from cracks that intercept underground water flow, long black streaks on cliff walls are caused by algae. The steep side of Half Dome has excellent examples of this discoloration. To return to lichens, not only do chemicals released by the plant aid in corroding the rock surface, its decaying tissues add organic material to soil particles slowly accumulating from the disintegrating rock beneath and fragments deposited by other means. Eventually, enough soil may collect to support mosses which thicken the tiny growing plot. They in turn decompose, and then a small bed is ready for pioneering hardy ferns, and grasses and other small flowering plants. The patch grows and may cover several square feet and be several inches thick unless a catastrophe removes it. A venturesome shrub takes root, then another, until the rock surface now supports a real thicket. Trees find foothold in the deepening soil and in convenient cracks in the parent rock below. Finally, all traces of the original surface become buried under soil and litter; climax vegetation has arrived.

Another type of succession begins in clefts. As gravel grains and other debris gather in them, higher plants can take advantage of any water held by accumulating rock fragments, dead leaves, and other organic matter. Hardy grasses and forbs become established without having to wait for lichens and mosses to work on the substrate. Such colonies in time spread out mats of vegetation that slowly cover the adjacent bedrock. Even trees, though remaining dwarfed, can begin and continue growth in cracks whose meager soils are enriched by discarded plant litter.

Mountain meadows are more than the flower-bright expanses of burgeoning green so pleasing to summer visitors. They are gracious pauses in ecological time, hospitable to a number of diverse creatures and rewarding to plants requiring light and moisture, open as they are to the energizing warmth of the high country sun.

Banner Peak and Mount Ritter, High Sierra

# 14. The Bluest Sky

Two natural communities are found at elevations of 9,500 feet and above, and one of these, unlike the other biotic complexes of California, cannot be reached by ordinary car. The motor traveler can look above the highest outposts of subalpine forest to true alpine country from several road-traversed passes, but these rock-bastioned rims and slopes are aloof. They are reserved for hikers and trail riders willing to expend energy, time, and in many instances money. Even with limited resources of all three it is possible to venture into the alpine world on your own. You should have at least a full day, a snack, a map of the area that interests you, and tennis shoes or good boots that have been broken in.

There are many places in the Sierra where all you need allow is a day in which to ascend from your car to timberline and above, and return. The Saddlebag Lake–Tioga Pass area is a favorite as two miles in any upward direction will take you to one of the numerous rock fields above tree limit. At the head of Rock Creek a stiff but feasible three-mile climb switchbacks up to Mono Pass. Several trails struggle above the Bishop Creek headwaters. On the other side of Minaret Summit, a vehicular crossing of the divide, the trails from Agnew Meadows quickly mount to spectacular alpine scenery via Shadow and Garnet Lakes. From trail head at the Virginia Lakes is another short but sturdy three-mile climb to Summit Pass. Sonora Pass, a motor highway, is rewarding; for only a mile or two up on each side of the summit, alpine gardens begin to carpet the rocky slopes.

Some clarification of terms is useful at this point. *Alpine* refers to mountain areas above timberline; *subalpine*, those at timberline or slightly below. *Timberline*, or *tree limit*, refers to the upper edge of tree growth. The two communities discussed in this chaper are subalpine forest and alpine fell-fields. Timberline, actually an ecotone, occurs between the two, as the upper limit of the subalpine forest is the lower edge of the alpine zone. There are a few areas in the Sierra where tree limit is just about road level—Minaret Summit and Tioga, Sonora, and Carson passes. These are the easiest places to become acquainted with the most typical timberline tree of the Sierra, whitebark pine.

Each of the vegetational zones of the range has characteristic pines adapted to certain climatic, edaphic, and topographical conditions. They extend from the thirsty slopes of foothill oak and digger pine to damp meadow floors ringed with the slender boles of invading lodgepole pine. Whitebark pine literally tops the group, with its lofty residence on many ranges throughout the mountainous West. At its lower limits in the Sierra it meets five other pines: Jeffrey, lodgepole, silver, limber, and foxtail. Two additional conifers—western, or Sierra, juniper and mountain hemlock—have the necessary stamina to exist on these storm-battered heights. The first is a loner, and one seldom finds specimens of this ruggedly good-looking tree within touching distance of another of the same species. Not only do they need full sunlight, their demanding homesites are responsible for solitude. Soil and moisture sources, scarce on high, rocky terraces, are hardly sufficient for one tree, let alone a number. Western junipers rarely grow taller than fifty feet; and when fortunate enough to be in a sheltered location, they have stubby but upright cinnamon red trunks. Where winter winds harry them, as on ridge tops, they are forced into the picturesque gnarling so typical of timberline trees. Hemlocks, on the other hand, are companionably shade tolerant, and one seldom sees isolated individuals. They are among the most graceful of subalpine trees, and their supple, small-needled branches bend readily under snow drift. A heavy pack in the sapling stage accounts for off-balance clumps thrusting out at odd angles to the slope on which they are growing. They do best in protected basins, around lake shores, for instance, and on shaded slopes, where the soils are moist enough for their needs.

Whitebark pines are capable of great endurance. On their hard-won castelations they do battle with an extremely severe climate. In growth habit they resemble no other western pines in that they often form multi-trunked thickets no taller than large shrubs. No one seems to know for sure whether several individuals group together in this fashion or if one trunk separates into a cluster of smaller stems. Though often curving together in lyrelike poses, their great flexibility bends them over in prostration where they are exposed to high wind. The white bark that gives them their name has a silvery luster rather than the chalky color of their meadow-edge confederates, aspen. They are scattered about—on rocky shelves high on the sides of a pass, in hedgelike masses on benches above glacier-parented lakes and meadows, and where natural windbreaks offer them some protection. Unlike lodgepoles they are not wet footed, but prefer well drained sites. Until the days of lightweight air mattresses, hikers were advised to spread their bedrolls on springy piles of whitebark pine branches, but improved equipment and good high-country manners have discouraged this destructive practice.

Those traveling the trails that traverse the crestline ridges find their paths leading to lakes and meadows of unsurpassing loveliness. Nowhere in California is there more beauty crowded into each square foot of scenery. Willow-bordered brooks wander through verdant patches of sedge, rush, and grass, spreading into small spongy marshes or tightening into rills edged with flowers. Many of the same floral types found below recur here—elephant's head, lupines, groundsel, monkeyflowers, shooting star, columbine, paintbrush, buttercups, orchids, and gentians. But some, like grass-of-parnassus, are unique and never move down from their high homes. Small shrubs of the heather family grow on the same fringing terraces where whitebark pine grows. The little magenta bowls of red mountain heather resemble those of a related shrub of high meadows, American laurel. Cassiope hangs elfin bells of pure white from tiny crimson star-point sepals. Sod-building sedges, spread out in coarse, compacted masses, or so-called dry meadows, are characteristic alpine dwellers.

The dwarfed plant cover above timberline has often been referred to as alpine tundra, not only because of its similarity to the treeless plains of the Arctic, but also because the two communities share a significant number of the same plants. Certain differences, however, distinguish the two types. Alpine tundra lacks the mosses and leafy lichens so abundant in the Far North; because of pronounced relief, its soils are better drained, and they are not underlain by extensive permafrost, or permanently frozen soil.

The two tundras were once contiguous, and there is considerable evidence that alpine tundra, as a community, is derived from the northern type. One theory holds that tundra was probably present on the foothills and plains surrounding the Rockies and other western ranges during the Ice Age. It retreated up the flanks of the mountains as the climate became warmer and forest reinvaded; now, its last isolated strongholds in temperate zones are high in mountain positions where the climate strongly resembles that of the Arctic.

A large number of these same alpine plants occur in the Far North, pointing to one-time continuity or connection between the two tundra communities. The author has seen the diminutive pink, moss campion, in several widely separated locations —up on Trail Ridge in the Front Range's Rocky Mountain National Park on a bright July morning when brown rosy finches were feeding on a nearby snowbank, at midnight when the sun was crawling through fog shrouding Norway's North Cape, and on a mountain flank overlooking a magnificent glacier during a typical Alaskan downpour.

It has been estimated that 42 percent of the tundra flora of Rocky Mountain National Park is circumpolar, that is, distributed in Arctic regions around the North Pole in Eurasia and on the North American continent, including the islands of the Arctic archipelago. In contrast, only 10 percent of the alpine flora of the Sierra is found throughout the boreal world. This is not to intimate that the remaining 90 percent is unrelated to tundra floras. Many of the genera are shared— *Gentiana, Saxifraga, Ranunculus, Pedicularis* (elephant's head), *Primula* (primrose), *Phlox, Polemonium*, and *Draba* (whitlowgrass), among others. The burgundy-red little succulent roseroot, Arctic pearlwort, alpine buttercup, mountain sorrel, pygmy bitterroot, willow herb, littleleaf huckleberry, Jacob's ladder, elephant's head, and shrubby cinquefoil are included in the list of those plants found in the Sierra as well as the Rockies and boreal areas. In addition the Sierra has many flowers that are almost identical to those farther east or north; they differ only in their specific status, and are similar in appearance—primrose, sky pilot, and alpine paintbrush are examples. But anyone who has memories of the gardens of the High Rockies with their exquisite one-inch tall clumps of unforgettably blue forget-me-not, moss campion, fairy primrose, goldenbloom saxifrage, and alp lilies no larger than a child's thimble will look for them in vain.

Differences in floristic composition are not the only distinguishing features of the two alpine vegetations. Richly developed tundra with thicker soils is poorly represented in the High Sierra which, essentially, has five alpine landscapes: (1) sheer rock walls, slopes, and ridges with isolated or clumped plants scattered sparingly in crevices over the mostly barren surfaces; (2) basin meadows; (3) rock-strewn flats, pass summits, and truncated peak tops; (4) lakes and ponds; (5) talus piles and scree slides. The most characteristic sites of alpine vegetation are small local meadows and fell-fields, stony stretches barren of much soil.

Why are there such dissimilarities between the alpine plant life of Colorado's Front Range, for instance, and the Sierra? Climate is an important part of the answer. The northern and central Rockies receive far more summer rainfall than the Sierra. It is an exceptional July day when one can roam up Colorado's Yankee Boy Basin in the San Juan Mountains, over Trail Ridge or Independence Pass without several showers falling in a 24-hour period. A soil-plant pattern has consequently evolved. It was set in operation by the presence of abundant moisture during the growing season. The more rain, the more plants, resulting in an increased supply of leaves, roots, and other remains that in turn deepened and enriched the soil. Summer precipitation has also made possible luxuriant herbaceous undergrowth at midelevations in the Rockies. Though at their best, Sierran wild flower gardens are impressive and colorful, sister ranges to the east have a superior display, with its famed blue columbine, coral tinted gilias, golden gaillardias, and violet harebells. Both floras have much in common; but there is a flamboyance, a spendthrift air about the flowered banks and slopes of the Rockies, in sharp contrast to the parsimony of Sierran hillsides in the summer, except where streams and drying ponds provide a continuing source of water. It has been pointed out that these wild gardens have contributed many dwarf forms to the alpine plant life of the Rockies. In addition, all but two of the high altitude species of the Front Range are perennial, whereas a number of Sierran alpine plants are annual. The accumulated root masses of the longer lived plants are important in constructing the sod of rich, well developed tundra formation. Another process may have been in operation. It has been suggested that many of the tundra species now shunning the Sierran heights were once present, and summer drought has driven them north, back to where reliable summertime moisture offers less rigorous habitats.

In the more barren areas of the Rockies, as in the Sierra, there are many fell-fields with their specially adapted plants. If wet-meadow-type tundra and its typical flora are scarce in the Sierra, the two great mountain systems of the West, the Rockies and the Sierra-Cascades, ought to share a number of rock garden alpine plants. To a point they do, but many alpine species common to both the Rockies and the Cascades do not even enter the Sierra, let alone make it all the way down the crest. There are several definite breaks in the Sierra-Cascade mountain complex—the Columbia River, the midelevation plateaus and foothills of the Klamath and Pit river drainages, around Lake Almanor, in the vicinity of Lake Tahoe and Donner Pass, Tioga Pass, and Minaret Summit to name a few. All of these areas are low enough to allow intruding arboreal growth between isolated alpine communities. According to a plant survey made many years ago by Frank Smiley, at each of these natural breaks a few more of the plants common to the Arctic and alpine Rockies drop out, and their places are taken by endemics peculiar to the Californian floristic province. Roughly 44 percent of the plant species of timberline or above are either endemics or are shared with the Great Basin and the Pacific Northwest. The remaining 56 percent are found in the Rockies; and of that, 10 percent are boreal in distribution. This means that slightly less than half of Sierran alpine material has little or no specific connection with either the Arctic or with the Rocky Mountains. Consequently, while California has many fascinating plants of timberline and fell-field, a good number are Far Westerners; and of those, 10 percent belong to the state alone. They have not only accepted the demanding regime of summer drought, but they are equipped to live in the punishing world of the high country.

A ride over any one of the higher passes of the Sierra discloses what happens to trees on the approach to timberline. They are smaller in size and fewer in number, and at last give up entirely. Those at the highest elevations exhibit many characteristics common to tree limit. Some take advantage of microclimates, small environments in which features of relief provide localized modifications from the general climatic pattern. Favorable microhabitats are quite numerous in alpine regions: sheltered pockets behind rocky projections where storm winds hesitate on their wild journey across the crest, and slopes comparatively warmer than others because of down drainage of cold air. Southerly or westerly aspects have the advantage of direct sun during the warmer parts of the day. Snow provides its own series of microenvironments, some more helpful to plant growth, some less so. Where it lingers in crannies or on north- and east-facing hillsides, it can prevent vegetation entirely if it does not melt until late summer. Where there is too little protective snow cover and meager meltwater, plants are also discouraged. Where snow lies in a thick blanket ready to disappear into the soil at the first signs of summer, vegetation effectively escapes the terrible pair, winter wind and cold. Temperatures may be much higher under insulating snow cover, and wind is practically nil. Many plants cannot live through the blizzards of alpine winter without this friendly quilt.

Prostration is a typical feature of timberline shrubs and trees. Anyone caught in disastrously high winds would do well to remember this and lie prone. There is much less wind pressure at ground surface, and trees permanently bent instead of standing upright profit from the decrease of force. The German language has contributed a useful word, *krummholz*, which means "crooked wood." It refers to copses of stunted, contorted trees at timberline. A little searching and one can find examples of this process carried to an interesting degree. Look for a boulder, perhaps not more than a foot high. You might find a little hedge of whitebark pine extending back behind it. At one time, a seedling took advantage of the protection afforded by the rock, and as it continued growth it was compelled by the driving winds to creep close to the earth, elongating horizontally rather than vertically.

Occasionally one will see trunks that are bravely tall, considering their winter ordeal. Very commonly the branches will be permanently pointed in one direction, giving rise to the term "flagging." It is easy to guess the direction of the prevailing wind, as the side of the trunk meeting it head on is bare of limbs or foliage. Though there may be some training by wind, most flagging is due to dehydration and the consequent killing of any twigs venturing growth on the windward side, but buds on the leeside can continue to grow. It is reasonable to suspect that snow and ice blast are also responsible for the damaged tissue. Compaction is another characteristic adjustment to cold and strong wind. Though unprotected tips of shoots are subject to wind shear, lateral or side buds form densely crowded masses pruned back to stiff hedgelike clumps that can actually bear the weight of heavy objects. When leaders, top-most twigs, project above the snow cover, they are often doomed to be killed by both chill and dehydration. Dieback or the death of most of the tree leaving a minimum amount of foliage and bark to continue food making and transport, is another adjustment to the harsh environment.

The trees and shrubs of timberline have other causes for stuntedness and dwarfing. Thin, gravelly soils, low in organic material, do not hold moisture well; in addition, at this altitude they are generally cold. Summers are short as well as cool at these elevations. Temperatures can drop below freezing any night of the year, and during winter they close down for eight or nine months of intense cold that rarely rises above frost. But for snowmelt and the only too occasional summer shower, it is an arid world as well. Not only is cold air dry, water in the form of ice is as unabsorbable by plants as the iron in a railroad track; only solutions can penetrate cell walls. Little rain falls in the Sierra during summer, and the first precipitation of the rainy season will probably be in the form of light autumnal snow. If it melts, it is but a brief interruption of a long drought for any timberline tree not fortunate enough to grow by a wet meadow. From September to late May, moisture is either scarce or locked up as snow and ice kept below melting point by the frost of winter air. Even if soil temperatures reach above freezing, cold substrates tend to significantly lower the metabolic rates of the plants of the community, even in summer.

This leaves but one open course, dormancy. The woody plants of the heights follow the same routine as those of the chaparral, except for a shift of season. Most food manufacture and water transpiration cease during the fall. When spring finally returns, which may be as late as July, full activity is resumed once again though still hampered by chill and the drought that follow when the melting snows have disappeared. All in all, the shrubs and trees of timberline do not have the time or energy to grow much. Even their cells are small in comparison to trees of more temperate regions. Trees whose soil resources are restricted, such as those growing from bedrock cracks or in shallow gravel beds, are subject to additional stress.

How do they maintain their vigor and, as in the case of California's most famed timberline tree, the bristlecone pine, live to incredible ages? If they anchor themselves to wind-harried, often unstable footholds, they could be sending down long roots which penetrate to water and soil pockets deep in bedrock cracks. The evergreen habit again proves useful, for no new foliage need be produced each spring. Already present, it is ready to go to work. Another helpful adaptation is known as hardening. The cell sap gradually thickens in fall. As if anti-freeze was slowly being added, the freezing point is lowered which prevents frost injury to what would otherwise be vulnerable tissue.

What about the herbs, the most fragile highland denizens? Most of them are perennials, for annuals have several strikes against them in the game of alpine survival. The flowers may be left unpollinated or the plant killed by frost before the seeds can mature. Suitable substrate may be lacking. By being perennial, the plant is assured of several years of life in which to produce successfully germinating seeds. Each year, however, the plant either dies back to root masses at the approach of winter or huddles in a little sofa-cushion hump. These densely foliaged mounds not only retain heat and moisture, they provide their own sheltering compaction. Buried under snow, they are well out of the reach of wind and cold. One of the buckwheats bulges up in tiny silver-leaved tufts so solid in mass that one can stand on them without much damage to the plant. Other plant pillows are phloxes, cushion-cress, podistera, sandwort, and glacial draba. A few species actually begin growth under snow and even open blossoms where melting carves out little hollows within the disintegrating banks.

Because closeness to the earth's surface is so desirable, many species are mat plants. A number of genera from lower altitudes have not only shortened their stems, but have also spread out, flattening themselves to the soil. High Sierran examples include sulfur flower, silver mat, pygmy *Erigeron*, and pussy paws. Several dwarf species, about as big as buttons, include a tiny bitterroot, pygmy *Ivesia*, an alpine willow and a dwarf aster. Tufts of small alpine grass, some growing in little hollow-centered circles, take root in the thin soils or between tumbled boulders.

Succulence is just as useful here as it is in lower arid environments. One of the loveliest alpine plants is roseroot, or sedum. It belongs to the stone crop group, a family known for its thick, juicy leaves and stems. Waxy or woolly leaves also deter water loss. The little white-flowered forget-me-nots, one of the globe gilias, and several composites, among them the striking alpine gold, have stems and foliage scattered over with a hairy coat. Other plants, however, seem to rely on no one set of features clearly adapted for survival in this harrowing environment. They bloom with all the aplomb and arrogance of less harassed relatives—flax, wallflower, rock fringe (a richly carmine relation of willow herb and often in protected crannies), sky pilot, alpine columbine, alumroot, and primrose, whose lush crimson flowers and juicy stems surprise rock climbers as they work along patches of scree. Plant life above the fell-fields is mainly comprised of lichens, those stalwart associations of algae and fungi that seem to defy all climatic regulation.

The animals of timberline and above are equally ingenious in coping with their inhospitable home. By their winter habits they can be roughly classified into migrants, sleepers, and cautious but courageous actives. When mountain sheep were more

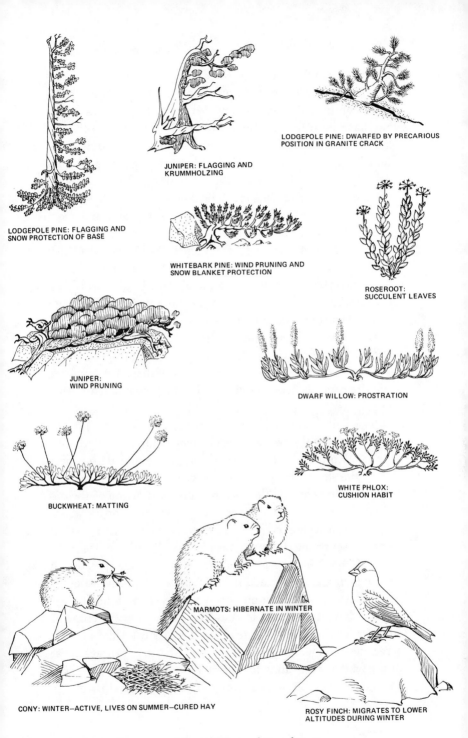

Figure 20. Adaptations to alpine climate

abundant than they are now, their yearly exodus down to winter range must have been impressive. Those still living in the Sierra continue the process and leave the high slopes where they have been feeding when the first snows presage the onslaught of winter. They slowly but steadily move down into friendlier climes. The deer of the Sierra, though no rock hoppers, also descend to less snowbound regions. The most typical alpine birds, gray-crowned rosy finches, forsake their fell-field summer quarters. They too seek the warmer sun and more easily obtained food of the lower levels.

Most alpine rodents sleep through the worst months; they include ground squirrels, various mice, alpine chipmunks, and marmots, roly-poly plump and plumy-tailed fellows of grizzled russet that sit sentinel on rocks and outcrops of the high country. During true hibernation, body temperatures lower considerably, and the animal falls into deep sleep. Though it may wake on occasion, for the most part it is in torpor, and its slowed rate of metabolism and cessation of most activity place little drain on its food resources, the fat accumulated during the summer.

One small creature, the pika (cony or little chief hare) of the rabbit group is the winter resident whose life habits provoke surprise. No migrant or hibernator, it goes about its business during the short weeks of summer, gathering herbaceous material growing close to the rock pile home. It is one of the delights of the alpine trail to see these little gray ghosts, about the size of a teen-age rat, tailless and with ears as round as buttons, scurrying between meadow and rock refuge with loads of "hay" in their mouths. Hay it is, for they spread it to dry and cure, and then add it to the piles each cony jealously accumulates in preparation for winter. When it finally descends, they move about in runways, feeding on the crops of summer and protected from blizzard and frost alike in their scree-slope home. Pocket gophers are also active through most of the winter, excavating tunnels in the surface earth and snow to reach vegetation or caches of food buried beneath winter's cover.

Few people have spent much time at timberline in the Sierran winter. We can only surmise what it must be like: gale-force winds hurling snow across crests and peaks; cold that could sting an exposed cheek to frozen whiteness in a matter of minutes; and days when the screaming stops and the snow, packed in stream head basins, lies smooth and unrumpled under the bluest sky.

Mono Lake in winter

# 15. The Other Side of the Mountain

The vast area on the eastern edge of the Sierra looks inland, not to the sea, the presence of which, even at timberline, considerably influences the natural landscapes explored so far. True, many winter storms from the ocean climb over the Sierran crest and move east to die or join those moving south from Canada or north from the Gulf of Mexico. But there is a transparency, a plate glass quality, to the atmosphere in these high interior rangelands seldom experienced near the coast. Distances no longer disappear behind blue gauze. They thrust up hills and mesas and lay down lakes and valleys that keep their details out to the horizon itself. Left behind are thirteen of the communities so far discussed. On the other side of the mountain, there are instead eight new communities, as well as variations of six already introduced.

Many Californians live some distance from the sea and may visit the beach, if at all, only once or twice a year; but still it is customary to speak of "coastal" fogs and "sea" breezes throughout a large portion of the state. Winter storms "come down from the Gulf of Alaska," and there is general awareness that the sun finally goes to rest beneath the waves of the Pacific. Now at the top of 9,941-foot Tioga Pass, a frequently used entryway to the eastern Sierra slope, it is as though another ocean pulls imaginations toward sunrise skies. What lies before the visitor is that great inland sea of mountain and valley, the basin-and-range province of the interior West.

Central California's small slice of it actually belongs to a major subdivision, the Great Basin. Not a lowland at all, though its name gives that impression, much of its floor is well above three thousand feet in elevation. It is so called because it has few outlets to the sea and is rimmed by high plateaus and ranges except at the extreme northwestern corner, which is partially drained by the Klamath and Pit rivers. It is really a complex of basins or sinks in which collected runoff either settles in permanent lakes, disappears into natural underground reservoirs, or evaporates into the desert air leaving the alkali-bedded dry lakes so typical of the region.

Those with standing water, in the main, are remnants of once much larger lakes, inheritors of the pluvial wealth of the Pleistocene. Great Salt Lake is one of the much shrunken offspring of Lake Bonneville. Pyramid Lake in Nevada is what is left of ancient Lake Lahonton; and Mono Lake, which we will explore more thoroughly later, is also a leftover. All three lakes have terraces of former shores which are easily identified.

Each sink is a valley between ranges that, chopping the surface of the Great Basin like storm waves in the open sea, rise three to four thousand feet above the basin floor. A few ranges reach impressive heights. White Pine Mountains, Wheeler Peak, Grant Range, Charleston Peak, the Ruby Mountains in Nevada and California's Inyo-Whites and Panamints all top 11,000 feet in altitude.

Any relief map of the Great Basin will give a fair idea of the topographical complexity of the region. On such maps, Nevada looks as if someone had filled a pint Mason jar with caterpillars and dropped them, aligning them so that they were all crawling, roughly parallel, either north or south. Though some ranges amount to nothing more than bumps on the horizon, most are respectable in size and unique for their universality of trend. Like the Sierra Nevada, they are fault blocks, upthrust masses of rock—sedimentary, metamorphic, and igneous with extruded volcanic material here and there—along cracks in the earth's surface. Through the centuries, erosion has deposited huge cones of detritus which flank the bases of these ranges. Where they coalesce, they form alluvial skirts completely surrounding inner sinks.

This corrugated landscape, covering thousands of square miles, could be presumed to have as varied a group of biotic communities as its relief features. Uniformity of climate, however, precludes the richness of natural scene common to most of California. To be sure, there are modifications owing to altitude, latitude, slope face, and drainage patterns; but much of it is characterized by the presence of one plant type which we now meet for the first time, Great Basin sagebrush. Preliminary acquaintance has been made with some of its relatives—coastal and beach sagebrush, mugwort, and alpine sagebrush, *Artemisia rothrockii*—but this is the book's first encounter with what may very well be the most numerous shrub in the West.

Traveling down from the top of Tioga Pass, one may not notice its quiet intrusion and, therefore, not truly realize its ubiquitous character until the road has dropped a thousand feet or so on the east side of the divide. The rapid eastern descent of roughly three thousand feet progresses with almost tobogganlike speed in contrast to the leisurely journey up the western slope. One can arrive at the foot of the range in less than a half an hour because of the nature of the eastern face. This is the escarpment along which movements occur that lift the Sierra from its heart-rock base.

Leaving the last of the alpine lakes, an artificially controlled but handsome body of water just east of the pass, those who are accustomed to the white granite of much of the High Sierra may well be surprised at the colorful slopes above. Extensive alpine areas of rust, buff, and yellow, brilliantly hued, typify the presence of metamorphic rocks. While wandering over some of the byroads in the vicinity of Mono Lake, visitors can note evidence of recent vulcanism, another feature of the eastern slope.

To return to the vegetation, if you have not had the opportunity to appreciate the dignity and charm of Sierra juniper, here is your chance. They can be seen on each side of Lee Vining Canyon, perched on their exposed sites. Several patches of dwarf juniper blotch the upper walls of the canyon head, just below the rim. Before the road was straightened and widened, tiny seeps encouraged charming gardens where rein orchid, monkeyflower, monkshood, red columbine, horsetails, and other streamside plants found congenial little environments. Aspen sprawled every which way among the currant bushes that were beginning to stabilize the scree slides of this precipitous terrain. But bulldozers rule the age. Now the winding little road with its breathtaking turnouts and heartstopping curves, its miniature gardens and thickets of willow has yielded to a broad highway whose building has all but obliterated the flowered nooks and crannies, the tiny cascades and waterfalls by roadside.

The steep, semibarren cliffs of timberline follow the road down until the shrubs of the Great Basin begin to crowd onto the more gentle slopes of the lower canyon. Aspen, understoried by sagebrush, makes use of the long, easy sweeps; Jeffrey pine and white fir thicken by the stream that tumbles to the bottom of the gorge. Quite suddenly, the canyon floor widens out to several large meadows, verdant in early summer with aspen, grasses, sedges, rushes, and scraps of iris as blue as alpine ponds. Many of the canyons opening out from the escarpment were glaciated in the Pleistocene; and small lateral, recessional, and terminal moraines still block their mouths to some extent. They are not difficult to spot if you look for dike-like ridges of boulders and rock fragments over and along which the roads penetrating the canyons must travel. The Lee Vining Ranger Station is located on one of these moraines.

Once out on U.S. Highway 395, the Great Basin with its sagebrush is firmly in command. By no means is this dominant shrub the only woody plant of the region. Climate, edaphic conditions, and other ecological controls limit its occurrence. Such circumstances are apparent approaching Mono Lake. Since it is highly saline, only salt-tolerant plants can live close to its edges except where freshwater trickles into it. Here mullein, thistles, and a type of ranunculus invade territory that otherwise would be held only by plants able to live in saline soils. Several weedy goosefoots, a salt-tolerant family in general, have managed to establish colonies on the encrusted white mud surrounding the lake. Willows, dock, grasses, sedges, rushes, goldenrod, and even wild roses and iris clumps cluster along concentric lines of hardened minerals which mark old shorelines.

Mono Lake's brininess is the result of its geologic history. During the Ice Age, a much larger body of water, Lake Russell, covered most of the Mono Basin. Its ancient terraces can still be seen six to seven hundred feet above the present surface. As it evaporated, its salts were concentrated, and today it is a veritable soup of many different substances. Only two organisms of any size exist in the saline solution—brine shrimp and black flies whose larvae were used by the Piute Indians as food and item of trade. The flies occur in such abundance they gather in living knots along the shallows, which burst apart when disturbed and then quickly reform. Many shorebirds visit this inland sea—avocets, stilts, California gulls, and Wilson's phalaropes whose habit of endless, rapid circling in place appears on the verge of dementia. Such seemingly pointless activity, however, is useful in that it keeps the water in motion and the brine shrimp, on which they feed, easier to find. On the south shore of the lake, dozens of tufa towers are scattered. These grotesque structures, sometimes fifteen feet or more in height, occur where fresh water seeps flow into the lake. Because of the action of calcareous algae, the calcium in the lake precipitates wherever it encounters freshwater.

The volcanic history of the area is evident everywhere. Lava and pumice floor the basin in many places, raising sections of it into tablelands often over eight thousand feet in elevation. Though the lake itself has two small island craters, one of the most notable features of the region's vulcanism is the group of small volcanoes known as the Mono Craters. South of the lake, they are inner cores of obsidian covered with pumice. Other craters, lava flows, hot springs, pumice flats, and cliffs of volcanic glass are indicative of the activity that is estimated by some to have ended but 500 years ago. On the north side of the lake, groves of aspen and huge aged willows, carpeted with grass, are green oases where streams flow down from the Sierra to partially replenish the slowly shrinking lake. One such set of trickles spreads little marshes along the western shore. Yellow-headed and red-winged blackbirds use the cover provided by tules and cattails and call out their ringing cries from snags of willows shading these wet places.

If one drives south the road dips and rises, undulating over moraine deposits, foothill spurs, volcanic tablelands, drainage channels, and basin bottoms. Looking west to the Sierran escarpment, faceted by the numerous canyons eroded into its face, one can begin to understand why the interior side of the range is so different from the Pacific slope. Not only does its precipitousness give the kind of dramatic and spectacular scenery seldom seen at 6,500 feet on the western side, but tree zones are much less obvious on the eastern face. The brush-covered slopes, sheer walls, and scree jumbles are barren of much arboreal growth, though strands of such vegetation wind down gullies and canyons where water and deeper soils allow more mesophytic trees and shrubs. Riparian growth here amid sparsely covered terrain is even more evident than it is in the foothills of the Great Valley. Decidedly this is the edge of a desert, a high, cold desert, to be sure, but a desert all the same where there is only enough rainfall, from 5 to 15 inches a year, to support low shrubs and scattered stands of drought-resistant trees. Contrast this scrubby growth to the Great Green Wall at 6,500 feet on the other side with its annual precipitation of 40 or more inches. Where stream flow or higher altitude provides enough moisture, there are many but not all of the conifers of the western slope—lodgepole, silver, and Jeffrey pines, white fir, and a few groves of yellow pine and red fir in certain restricted localities. In the streamside growth, a very handsome tree, water birch, is frequently conspicuous. Though it does occur on the Pacific side of the range, it is not too common; almost any stream on the east face, however, is bordered by this relation of the well-known paper birch of northern woods. Various willows, black and, more rarely, Fremont cottonwood, and aspen are its usual companions.

Where the stream courses of the escarpment widen into upland valleys containing lakes, as those on the June Lake Loop, in the Mammoth Lakes, Virginia Lakes, Convict Lake, and at the head of Bishop Creek, coniferous forests are more extensive, particularly on shady slopes. One can imagine himself back at Tuolumne Meadows or on the road to Glacier Point. High at road end in the more accessible canyons (many have mining roads that, though narrow, steep, switchbacked, and dirt, are negotiable by ordinary car) where trailheads promise high-country adventures, several trees approach timberline—

whitebark pine, mountain hemlock, lodgepole pine, and two mentioned casually before, limber and foxtail pines. Though both of the latter are confined to the high country in the central and southern Sierra, foxtail pine, a California native, occurs at lower altitudes in the northern inner Coast Ranges and the Siskiyous. Limber pine has a much wider distribution. It extends from southern California to the eastern Rockies. Both have stiff, short-needled foliage covering the flexible stems like coarse fur. Foxtail pine appears to be more numerous on the west side of the divide, while limber pine is more common on the east.

Down on the sagebrush tablelands at the foot of the range, only two forest types are encountered with any frequency. Pinyon pine, another species new to the transect, forms woodlands above 5,000 feet; and Jeffrey pine occupies higher elevations or more mesic sites with open spicy-scented forests. Many of the dry hillside shrubs move in as understory to these two conifers—rabbitbrush, sagebrush, buckwheat, bitterbrush, manzanita, ceanothus, service berry, granite and other gilias, desert sweet, desert peach, wild currant, shrubby cinquefoil, wild rose, and horsebrush. Growing with Jeffrey pine on rocky ledges or steep, thin-soiled hillsides, are Sierra juniper and large shrubs of Great Basin mountain mahogany, almost tree-like in size and stance. All three make use of rock-trapped under-surface water. Out on meadows that remain in some of the moister basins of the rolling tableland, lodgepole pine usually persists in moving in first, just as it does in meadowlands on the western side, while the drier-footed Jeffrey follows closely behind. A broken line of contact wavers across the tableland east of the Sierran base. This marks the shift from Sierra juniper to Utah juniper, a smaller species of lower elevation and much wider range. Pumice flats, patches of barren volcanic debris, are being invaded by trees and shrubs just beginning their encroachment. Water drains down quickly through the porous rocky surface; consequently it is quite dry and cannot support much vegetation. Ecological succession will encourage soil building in toward the hearts of these sterile pockets, and forest or shrublands will eventually cover them.

Flowers are about as abundant here on the drier side of the Sierra as they are to the west. Early summer offers displays of prickly poppy (like perfectly poached eggs with their large white petals and brilliantly yellow centers), pink pentstemons, scarlet bugler, evening primroses, scarlet gilia, mariposa lilies, and lupine. In late summer, rabbitbrush, a gorgeous plant despite its unflattering specific name which means "nauseating," lines the highways and clusters in clumps between the sagebrush with a striking combination of golden flowers and silver-green foliage.

Some of the same factors or related ones enforcing tree limit at high altitudes are at work here, where the trees of the eastern face finally yield to the shrubs of the Great Basin. Even the hardier trees such as Jeffrey pine and western juniper cannot live below this ecotone, with the exception of riparian sites and a few isolated upland islands. The primary factor precluding tree growth is scanty precipitation, the effect of which on the habitat may be intensified by low winter temperatures, thin soils, and strong winds, potentially difficult conditions in themselves.

Where organisms attempt life in a marginal area, the hazards to which they can succumb are greatly multiplied. Take, for instance, Jeffrey pines, the last tall trees encountered if one travels east over the Mono Basin. What were all the circumstances that governed the establishment of the groves in the first place, and what are the possible threats to both individual and stand? The most important influence operating in natural communities is chance. It certainly plays a determining role in the distribution of organisms whose introduction to an area depends largely on the happenstance of their presence close enough to permit colonization of the new territory. Having entered, if they do, their continued presence, or ensuing disappearance, rests on environmental factors and the tolerance ranges of the species for these factors. Chance, however, continues to maintain its grip. Its cold impartiality has no regard for the effect of such circumstances on the well-being of the community. An unusually hard winter, a decade of drought, or a summer of fire, and no Jeffrey pines may be left to propagate. In 1936–1937, intense cold killed many young pines on the east side of the Sierra. Many mature trees live through such catastrophes, but cone-producing buds are often destroyed. Insect damage, destruction by larger animals, and fungal infestation of cone-bearing tissue also interfere with seed production.

In common with most species of the genus, the cones of Jeffrey pine take two years to develop. There are many hazards for the slowly growing cones—storms, fire, and hungry chickarees, crossbills, and insects such as cone beetles and pinecone moths. If fate allows, the cones will ripen and open to drop their seeds. Then the crop is attacked by hordes of ground-feeding birds and rodents anxious to fatten themselves for migration or hibernation, though many rodents aid dissemination by hording forgotten or never fully exploited caches. If the seeds escape destruction, fate still has the upper hand. They may fail to germinate because of lack of moisture or by falling on bare rock and other unsuitable substrates where they desiccate or decompose.

If all these hurdles are successfully passed, and the pine seed remains viable, it will burst one warm day when the ground is moist, and a tiny sprout will work up through the soil, living on the stored nutriment within the seed itself. After roots begin to penetrate the soil and the first few needles start photosynthesis, it is still at the mercy of its environment and chance. Intense frost and drought will always threaten it. Fire is never improbable. Winds and flood may topple it. Other plants could prove more competitive for soil moisture and minerals. Nutrients may be lacking as well as beneficial soil organisms. Cutworm attack is possible. Shade may doom its initial efforts. If they crop it, browsing and grazing animals will make very short work of its tiny attempt to live, and their hoofs can prove as destructive. If, almost miraculously, it escapes these fates and continues life to full maturity, its enemies seem to multiply. Porcupines, excellent climbers despite their clumsiness on the ground, eat its outer bark and destroy its food- and water-conducting tissue. Lightning plays around it during the summer months. Winds shriek past in winter. Man himself judges it for potential timber harvest or may cut it down to build roads, homes, or resorts.

Even if it escapes all these disasters, at some time an irreversible process will begin, and the end result is finally death. Mistletoe often begins the trend. This semiparasitic pest weakens the tree and prepares it for invasion by bark and other beetles, needleminers, flat-headed borers, and weevils. Roots damaged by rot and other fungi are open to additional attack. One of the rusts, also a fungus, infects the limbs of Jeffrey pine, while Oregon pine engraver, a beetle, confines its activities to the tops of mature trees.

One of the most deadly rusts is white pine blister rust which has a complex life history. Brought unwittingly from Europe, it found a remarkable set of biotic circumstances allowing it to flourish in the Great Green Wall. It requires two hosts for its existence, shrubs of the genus *Ribes* (currants and gooseberries) and pines of the white pine group—sugar, silver, whitebark, foxtail, and limber. Alternating between the two hosts, it has spiraled out until it threatens most of the white pines in the range. After parasitizing a pine, where the fungus invades a vital layer of tissue just under the bark to live off the tree, it produces sacs that release rust-colored spores into the air. Some spores settle on leaves of *Ribes* plants and after several months and stages of spore reproduction, a final spore is released which returns the infecting fungus to needles of other white pines, and the cycle continues. Control of this disease is managed mainly by eradicating the *Ribes* clumps within the vicinity of infected white pines.

Every conifer in the Sierra is threatened by some type of fungus or insect damage, though some species such as the big tree are remarkably resistant. Even Jeffrey pines have chemicals in their sap and tissues which aid in their defense against infection. Sooner or later, however, all the trees in the range will succumb; then the various processes of soil making will contribute to their distintegration, reducing their remains to basic materials only then ready for chance to assign them to another living plant.

Map 2. The deserts of southern California

International boundary
State boundary
County boundary
National monument or state park boundary
Highway
Dry lake

0        25   Miles

Bristlecone pines, White Mountains

# 16. The Short Forests

Owens Valley is hot in the summer—undeniably, forthrightly hot. By nine o'clock of a July morning the already apathetic breeze is almost too bored to continue; and the mercury has soared to 90° F., even under the cottonwoods and poplars holding back the worst of the sun. When the clouds are large and thick enough for thundershowers, the rain only adds humidity to the ovenlike atmosphere of this great, walled-in trench, a topographical feature known as a graben or valley dropped between two parallel faults—in this case, those responsible for the Sierra Nevada to the west and the Inyo and White mountains which border the valley to the east. Such a term, however, conveys little impression of this part of California, one of the most spectacular rises of land anywhere in the country. Driving from Lone Pine to Bishop on a bright, cold December morning when fresh snow has sugared the Sierran crest, and the willow stems are cranberry red down in the bottomlands, one sees the valley at its best—that magnificent western wall of cream-colored granite rising full into the low winter sun. The candle-flame yellow of Lombardy poplars and cottonwoods traces the creekways draining the pediments, and the shadowy outline of the Inyo-Whites breaks the eastern horizon.

One can enter Owens Valley from the north on two major routes: along the foot of the Sierra and down Sherwin Grade from Lake Crowley via U.S. Highway 395, or on U.S. Highway 6, coming into California from Nevada a few miles east of Benton and following its own valley between the White Mountains and the volcanic tablelands that tip into Mono Basin. A connecting road, State Highway 120, takes off from Benton Station to the northwest over an undulating plateau and, rounding the Mono Craters, cuts into U.S. Highway 395 just south of Lee Vining. Regardless of the route chosen, U.S. Highway 395 or State Highway 120–U.S. Highway 6, the traveler, dropping from the central High Sierra, invariably passes from aspen and Jeffrey pine, through stands of pinyon pine, and crosses long alluvial, scrub-covered slopes to the valley floor with its winding riparian corridors of rich summer green.

Though State Highway 120 is the longer, less traveled route, it is an interesting introduction to a new type of mosaic, that of the Great Basin, with its own set of climatic and edaphic characteristics with which we made acquaintance in the last chapter. Once the Mono Craters are to the west, the Sierra, a dominating feature throughout much of eastern California, somehow becomes less important. On the threshold of this vast interior realm of ranges and basins, one leaves behind the stands of white fir and sugar pine which thrived so well at the same elevations to the west. The rainshadow of the Sierra continues to operate far to the east, just as the influence of what is termed a continental climatic regime is felt as far west as the Sierra's eastern slope. Summers are warm, at middle and low altitudes, and winters are cold. Precipitation is much less than that of comparable elevations on the western Sierra, ranging from eight to twenty inches and falling mostly in the form of snow. Summer showers, nevertheless, can be expected, but there is much variation in number and intensity from year to year. It is a harsh climate, but very seasonal—a wonderful region for homesick easterners to visit when they complain of the climatic placidity of coastal California.

This lack of climatic coddling is much in evidence as one drives east over the uplands southeast from Mono Lake. Much of the way is across the gray-green monotony of rolling, sagebrush-covered plains, modified by three vegetational interruptions:

(1) Where rocky outcrops push up like rubble heaps, pinyon pine, juniper, desert or curl-leaf mountain mahogany, and even occasional Jeffrey pines suddenly appear in a dark green rash, in striking contrast to the quiet colors of the sagebrush slopes. Once again, broken bedrock and probing roots enable larger vegetative forms to compete successfully for their share of water. Sagebrush sometimes continues into these outposts as understory to the taller plants. There is some evidence that the

trees of the rocky islands are protected from range fires by their isolation.

(2) Many brushy slopes have streaks of olive green where bitterbrush, a browse species highly preferred by stock and ruminant wildlife, has intruded into the almost solid sagebrush cover. Though commonly found in an intermixture, it also occurs in relatively pure stands, pioneering on recently deposited volcanic material, roadcuts, and mud flows. Bitterbrush appears to require porous, well-drained, coarse-textured soils, whereas some species of sagebrush are tolerant of heavier soils. It recovers very slowly after fire, however, unlike big (Great Basin) sagebrush which may take its time but eventually reinvades its former terrain.

(3) Depressions and drainage ways, scattered over the tableland, nurture pockets of plants characteristic of more mesic environments, particularly where water is more or less present the year around. Unexpected little ponds are delightful in this arid landscape, with their grasses, sedges, rushes, willows, and other moisture-requiring species.

By the time one has reached the long, straight stretch of road between Benton Station and Bishop, sagebrush, constant companion since the top of Tioga Pass, has given way to another major scrub community, characterized by certain species loosely termed "scale bushes." Not only are their pale leaves usually covered with small scales, but their fruiting stalks often look like collections of fish scales glued along a central stem as each carpel or seed is enclosed between two flaky bracts. There is a surprising variety of color among the scale bushes, their relations, and associates, in foliage as well as fruit bracts and flowers. Such differences are often subtle to be sure; but an aware eye can see attractive notes of rust red, rose, gray, pink, tan, and various pale greens and lavenders blending in a pastel-tinted tapestry when seen from the window of a speeding car.

Once on the floor of the Owens Valley itself, the mountains to the east provide an introductory lesson in Great Basin ecology. The Inyo and White mountain ranges are fairly typical of the larger range or range complexes of this inland region.

They are somewhat higher in elevation (White Mountain Peak is over 14,000 feet), are closer to the Pacific Ocean, and may have suffered more of man's disruptive influences than sister ranges to the east; but they demonstrate the outstanding vegetational theme of the arid west: zonation. This is the striking feature of the mountains of the Great Basin. We encounter comparable altitudinal belts on the western Sierra, but the impact is less pronounced as one progresses up through conifer forests that seem all-of-a-piece to the uninitiated. It is only when one learns to tell the typical species apart that the various belts can be distinguished; they intergrade with few sharply defined boundaries.

The zones of vegetation are quite obvious on the western slope of the White Mountains, as the indicative species differ noticeably in appearance, given a little study. Their occurrence results from the same physical condition that produces vegetational shifts on the Sierra: adiabatic cooling. For each gain in altitude of a thousand feet, the temperature drops roughly 5.5° Fahrenheit.

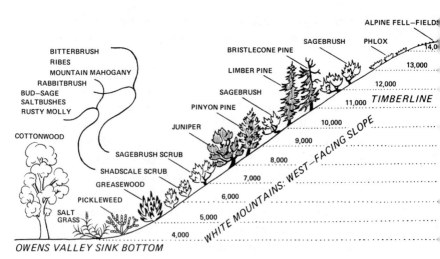

Figure 21. Altitudinal zonation on the White Mountains

Such cooling affects storms managing to overreach the heights of the Sierra, and there is consequent buildup of rainfall on the upper slopes of the White Mountains. The gradual decrease of temperature also influences plant cover.

Sagebrush, so extensive and ubiquitous, is the integrating background, the matrix, as some botanists term it, for many plant patterns superimposed on it by climatic and edaphic variation. It is absent, or nearly so, from only two Great Basin communities; but it is a prominent member of the others. From basin floor to the lower edges of alpine rock-fields—where, however, there are modifications such as an edaphically influenced and spotty distribution in the bristlecone–limber pine stands of the White Mountains—sagebrush is as domineering a plant group as one will meet anywhere.

Because of its major role in the biota of the Great Basin, the group deserves a more detailed account and description than we have given it so far. It belongs to the genus *Artemisia* in the sunflower or composite family, though its inconspicuous, almost insignificant flowers are hardly what the botanically unsophisticated would consider typical of the family. Other members of the genus have already been introduced—the rank-growing mugwort of riparian sites, the feather-foliaged beach sagewort, and the subshrub, California sagebrush, of coast and sage scrubs. Outriders of a near relation and look-alike of Great Basin sagebrush, Rothrock or alpine sagebrush, drift over the Sierran divide down into the subalpine forest zone of the western slope. At this point we are confronted with a taxonomic puzzle that has plagued many botanists. Should the last plant and the dozen or so other closely related sagebrushes really be separated into species, or should most of them be considered varieties or subspecies instead? Like the oaks, they cross easily, which confuses the picture considerably. Current thinking has divided them; those listed below occur in California along with their approximate distribution and ecological limitations:

(1) *Artemisia tridentata* (Great Basin, basin, big, or common sagebrush) extends north to Canada, east to and beyond

the Rocky Mountains, and down into Baja California. It is one of the larger species, ranging to fifteen feet in height in better sites. Though it has a relatively wide tolerance for many edaphic conditions, as it is found in dry areas and moist, in valleys and on mountain slopes, in alkaline as well as non-alkaline situations, it does best in deep, well-drained soils and sheltered locations. There are several subspecies which seem to exhibit locational preferences, one of which, *vaseyana* or mountain big sagebrush, is restricted to higher elevations, as implied by its common name.

(2) *Artemisia bigelovii* (flat sagebrush) is scattered throughout the Southwest from Colorado and Texas to California at altitudes of from three to five thousand feet. This is a very drought resistant, small or dwarf shrub, well suited to drier sites, such as limestone substrates.

(3) *Artemisia nova* (black sagebrush) ranges from five to eight thousand feet through the West, from Montana south to California and northern Arizona. In its darker form it is relatively easy to distinguish from other sagebrushes. Evidently it is a species that does well on shallow soils.

(4) *Artemisia arbuscula* (low sagebrush) is another dwarf species, and it grows from 5,000 feet to timberline, and from Washington south to California and east to northern Utah. It homesteads where many other species of sagebrush do not, on dry, sterile sites that are often alkaline in nature. A subspecies is common on soils of volcanic origin.

(5) *Artemisia rothrockii* (Rothrock or alpine sagebrush) is a low-growing shrub which seems at home in high mountains (up to 11,000 feet) from the Sierra to Wyoming and Colorado.

(6) *Artemisia cana* (silver or hoary sagebrush) has a wide distribution, but only one subspecies, *bolanderi*, enters California. It is one of the group tolerating very alkaline conditions and is common in many of the basins of that nature in Oregon and California.

Few readers will worry much about differentiating between these six species in the field. The best that can be done here is to note the large forms and the dwarf types, those that can take alkaline and other less fertile sites, the forms characteristically found in high mountains, and those that occur at lower levels. In general their appearance is much the same. They all have aromatic silver-gray-green leaves of small size decidedly three-toothed in some species, in others less so. The foliage typically bursts from gnarled woody trunklets in attractive tufts. In flowering season dozens of straight-stemmed stalks thrust up from the leaf masses and bear minute blossoms. Sagebrush is at its best during or just after a rain. The colors deepen slightly, and the world seems suspended in rich, pungent odor.

Other shrubs are by no means excluded from the community. Buffaloberry, bitterbrush, several *Ribes*, mountain mahogany, and cotton thorn are common associates. Two other shrubs deserve additional description. One is blackbrush. Its presence usually indicates the approach of the southern edge of the community to warmer and drier climatic conditions. It is frequently found in sandy soil. The other is rabbitbrush. Blooming in late summer, this striking plant is a flamboyant harbinger of the autumnal colors one can expect from the higher elevations of the Sierra and Great Basin mountains. It is often found growing between clumps of sagebrush, particularly on disturbed soils. It invades newly heaped roadside gravel piles and recently flooded sandy washes. Somewhat sub-shrubby, it quickly covers such areas with great bouquets of sunny color. Another composite, goldenbush, is almost as richly yellow. Herbs such as paintbrush, pentstemon, blazing star, lupine, locoweed, monkeyflower, buckwheat, and many perennial or annual grasses flourish throughout the community unless the shrub cover is too dense.

From the discussion of the interior sagebrushes, it is apparent that the group, as a whole, has the capacity to live over much of the intermountain West. Given certain limitations and compensating tolerances, both of which vary from species to species, it may be found alone or with other shrubs, and as understory to most of the trees of the region. It reaches from chill mountain heights to hot valley floors; from moist, streamside sites to dry, thin-soiled slopes; from alkali clays to lithosols (literally, rock-soils). In common with most other shrubs of the arid West, it has certain features which enable it to struggle along under adverse conditions, yet to thrive where the environment is genial. Small size, light color, and hairiness of the leaves suggest drought resistance. Long and extensive root systems aid in the search for water. Hence its universality within certain limits discussed below.

In recent years, the sagebrush group has enlarged its territory at the expense of the perennial grasses, which formerly were in favorable balance. Stock and wildlife forage preferences are of great importance. Sagebrush with its stiff twigs and small aromatic leaves is less palatable than grass. Though it is browsed when tastier food is scarce, it is usually left alone. Overgrazing and, according to some investigators, frequent range fires proved a two-headed nemesis for much of the Great Basin's better range, weakening the bunchgrasses—wheatgrasses, wild ryes, Indian ricegrass, and some of the bluegrasses—that for thousands of years had lived compatibly with the sagebrushes. They grew between the shrubs and under the taller plants until forced out of the range by grazing and fire stress. Introduced annuals, repeating their success in the Central Valley, took advantage of the vacuum. As they can use the skimpy and shallow soil moisture untapped by the sagebrushes, they managed to establish a working relationship with the dominant shrub which also took advantage of its weakened ex-partners and enlarged its territory. Ranchers, in an attempt to return the range to its former productivity, have begun to destroy many acres of sagebrush by deep ploughing, fire, and other means. Actually, the Great Basin bunchgrass species have suffered less, by and large, than those of the Central Valley and surrounding foothills. It is still possible to find good representations of them, here and there.

Sagebrush may be considered undesirable by stockmen, but the community shelters many animals using its thickets for cover and its resources for food. Several are completely dependent on it, and are found nowhere else. The sage hen, related to sooty (blue), ruffed, spruce, and sharp-tailed grouse, is peculiar to sagebrush plains. Though it has a smaller distribution than the others, it is the largest of the American grouse. Cock-of-the-plains is another name for the bird that boasts a courtship behavior considered to be the most spectacular of the group. In spring the strutting grounds echo with the drumming of the males. They inflate the air sacs of their necks and, spreading their pointed tail feathers and stiffly positioning their wings, they strut jerkily, producing a variety of sounds that have been compared to rusty pumps or cracking whips, depending on the observer. Undoubtedly they are well suited to their environment. Not only does their mottled plumage blend well with the quiet colors of their habitat, but they are one of the few animals that live almost exclusively on the leaves of sagebrush, augmented by occasional insects, fruits, and shoots of other plants, particularly locoweed, wild vetch, and goldenrod.

Another bird whose streaked front and gray-brown back fit him nicely into shrubby cover is the sage thrasher. Smaller than his cousins, he appears to alternate, as they do, between insects, when they are plentiful, and seeds at their time of ripening. Many sparrows find these open, rolling plains with their grasses and other seed-producing plants a desirable habitat—vesper, black-throated, black-chinned, song, Brewer's, and savanna. One species is confined to sagebrush, Bell's or sage sparrow. It forages between the bushes, using the tops of them for lookout posts and scurrying to safety under their cover when disturbed. The green-tailed towhee is smaller than the brown or rufous-sided towhees of the foothill brushlands. With his white and gray streaked face, reddish cap, and green tail, he blends well with the delicate shades of his habitat. Searching for prey, poorwills, prairie falcons, Swainson's hawks, and ravens drift back and forth over these gray-clad uplands.

Many mammals of the sagebrush plains—chipmunks and antelope ground squirrels—are day active; but at nightfall, numerous nocturnal species trade places with them, taking over feeding sites vacated by diurnal forms. Kangaroo rats, wood rats, and deer and pocket mice rely on seeds and fruits gathered in the darker hours. The sagebrush vole (meadow mouse) is another animal limited to the steppe interior. Shorter and smaller tailed than most of its relatives (none of which is distinguished by long, graceful tails), it is also the most "desertized." It lives on any green stuff it can find and needs no other source of moisture than that present in the food it eats. Elaborate runways are the hallmarks of this little fellow, and by remaining hidden in them a good part of the time, it escapes being dinner for coyotes, gray foxes, badgers, and other predators of the arid plains.

Almost unchallenged, sagebrush rules from alluvial slopes that apron the high-desert ranges to timberline and even above. Four factors, however, control its lower limits: temperature, rainfall, salinity, and soil structure. With the approach of warmer, drier climatic conditions, shadscale scrub frequently shares a broad ecotone with sagebrush and then supplants it. This rather desiccated-appearing cover of shrubs is remarkably uniform in size and appearance, considering the many families represented here. Not only tolerant of the so-called alkali soils characteristic of the floors and lower sides of the platterlike basins that abound in the region, it is very xerophytic with many of the adaptive features such as small, light-colored, hairy or scaly leaves, and extensive roots common to plants of arid regions. Wide spacing between shrubs is the result of intense root competition for soil moisture. Where rainfall drops below seven inches and both summer and winter temperatures are higher than those of the sagebrush zone, these small, stiff, often spiny bushes are spread thinly over the lower alluvial slopes. Many of them belong to the goosefoot family. One genus, *Atriplex*, contains the scale bushes—shadscale, lenscale, wedgescale, etc.—for which the community is named. Another common name for the genus is saltbush, reflecting its ability to tolerate saline soils. In the same family are hopsage, winter fat, and rusty molly, while the composites contribute broom snakeweed and horsebrush, names intriguingly zoological. Several *Daleas*, a typical desert shrub genus, occur here. Cotton thorn and boxthorn testify to the general spininess of the shadscale community, a feature of another sagebrush very common to the shadscale association, bud-sage.

Its Latinized name, *Artemisia spinescens*, is indicative of its bristly character, a decided departure from the growth habit of its relatives. Its position in the shadscale landscape and away from the other sagebrushes emphasizes the eclectic nature of the genus throughout the Great Basin.

Apparently not only a climatic shift accounts for the presence of shrubs even more xerophytic than those of the sagebrush community, but edaphic factors are of prominence. Though some of the desert sagebrushes can stand soils that are moderately to heavily alkali, for the most part they need well-drained substrates that are not conspicuously saline. The shadscales and their neighbors, on the other hand, appear to thrive where salts are present in moderate concentrations. Desert pavement, a stony surface often found in arid regions, is rare in sagebrush areas, but frequently occurs in the shadscale community. Soils vary from sandy gravels to heavy clays, and hardpans occasionally occur. Considering that climatic drought is reinforced by edaphic conditions of soil salinity, resulting in physiological drought, it is not surprising that these little shrubs often look as though they were crafted from cornflakes.

Taking one of the many dirt roads crisscrossing the floor of Owens Valley south of Bishop, one encounters sooner or later the other scrub community of the steppe interior which replaces sagebrush—alkali sink. Where the water table is high in arid regions, capillary rise brings up dissolved material. Evaporation concentrates the minerals accumulating on the surface because of this upward pull, and those deposited by water draining off surrounding hillsides. Many basins in this landlocked region have playas, permanent or transient lakes, floored with minerals collecting through the thousands of years during and since the Ice Age. Trapped here because of the absence of sea-destined drainage, there has not been sufficient rainfall to leach these solutes below subsurface depths. Such collections are widely but somewhat incorrectly termed "alkalis." They may be alkaline, that is basic in nature, but many of these accumulations are on the neutral side. Strongly alkaline substrates are infertile for numerous species, just as highly acid soils discourage many plants. However, whether alkaline or not, the major reason for barren playa floors is the salts concentrated here. One highly alkaline soil is the infertile black alkali. A high percentage of sodium on clay particles not only results in alkalinity, but this soil type is very saline, as well.

After heavy rains, the heart of the sink is underwater for intervals ranging from days to weeks. Eventually, however, the water evaporates and the center dries out completely. Then mineral-impregnated surface clays are split by crisscrossing cracks. Such substrates are often underlain by claypans or other impervious layers. They concentrate the standing water, high in solutes, in shallow depths at and just below the surface. Such a combination of features is disastrous to any plant life, and the central portions of most sinks are quite sterile. American deserts have many mineralized basin floors scattered between their ranges: Bonneville Salt Flats, Death Valley's Devil's Golf Course, and numerous places where commercial mining of the more valuable minerals has been undertaken, such as Owens Lake at the southern end of Owens Valley and Searles Lake in the Mojave Desert. Though most are usually dry, mirages playing over these white expanses give them the appearance of having reflecting water.

In the northern part of the Owens Valley, muddy marshes rather than large playas are present. Their heavy moist soils are highly saline. As the shrubs of shadscale or sagebrush scrub approach these sumps, greasewood, a fleshly-leaved goosefoot, makes its appearance, usually in company with the more salt-tolerant species of *Atriplex*, such as shadscale itself. Where, finally, permanently wet soil is encountered, these plants give way to the same succulent types met in the salt marshes of San Francisco Bay—pickleweeds with their fat little "sausages" tightly strung together. One can find alkali blite, related to the coastal sea blite, along with desert salt grass, a close cousin of the salt grass of tidal flats. Alkali sacaton, another grass frequently found in these sinks, salt-adapted rushes, sedges, and bulrushes fill out the tangles of growth which, having adjusted to a potentially inimical substrate, can take good advantage of that desert rarity, a permanent water source. Like the seaside halophytes, they have made physiological and anatomical changes which protect them from the water loss threatened by reversal of the normal osmotic process.

One other community literally graces the floor of the Owens Valley, the riparian woodlands of welcome shade lining what is left of the Owens River and its tributaries. Up on the pediments or fans above the valley bottom, running water allows conifers such as Jeffrey pine to invade lower elevations. On the floor itself, willows and cottonwoods are the principal streamside trees along with locusts, poplars, and other alien trees introduced by early settlers. High in these verdant tunnels, Bullock's orioles, Wilson's and yellow warblers, black-headed grosbeaks, and several flycatchers find the food resources of the green arcades particularly rich. The whole valley is a birder's paradise. Black-billed magpies perch on every fence post, and no lawn is complete without a contingent of cocky robins.

As the warm season progresses, spring wildflowers—apricot mallow, evening primrose, and desert dandelion—give way to those of summer, particularly where irrigation augments the natural water sources. Prince's plume waves golden tufts in the hot breeze. The fences are so rich with bee plant, that a solid lavender wall may line the roads. When mixed with sunflowers, the effect is that of unending floral arrangements of unabashed color.

To really appreciate the vegetational zonation on the slopes of Great Basin ranges, drive from Big Pine to Westgard Pass and turn left to the bristlecone pine reserve high in the White Mountains. The shadscale scrub begins admitting a few sagebrush scrub species, and towards late summer, rabbitbrush flourishes in golden splendor. Suddenly, there are no more scale bushes. Sagebrush is king again, but it does not rule alone for long. It begins to share its reign with pinyon pines and, slightly higher, Utah junipers. Where the now improved road to the White Mountain bristlecone pine forest departs from the main road through the pass, one could be deep in Arizona and expect to see a Navajo hogan tucked in the grove of small

trees at the fossil trail turnout. This is one corner of California
that should be elsewhere. The dwarfed forest somehow doesn't
seem to really belong here, though climatically it has every
right to be present. The tree-screened hills should widen out to
the mesas and buttes of the Indian country, for this is their
kind of natural landscape—pinyon pines and Utah junipers in
their own dry, pitch-scented air. In California, only along the
eastern base of the central Sierra and the western outliers of
the mountains of the Great Basin can one find this tail-end
extension of the coniferous woodlands of the Southwest.

What strange little trees they are. They have none of the
grandeur of their taller relatives, nor the scarred dignity of the
old fellows of timberline. Though young junipers are typically
conical, and some mature individuals branch from the base in
full-bottomed plumpness, many are grotesquely twisted, with
tufts of foliage at the ends of posturing branches. Pinyons
sometimes open out in canopies surprisingly wide for so short
a trunk. On close inspection, it is simple to tell apart the two
main species. Pinyons have needles (one, two, or four to a
bundle depending on species), and junipers have scales. It is
somewhat more difficult to distinguish between them from a
distance. The pines seem a little on the blue side, the junipers
slightly more yellow, but both have gray tints which darken
on far hillsides so that the trees appear almost black. In the
southern part of the state, California juniper is the semidesert
companion of pinyon pine; however, it often occurs alone, particularly at low elevations. Utah juniper, on the other hand, is
rarely without its associate though both species can and do
grow in relatively pure stands, undiluted by each other.

The zone occupied by this coniferous woodland receives
more moisture than those of the two Great Basin scrubs. Higher
in elevation—5,000 to 8,000 feet—its rainfall averages from
12 to 20 inches. The trees have the deep-spreading roots typical
of semidesert woodland, and the scattered spacing is indicative
of active competition between individuals of the stand. They
often avoid basin floors or the lower skirts of alluvial slopes.
Like the shrubs of the chaparral, they seem to be most at home

on shallow-soiled, rocky, hill and mesa sides where long roots can effectively probe for underground water. Yet they make a scattered appearance on the ochre and vermillion sands of the Navajo country, indicating a wide amplitude of substrate tolerance. Topography influences their distribution. At lower elevations on the west face of the White Mountains, the more mesic north exposures have well-developed pinyon–juniper woodlands, while the southern exposures are characterized by shrubs of the sagebrush zone. In more moist and sheltered areas, the trees are tall and crowded so that one has the feeling of a real though dwarfed forest rather than a woodland.

Through it all runs a tide of sagebrush, lapping up against rocky pinnacles, flowing out over tree-dotted ridges and across rolling plains. There is moisture enough to go around, it seems, and many plants of the sagebrush scrub have joined the community—mountain mahogany, bitterbrush, desert sweet, squawbush, blue sage, with its little bright purple balls, golden-bush, spiny phlox, desert peach, snakeweed, desert snowberry, several cacti, and Mormon tea. The last species has a wide distribution throughout the arid west, true as well for various buckwheats which range from the soft-tinted monotony of the shadscale scrub to the timberline forest we shall shortly visit. The herbaceous layer features a surprisingly large number of perennial grass species, considering their fate in many areas of California, and numerous bright-hued wildflowers—pentstemons, paintbrush, and lupine.

Birds work back and forth through the little forest, but the general aridity and lack of variation in plant cover limit the number of species usually found here. Many birds active in the coniferous forests of the Sierra also use the woodland. White-breasted nuthatches, chickadees, and black-throated gray warblers are not uncommon. Hairy woodpeckers are seen frequently, and one bird is very characteristic of the coniferous woodland, the pinyon jay. As its name indicates, it is seldom found elsewhere. It is a social bird. One cannot be long in this short forest without hearing peculiar angry-catlike calls as the flocks wing by. They are much duller in color than scrub or crested jays. The plumage is mostly dark gray with a faint blue wash over the wings and back.

A large number of rodents have settled here—Beechey and golden-mantled ground squirrels, several chipmunks including one confined to eastern California, gophers, Great Basin kangaroo rats, porcupines, wood rats, and mice of many species. Though named for one of the dominant trees of the woodland, pinyon mice also live in the foothills bordering the Central Valley. They belong to the deer mouse group and have its characteristic white feet, large ears, and lightly haired tail. The larger mammals of the sagebrush scrub—mule deer and pronghorn antelope, among them—continue to accompany it where it slips in as understory in the coniferous woodland. Coyotes, gray foxes, bobcats, and mountain lions use the cover provided by brush and tree as they search for their prey.

Above 9,000 feet, pinyon and juniper open their ranks and finally give way. The road now winds through sagebrush scrub, retaking full command. As the vegetation cover decreases in height, sudden views shape themselves. The Sierra looms to the west, and steep canyons drop on all sides. The intimacy of the woodland has been replaced by wide horizons uncluttered by trees. But not for long.

At 10,000 feet, the first limber pines descend to road level, and the visitor enters the most amazing forest in the West. The trees of this area were living when the pyramids of Egypt were being built—and look like pieces of driftwood. Not a few Californians felt a sense of loss when it was discovered that the superb groves of big trees had lost the privilege of claiming the oldest living organisms to collections of battered snags, no more than thirty feet tall, high on some barren ridges hardly anyone had ever seen before—that is, until the photographers arrived. Any camera enthusiast can tell you that the big trees are tough subjects. They are just too large, too straight, and too much a part of a heavy forest to make exciting pictures. But those bristlecone pines! They are among the world's most photogenic trees, half the time resembling something else. Those with imagination can see a host of figures—

tragic, joyous, pensive, pleading. Trees they may be, but there is something so unique here that no other timberline area, where grotesquely twisted trees are to be expected, approaches it for wonder.

Aside from the fantasy and charm of their shapes, color sings out from both environment and tree. An intensely blue sky mates with soils as white as chalk in places. The exposed wood varies from cream to gold through rich brown. The seed cones are deep purple-brown, and the staminate cones a lovely rosy-red. Mat plants underfoot range from the delicate pink and white of alpine phlox, to purple locoweed, and yellow flowers of the daisy family; from rosy rock cress, to lavender phacelias and blue pentstemon.

Though bristlecone pine continues to associate with its coniferous companion throughout much of the community, it has its densest and most pure stands on north-facing slopes and where snowbanks tend to accumulate. Both look a good deal alike, but limber pine needles tend to tuft the ends of the supple branches, whereas those of the bristlecone pine grow in a bottle-brush effect, and are much stiffer in manner. The cones differ as well, since the bristles at the tips of the scales are a sure means of identifying the more famed species.

The story of their discovery is one of the fascinations of the forest. Though bristlecone pines were known to grow on the White Mountains, they had never aroused much interest until a scientist happened to drill deep within their boles in an effort to learn more of the climatic past of the Southwest. He was looking for trees, living and dead, which would enable him to extend the tree-ring story back to dates as yet unreached at that time. Certain trees are more sensitive to climate than others, that is, they react pronouncedly to variations in rainfall and temperature, with corresponding variations in the width of their annual rings. By correlating a series of tree-ring patterns, gathered from all over the Southwest, scientists were beginning to discover fluctuations in climate that had taken place in the prehistoric past. To Dr. Edmund Schulman's surprise, not only did he come across a bonanza that was destined to extend the tree-ring series to cover 6,000 years, but he found he had discovered the oldest living plants, and in one of the most cruel timberline areas of the West at that.

At 11,400 feet, on a rain-shadowed range receiving roughly twelve inches of annual precipitation, hammered by gale-force winds sweeping unhindered over the high plateaus, with a growing season measured in weeks and substrates that vary widely in their fertility, it is amazing that trees are here at all. One would think, under these circumstances, that the bristlecone pines would claim the better soils and thus account for their occurrence *and* their almost unbelievable longevity. Not at all. On the White Mountains, they are usually confined to dolomite, a very light-colored type of rock which weathers into shallow soils, alkaline in nature and lacking in some important minerals. Looking across at bristlecone–limber pine covered slopes—and there are many for they are not restricted to the two best known groves—the edaphic story of this fantastic landscape is clearly told. In fact, it is a classic example of the soil control of community distribution. Where the ground is white indicating a dolomite foundation, the bristlecones are scattered about in open groves. Where sandstone or granite occurs, limber pine and several shrubs take over—low sagebrush, which replaces most other sagebrush species at this elevation, mountain mahogany, desert sweet, rock spirea, and *Ribes*. It should not be implied that shrubs are missing from the bristlecone pine forests. Low sagebrush occurs in a very sparse and sporadic undercover along with a number of perennial grasses, mat plants, golden currant, and rabbitbrush.

The dolomite of the White Mountains has many properties distinctly discouraging to plants. It reflects light and heat because of its color and, therefore, is cooler in temperature—a distinct disadvantage to alpine plants. Not only does it erode into thin soils, but a hardpan is typical about two feet beneath the surface. Lack of minerals and high alkalinity are additional undesirable features for the well-being of most plants. On the other hand, those able to grow under such adverse edaphic conditions suffer little competition from those avoiding it, and here is much of the reason for the natural landscapes of

timberline in the White Mountains. The pines are so remarkably adjusted to tree-limit hardships and infertile dolomite
outcrops that they live the longest of any plants in the world.
The dense wood is made of small insect- and decay-resistant
cells. This lignification is partly responsible for the slow
decomposition rate of dead tissue and accounts for the litter
of "driftwood," rich resource of tree-ring data that has pushed
back our knowledge of past climates to a span of thousands
of years. The needles tend to remain for decades on trees in
poorer sites, thus maintaining photosynthetic capacity without having to drain energy sources during times of severe
stress.

Another important adaptation is the ability of the bristlecone pine to maintain metabolic equilibrium with available
water. Though photosynthetic activity drops sharply during
cold-season dormancy, respiration continues well into late winter. Needle leaves have many drought-resistant features; nevertheless, some water loss is inevitable during the gas exchange
involved in respiration. Trees of the tropics can afford to have
huge masses of thin, large leaves with high evaporation rates;
trees of the arid timberline cannot. They need no more foliage
than that necessary to keep alive a minimal portion of the tree.
More leaves would make more food but would also increase
water loss. Much of an older bristlecone pine is dead—beauti-
fully and esthetically dead, but dead all the same. Many of the
trees, particularly those on more exposed sites, have but one or
two foliated branches connected to the roots by a thin strip of
living bark that carries the necessary ingredients of life up and
down the trunk. The dead bark is scoured off by storm and
sand blast, exposing the lovely wind-polished wood beneath.
The bare branches slowly erode to picturesque snags, and old
exposed roots writhe with appropriate gestures.

The Patriarch Grove, the higher of the two most commonly
visited areas, is the archetype of such a landscape. Though
many trees are still quite heavily needled, some with multiple
trunks supporting thrifty, well-foliaged branches, the gently
sloping plain could have inspired Salvadore Dali to his most
extravagantly creative moods. A large number of the trees look

as though they had been stripped clean, sawed off at the base, placed in position by some giant hand, and then carefully re-arranged for best effect. Many of them lean slightly which gives them the look of being purposefully organized. Probably no other living landscape so much resembles an art gallery.

Driving higher, and it is possible to do so if your car can take it, the pines are left behind. Low sagebrush and other alpine shrublets are once again unchallenged. This species is very similar, superficially, to the sagebrush so typical of the hillside slopes seven thousand feet below. How consistent the sage-brush group has been, giving way only when soils proved so difficult it could not compete with better adapted vegetation. It has encompassed two short forests, besides creating one it-self, where optimum conditions allow the largest of the species to grow tall in fine disregard for the rigors of the surrounding desert. It has played host to countless creatures dependent on its food and shelter. It has been gracious to bright flowering species enlivening its quiet green. It is, regardless of its extent and ubiquity, a favorite desert shrub to those who love its wide gray distances, reaching for the sky.

# 17. Wash and Oasis

Deserts may be cold—Antarctic—or hot—southern Sahara—but only the sterile wastes of the highest mountains equal them in the hostility of their environment. In some respects, the des-erts of California are more alive than many comparable regions of the world. A brief description of the earth's climate complex may be useful here, not only in an attempt to explain the *why* of deserts, in general, but to compare the dry regions of the state with others of the same nature. Leaving out the polar des-erts, plagued by generally low temperatures and scant precipi-tation throughout the year and long, dark, bitter winters, most true desert regions are semitropical, occurring roughly between

Palm Canyon, Anza-Borrego State Park

the latitudes of 15 and 40 degrees on either side of the Equator. They occupy zones of calm descending air between the trade winds, on one side, and the storm-bearing westerlies, on the other. Having lost moisture before and during its descent, such air is usually dry and sponges up water vapor rather than releasing it. Huge high-pressure cells are common meteorological features of these latitudes. They divert storms that might have drifted in from adjacent rainier regions and sit, more or less permanently, over large areas, further reinforcing the scanty precipitation regime.

Certain localized conditions may intensify patterns of aridity. When moist air flow is generally from one direction, intervening mountain ranges block advancing storms and rob them of their moisture. Rainshadow accounts for the great deserts of Africa or the Middle East only in part, but it definitely influences many local areas. It is very influencial in the climatic spectra of the Pacific states. It even operates as far north as western Canada, whose mountains are directly in the path of storms moving across the continent from the Gulf of Alaska. The lee sides of British Columbia's coastal mountains and the Rockies are much drier than those to the windward. Distance from the sea, major source of atmospheric moisture, is an additional cause of aridity in areas deep within land masses.

For considerable distances along the western edges of most continents, cold currents upwell, chilling the local onshore winds and condensing their meager moisture. Fog, not rain, results, and it may modify the immediate natural landscape to a significant degree, particularly in terms of plants able to benefit directly from the increased atmospheric humidity. Patches of withered, shriveled cactus, apparently enduring prolonged drought, grow on bluffs overlooking Baja California's Pacific shore. Yet they are tufted with tatters of epiphytic lichen. Of little use to the cactus, the frequent coastal fogs have permitted flourishing growth of plant types characteristically at home in mist-wrapped forests atop the Santa Cruz Mountains, just south of San Francisco.

We should not imply, when we speak of zones of subtropical calm, that winds are absent from desert lands. On the contrary, strong wind, usually of a local nature, is a feature of desert climates. Unhindered, it sweeps through passes, down draws, and over dunes and bleak plains, further drying the already thirsty landscape. Nor is rain impossible. Thunderstorms, generated by warm-season convection air turbulence, account for spotty but often torrential downpours. Where deserts are peripheral to regions of greater rainfall, the highs occasionally break down, particularly when the world's climate belts have shifted because of the change of season. During summer, surges of humid tropical air slide northward, bringing rain squalls to the Southwest. Conversely, winter storms from higher latitudes occasionally ride down across the Mexican border, with welcome precipitation for northern Baja California and Sonora.

The closer an area is to the Equator, the milder the winters become. Deserts of low elevation and latitude rarely experience severe winters, but they all blister under truly torrid summer temperatures. At their worst, arid regions are very hostile environments, with a pattern of extremely meager and erratically distributed precipitation, low humidity, gusty local winds, many hot days, and intense insolation. Marked diurnal temperature fluctuations are characteristic of regions of low humidity. Air moisture not only retards absorption of solar heat by ground surfaces but slows the loss of this warmth to the upper atmosphere. Where such buffering is absent, air temperatures soar and descend with little hindrance.

The arid lands of the North American continent are semitropical or southern temperate, occurring for the most part in the dry latitudes, slightly below or within 20 degrees north of the Tropic of Cancer. They are dominated by a rainshadow extending east from the Coast Ranges and the Sierra-Cascade mountain chain. Though isolated from the sea by this mountain barrier, they receive occasional gifts of moisture from the Pacific Ocean, and the gulfs of California and Mexico to the south and southeast.

Two conspicuous desert types are distinguishable, cool and warm. Sagebrush plains are typical of the colder arid lands and extend as far north as eastern Washington. Locally shadscale scrub first infiltrates and then takes over on descent to warmer and drier environments; but in general, the key indication of the Southwest's variant of warm deserts is the presence of creosote bush, a shrub as characteristic of this type of arid landscape as sagebrush is of cooler drought-bound regions.

Confining our discussion to California and its neighboring states, it is customary to refer to high and low deserts. Altitude is a determinant of prime importance. We might go a step further and individualize three types: high, middle, and low. The first is California's portion of the Great Basin, roughly over 4,000 feet and dominated by big sagebrush. The middle desert approximates the Mojave, from the western end of the Antelope Valley northeast to a basin-and-range complex that includes Death Valley and south to what is an admittedly arbitrary boundary, the Riverside County line; altitude ranges from below sea level in Death Valley to 4,500 feet. Average annual rainfall is from 4 to 15 inches and varies from place to place, and year to year. Over much of the middle desert, summer temperatures of 95° to 100°F. can be expected, and night frost is common through the winter months. The third type drops from 2,000 feet to below sea level and comprises the Colorado Desert, California's part of the Sonoran Desert which extends east into Arizona and south into Mexico. Summer temperatures are often considerably higher than on the Mojave. Rainfall averages are somewhat lower (1 to 5 inches). Its topographic barriers are decisive only on the west and north. The Coast Ranges of southern California swing east from the ocean in the vicinity of Santa Barbara and, with the exception of a few passes, form an unbroken wall until they pivot around Mount San Gorgonio and thrust south to the Mexican border. The east-west trending mountains are termed the Transverse Ranges, and they are one of the few that show such marked departure from the usual direction of most of our continental ranges. Those extending south of Mount San Jacinto, partner peak to the taller San Gorgonio (Old Grayback) on the other side of the pass, are called the Peninsular Ranges as they form the backbone of northern Baja California. They are the relief features that not only bound but help account for the Colorado

Desert to the east. Extensions of the Transverse Ranges, the Little San Bernardino and Eagle mountains, divide the Mojave from the Colorado Desert. East of these ranges there is no topographical boundary separating the two deserts. Though each has typical floristic components, tongues of low desert plant life lick into some southern sections of the Mojave. In general, the colder winters of the middle desert deter many species of the Colorado from establishing themselves farther north.

For the most part, rainfall increases as one goes north to the Great Basin or higher in altitude. The eastern portions of both low and middle desert are at the edge of the summer rainfall pattern of the intermountain West. What winter storms escape past the capturing peaks of the Coast Ranges and Sierra Nevada are supplemented by summer showers from moist air masses from the south and east. These storms, though local in nature, influence the structure of the plant communities of the eastern edge to some degree, and they occur as far west as Palmdale in the Mojave, and Palm Springs in the lee of Mount San Jacinto. It is normal for southwestern deserts to receive some rain during the warmer months; however, it is very undependable and localized and usually arrives in deluges with flash floods and high runoff.

On both sides of the mountains that abut the deserts to the west, many of the natural communities have been modified and their species rearranged to a bewildering degree. Alder thickets are small jungles along Whitewater Creek, which drains the desert side of Mount San Gorgonio. Brittle bush, one of the common plants of the lower deserts, drifts as far west as Lake Elsinore, only several dozen miles from the ocean. Great Basin sagebrush and digger pines are unlikely companions in the mountains west of China Lake. California juniper, chamise, coast live oak, and cholla cactus, all distinctive members of four different natural communities, are closely associated in Big Tujunga Wash, a finger of semidesert that slips over a low ridge into the Los Angeles Basin. Another anomalous extension has found its way to the Coast Ranges, southwest of Bakersfield. Sagebrush, Mormon tea, pinyon pine, juniper, and rabbitbrush—all typical plants of the Great Basin—come within shouting distance of the sea. Driving through this landscape on the winding road that skirts Mount Pinos and runs west to the Cuyama Valley, one can scarcely believe that the ocean is but fifteen or so air miles away.

The Mojave Desert itself is a meeting ground for many different floristic elements. A number of plants characteristic of Arizona are present in the New York, Providence, Old Dad, Old Woman, Granite, and Whipple mountains in the eastern section. Cliff rose, little-leaf palo verde, Apache plume, smooth menodora—one of California's few representatives of the olive family—a southwestern ash, and desert scrub oak have made their way here, perhaps because of the summer rain. A small number of saguaro cacti have ventured across the Colorado River. From the north, big sagebrush and bitterbrush, though scarce on the plains of the middle desert, have wandered down in broad gray stripes along the flanks of the ranges on the deserts' western border. Where the low desert intergrades with the middle in the eastern part of southern California, smoke trees and ocotillo have crept up from their usual haunts. Two native palm oases, on the north side of the Little San Bernardinos, are far from similar communities in the Colorado Desert to the south.

There are many instances of east and west, north and south meeting quite compatibly in the mountains of eastern Kern and Los Angeles counties. The southern Sierra, the Tehachapis, the Coast Ranges, and the Mojave Desert all come together in a welter of canyon and ridge. In addition to the unusual associations already mentioned, we find other interesting and peculiar assortments. Valley oaks, of all things, have crept through the Tehachapi Pass to the desert edge where they grow with Joshua trees and cactus. This and other odd combinations have been noted by Ernest Twisselmann in his *Flora of Kern County* (San Francisco, 1967), a very useful guide to the biotic communities as well as the plants of this ecotonal zone. He points out that quite a number of species commonly thought exclusive to the Pacific slope have leaked over to the desert—for instance, Chinese houses, California poppy, and owl's clover. In fact, one of the places in which one can still see profuse displays of the last two wildflowers is on the west side of the Antelope Valley where Joshua trees form thick groves. Low passes, ranges of moderate elevation, and a climate of fairly uniform aridity permit such strange floristic goings-on. In the central Sierra, the montane barrier is too high for this commingling.

The Mojave and the Colorado deserts share a matrix plant which not only ties the two areas together ecologically, but serves to give the sear plains a uniform appearance. Creosote bush is so well adapted to its arid home that it dominates the flora almost as undisputedly as big sagebrush, fellow tyrant to the north. With various cacti and a number of other shrubs— pygmy cedar, sweetbush, cheese bush, brittle bush, desert trumpet, bur-sage, rabbitbrush, a few buckwheats, desert thorns, and several *Daleas*—it covers thousands of square miles in a sparse scrub. Like sagebrush, it tolerates moderately saline soils, and it yields to interruptions, determined by sub-stratal and climatic modifications. Though not as corrugated as the Great Basin, the Mojave Desert has its share of sink and mountain topography with characteristic zonation. Most of the ranges are fault-block in origin, but several extinct volcanoes and associated lava flows are intriguing relief features east of Barstow.

Components of the shadscale scrub occur sporadically over the desert plains, but the community begins to exert itself as such where the soils become increasingly alkali around the edges of playas. By no means is the shadscale community structure identical to that found in the Great Basin. Several species are new, extending no farther north than the Mojave. One is allscale and the other is a handsome member of the goosefoot family, desert holly, named for its creamy green, deeply toothed leaves. Quite a number of typical Great Basin species occur in the Mojave but are rare or missing from the lower desert—arrowscale as well as a number of other scale bushes, spiny hopsage, winter fat, green molly, and greasewood. On the beaches around the Salton Sea, a definite zonation is recognizable. The creosote thins out, giving way to allscale which in turn yields to sturdy halophytes—saltbush and inkweed among them. Finally, just edging the shore are patches of salt grass, cattail, and pickleweed.

Out on the plains surrounding the isolated ranges like a tawny sea, creosote bush and its associates are ubiquitous. Only where washes course in sandy winding trails does this cover break. Then other desert plants are given an opportunity to challenge the monopoly of the reigning species. A famed plant of the Mojave, Joshua tree, is largely confined to the upper alluvial slopes. Instead of replacing creosote bush, it thrusts up through the scrub, much like digger pine towering over a hillside of chaparral. A smaller relative, Mojave yucca, is widespread over the intermediate elevations of the desert for which it is named. It is not restricted to this region, however, as it is scattered down through the eastern Peninsular Ranges. Much less branched than its arboreal relation, it is similar in appearance because of its clusters of white flowers at the end of spike-leaved stalks.

The smaller hills, some almost buried in their own broken bones, as it were, show little or no plant zonation. Steeper faces of exposed and weathering bedrock are almost barren, but gentler slopes carry the shrubs common to the surrounding landscape. The taller mountains and those flanking the deserts to the west have routed down, at altitudes from 3,000 to 6,000 feet, southern extensions of plant types familiar from the short forests—rabbitbrush, cotton thorn, blue sage, horsebrush, sagebrush, pinyon pine, and juniper. Above this zone, montane conifers—yellow and Jeffrey pine, white fir, and lodgepole pine—form islands of cool green on the Transverse and Peninsular ranges, overlooking the hot plains below. The highest peaks of these mountains reach to timberline with stands of limber pine 9,000 feet and above.

Just as certain species are typical of the Colorado Desert, there are several whose distribution is centered in the Mojave. Both common and Latinized names indicate this geographical pattern: *Mojavea* or ghost flower, Mojave sage, Mojave aster, Mojave *Dalea* which is related to indigo bush, Mojave yucca, Mojave monkeyflower, and Mojave prickly pear cactus. One of the most outstanding wildflowers of the middle desert is an eye-striking mariposa lily of Chinese red. Its little cups of flame usually sit close to the ground on short stems surrounded by several green-gray, slim, elongated leaves. When the winter rains have been good, the Mojave has as lavish a wildflower show as the Colorado. Many species occur on both deserts, but a few are more characteristic of the Mojave: thistle sage—an exquisite flower that looks like bouquets of tiny lavender orchids—bird's-eye gilia, pennyroyal, and paintbrush. Desert candle or squaw cabbage is an oddity that once seen is seldom forgotten. Its inflated yellow-green stems look as though the plant had swallowed golf balls and are topped with absurd little tufts of purple flowers.

The Colorado Desert is much smaller in size than the Mojave. It has two quite distinct sections—a large trough to the west and a chunk of basin-and-range topography to the east. The northern part of the trough is called the Coachella Valley, cupped between two upturned hands whose thumbs are the Peninsular Ranges to the west and the Chocolate-Orocopia Mountains to the east. The bent-up fingertips are the Little San Bernardino and Eagle mountains on the north. In the gap, where the two palms are joined, lies the landlocked Salton Sea, the last in a series of lakes that periodically flooded this low-lying area because of overflow from the Colorado River. This large lake is a prime but problem recreation area for water-hungry sports enthusiasts. For a time, irrigation drain-off threatened to raise its surface until seaside resorts would be inundated. Now, constant evaporation is concentrating its dissolved minerals. Soon the water will be so briny that nothing will be able to live in it, and the fish population will disappear.

Below the Salton Sea, in the southern extension of the trough or the Imperial Valley, intensive truck farming is possible because of deep silt soil, level land, year-around mild temperatures, and availability of irrigation water. To the west of this rich valley, the Anza-Borrego, a desert-within-a-desert, is a tangle of much eroded badlands, plains, and steep canyons complicating the eastern base of the mountains in back of San Diego. In this broken country close to the Mexican border, one can find several plants that one would expect only in northern

Mexico or southern Arizona. Desert apricot has worked as far north as the Palm Springs region. The Anza-Borrego country lays claim to fairy duster with its delicate puffs of pink and an arboreal oddity, the elephant tree. One of several species called by this name, it is a *Bursera* and belongs to the torchwood family, which has few nontropical members. Like many desert trees, it is a bit peculiar in appearance, with branches tapering rapidly to resemble the trunk of an elephant. They are covered with white, papery bark which, when injured, exudes a blood-red juice. The tiny leaves do little to improve the looks of this short, stiff-jointed tree, which—while fairly common in Baja California, Sonora, and the mountains of the extreme southern part of Arizona—in California is restricted to one small grove near Fish Creek in San Diego County. A number of shrubs more commonly encountered on the Arizona desert have pushed as far west as the mountains east of the Salton Sea—gray thorn, California snakewood, and crucifixion thorn—among them.

The eastern Colorado Desert looks much like the Mojave, and it is difficult to delimit the two areas. The same gaunt hills stand as though freshly quarried amid the chips of their shaping. The wide plains between them gradually lower in altitude, dropping steadily to about 300 feet above sea level at the Colorado River, which is now little more than a canal between reservoirs. There are few playas in the Colorado Desert, but many sand dunes. Excellent examples of this type of terrain run parallel to the Coachella Canal, on the east side of the Imperial Valley.

From the highway, the battered mountains look inhospitable to anything but the few desert shrubs that have footholds on their scarred flanks. But they hold surprises. The desert can be both a verdant garden and as barren as an airport runway, depending on season and substrate. Not all spring seasons have good wildflower shows. Rain must be adequate and correctly spaced for the maximum display. One four-inch cloudburst in September does not equal four storms bringing one inch each, several weeks apart, from late November through February. The more rain the better, of course, but timing is almost as important as amount. When there have been heavy, widespread, soaking rains and the desert is at the height of bloom, the highways push through masses of flowers lining the road on each side. Large white evening primroses, like little moons, gleam over variegated carpets of deep rose sand verbena, sunny desert dandelion, and desert sunflower, which are often joined by desert marigold, coreopsis, and less showy daisy family species. Where desert pavement is encountered, the display ends abruptly, and only occasional flowering annuals and the dropped blossoms of the undaunted creosote bush, little golden windmills, brighten the hard, rock-mosaic surface. If the winter rains have been kind, on the road that takes off to the hamlet of Rice from the main Los Angeles-Phoenix highway it is possible to see one of the queens of the desert, the wild "Easter lily," a miniature of the commercial lily of Eastertide. Though they are usually but a foot or so high with five or six blossoms, they can grow to 5 or 6 feet tall and continue bearing flowers along this towering stem.

A few miles east of Indio, turn south via State Highway 195 for a quick look into Box Canyon. On the alluvium of the upper wash, springtime annuals may be sparse but still thick enough to be impressive. Here the outstanding plant is ocotillo, at this season tipped with flaming red flowers and green with new leaves. Decked with such rich colors, it is quite different from its fit-only-for-kindling appearance during the rest of the year. Desert plant oddities are by no means uncommon, but this shrub is still one of the most peculiar in appearance— bundles of needle-spined, whiplike rods tied together at one end and thrust into the soil.

Where the wash sides steepen to cliffs, arboreal forms, though rare in much of the California desert, either cluster in webby thickets against the gorge walls or string out along the gravel bars of the canyon floor. Palo verde, ironwood, and desert willow (not a true willow but a member of a large tropical family) all grow to small tree size. When fully flowered, each is alive with color and bees. The first is a cloud of yellow, and the other two are pink, the last species having sprays of large trumpet-shaped blossoms. They are joined by the charming but aggressively spined smoke tree whose filmy gray contrasts with the harsh desert landscape. Other small trees frequently encountered here include mesquite and catclaw, a true acacia. They are related and both have fuzzy caterpillar inflorescences of pale yellow. Chuparosa or beloperone, a stiff little shrub with tubular scarlet flowers, is an inhabitant of the wash community and is much visited by the hummingbirds for the nectar obtainable from its blossoms.

After good winter rains, wild gardens brighten the wash floor and lower slopes—apricot mallow, clumps of coral tinted bells arranged along bending stems, fivespot, a graceless name for little pink bowls as fragile looking as Dresden china, suncups, a type of evening primrose, wild-Canterbury-bell phacelia, silk-sheened blazing stars, and ghost flowers. Many desert annual plants, typified by extremely small size, are referred to as "belly plants" as that is the portion of one's anatomy on which one must rest in order to see them at close hand. Some common wildflowers of this group are *Eriophylum* (a tiny bouquet of yellow flowers), calico plant, rattlesnake weed (its milky juice places it in the euphorb group, distant cousin to Africa's great candelabrum trees), Bigelow monkeyflower, desert star, and nama, a magenta blotch on the gravel as though wine had been spilled and had congealed.

Jeep tracks wind up any wash wide enough to permit them. When they are forced to stop by deepening sand or enclosing boulders, foot trails take over, some almost indiscernible, and meander up the canyon. Those that follow the floor often require hopping and clambering up steep staircases of large boulders, a strenuous type of exercise if one is out of condition. One can also skirt the gully rims on none-too-obvious trails that tack back and forth across the hill faces. Both above and below, one can see that water is the sculptor of these desert ranges, scarce though it is at times. It has tossed down the chunks of rock, large and small, littering the canyon bed, cut the great V the hiker is ascending, and created cliffs for miniature waterfalls when their streams are flowing.

Hillside vegetation often differs from that of the gully floor. On the rim sides grow cacti and low, scant, and often prickly shrubs—ratany, goatnut, Mormon tea, turpentine broom, bladder sage (sometimes called paperbag plant because of its inflated, thin-walled fruit) and desert almond. There may be squaw bush, on an east-facing slope in the shade of a rocky prominence, and many species that have straggled up from the fan slopes below such as brittle bush and indigo bush. In such rocky areas south of Palm Springs, century plants are common. They begin to bud in early spring, thrusting up from thick, needle-tipped leaves giant asparagus-like stems which later break into clusters of rich yellow blossoms. Nolina, belonging to the yucca group, has a similar growth form, but its stalks bear elongate puffs of creamy white. Cacti are forever underfoot, as any desert hillside hiker knows. Fishhook and young barrel cacti tuck into the rocky hillside like small spine-covered boulders.

The canyon floor has protected crannies—under overhangs and against boulders—which shelter numerous plants. Apricot mallows and phacelias, four-o'clocks and bladderpod spray out lavishly. The last is a plant of the pea family which has distended, swollen-looking seed pods, hence its name. It is a frequent shrub of the sand patches, level places between the boulder clutches where mesquite, catclaw, palo verde, and desert willow continue to find foothold. In most desert hillside canyons, rim trail and gully staircase gradually converge. Continuing still higher, they often lead to the most dramatic living feature of the Colorado Desert, a lush oasis, complete with springs, in the heart of a lifeless-looking, seemingly barren desert range. A number of these groves of welcome green shade not only have wild palms but true willows, cottonwoods, and cascading masses of pink and gold stream orchids in late April or May. To come unawares on such rich vegetation is a memorable experience, one which often leads to speculation about desert plant growth in general. Among the many questions often raised is: Why do plants even occur in the desert at all? It seems to be universal that where conditions are not so severe as to preclude all possible plant life, enough species will adapt, in one way or another, so that a true community exists: congregations of plants and animals that can live even under ruggedly adverse circumstances. Only on polar ice fields, the most unstable parts of large shifting sand dunes, the hearts of alkali playas, the few really rainless deserts, ocean depths, the punishing heights of the tallest mountains, and uncongealed lava flows is plant life in some permanent form virtually impossible.

Desert plants can be categorized according to several primary types of growth behavior. There are as many versions of such organizing as there are naturalists who think them up. For simplicity we use three: those whose way of life announces that water is available the year around; those that retire from active metabolism during adverse conditions; and those that continue to struggle along. To put it another way, plants living in a desert are either water users, ephemerals, or drought-adapted perennials. The first two have made the least changes to their demanding environments. Where water is permanent—along mountain-draining or spring-source streams, around seeps and pools, and in the vicinity of the larger rivers such as the Colorado (or near present-day irrigation ditches)—waterside growth common to other parts of California and the Southwest is much at home. In moist soils where the water table is at no great depth, willows and cottonwoods, though not typical desert plants, are joined by mesquite, catclaw, and tamarix, a pink-plumed, salt-tolerant tree originally from the Near East. Reeds, seep willow, arrowweed, sedges, and various rushes are in the damper places, and tules and cattails where open water is constantly present. In areas of salinity and heavy mineralization, resident species are essentially halophytic. Salt grass and alkali sacaton are commonly found in such habitats. Shrubs such as saltbushes and inkweed are frequently found in the transitions between the oasis and the drier desert.

The oasis plant that deserves star status is the native fan palm. A relict of once much larger distribution and wetter climate, it has maintained precarious membership in the flora of the Colorado Desert. Two oases, however, are at the southern edge of the Mojave Desert, slightly misplaced. One very striking group remains in Arizona—Kofa Palms. Both the fan palm and a good-looking relative, the blue palm, are present in large numbers in northern Baja California. For the most part, fan palms are restricted to areas of permanent surface or subsurface water. Many groves are located in canyons on the flanks of the mountains to the west and north of the Coachella and Imperial valleys. Palm Canyon, for which Palm Springs is named, is one of these oases. Several small groups are in open desert where seeps and pools occur, such as Seven Palms, Dos Palmas, and Twentynine Palms, the latter being one of the two north of the Colorado Desert. A group of groves is strung along the base of the Indio Hills, whose south face is a scarp created by one branch of the San Andreas Fault which splits east of Pearblossom into two great cracks. One runs just north of San Bernardino and divides into a complex of smaller faults near Banning, recombining as one fault east of the Salton Sea; the other drops south near Hemet and slices down through the Anza-Borrego country, west of the Imperial Valley. At various points along the Indio Hills, groves of wild palms dot the otherwise almost barren slopes. Thousand Palms, Pushawalla, Biskra, Willis, Macomber, and a number of other oases draw on moisture sources where the water table has been forced to the surface by the fault.

In the pastel-tinted Mecca Hills, cut through by Box Canyon, a much dissected landscape cradles several little oases, including one that is a gem, Hidden Springs. They are difficult to reach now as the aquaduct has cut off vehicular access. Hiking to them is adventurous but rewarding. Water erosion in these soft rocks, mostly mudstone and conglomerate, has carved out labyrinths of winding, steep-walled, narrow passageways, some in permanent shade, where dry waterfalls, tunnels, and alcoves crawl about in secret-dungeon complexity. Palm hunting in this odd geological pocket of the California desert is even more of a challenge as corridors narrow, and one must edge sidewise past sharp-rocked walls; or they widen out to charming canyons, often surprisingly thick with desert vegetation.

Camping in a canyon oasis has its own delights. Then one can catch memory-enriching details that a hurried visit usually misses: the golden hue of both surrounding rocks and palms in the light of late winter afternoon; the dry rustle of the fronds in the endless desert wind; the skirts of dead leaves that from a distance have the color and texture of the basketry made by the Indians that once lived in these oases; the faint smell of alkali which sometimes encrusts the ground with white crystals; the fruiting stalks hanging down from the masses of huge accordion-pleated palm leaves, heavy with sweet but tiny dates; and the sheer splendor of the palms themselves, towering into the blue sky, hemmed in but never dominated by the crags that rise around them.

When dates drop from the palms, these sugary morsels are eagerly sought by coyotes, carnivores with extremely wide food choices; they appear to eat almost anything edible, with the exception of grass and leafy material in general. Their footprints are often seen in the soft earth around springs and along desert streams. Among other mammals one can hope to glimpse in the vicinity of oases, particularly those in canyons away from the desert floor, are mule deer and bighorn sheep. The latter is the desert variety of an ungulate occurring in mountain areas from Canada to Mexico. True sheep, they browse on Mojave yucca and the leaves of many shrubs and small trees. One of the most fascinating experiences desert mountains can offer is the chance of observing a group of bighorns stepping, Indian file, along a game trail led by an ewe. Sheep, used to following their mothers while young, continue the habit of remaining behind a female leader when mature. Observation chances are best near waterholes, as these animals must drink regularly.

A number of reptiles are typical of arid rocky hillsides. Collared, and desert and granite spiny lizards sun themselves on exposed boulder surfaces which they desert for protected niches when they are startled. California's largest lizard, the chuckwalla, is, without exception, a rock dweller. Though much of its body is black or gray, individual color variations of red and yellow are not uncommon on its back and tail. "Chucks" are vegetation eaters, a habit not common in the lizard world. Thus they make good pets as they are easy to feed. But catching one is not too simple. They appear to be lethargic and slow moving, but they are wary and elude their would-be captors by resorting to strategy. They escape into small crevices, and when cornered by threatening hands or capture devices, they inflate themselves, wedging in so that it is amost impossible to pull them out.

Black-tailed gnatcatchers, desert song sparrows, and ladder-backed woodpeckers are year-around residents of an oasis environment. In summer, blue grosbeaks, hooded orioles, goldfinches, and kingbirds seek either insect or plant food, depending on their tastes. Along the Colorado River, brick-red summer tanagers work through the cottonwoods, west of their usual territory. In spring, chats, yellowthroats, and Wilson's and yellow warblers pause in their favorite habitat before going on to riparian woodlands north and west. White-crowned, Lincoln's, and chipping sparrows take their places in winter.

To return to the story of plant survival in this arid region, the ephemerals are short-lived annuals carrying dormancy to an advanced degree. They are, strictly speaking, alive as plants only a few weeks of the year; they remain in seed form, needing neither food nor water for indefinite periods of time. When rain occurs, either in summer or winter, some, but by no means all, will germinate and grow a tiny tuft of foliage and stem. Whether they succeed in producing spectacular wildflowers depends on the ensuing weather. In dry years, plants remain stunted and, at best, grow only a blossom or two. In optimum years, when the desert as a whole receives a great deal of well-spaced rain, then blooms the showy display. A large number of plants and seeds, however, are harvested by rodents and birds. Regardless of weather fluctuation, most of these plants have the characteristic juicy stems and green leaves of water wasters. Quite a number do have some moisture-conserving features—hairy or sticky foliage, small size, and so forth—but in general the ephemerals behave as though moisture were plentiful, as it may be for the three or four weeks of their life. If all goes well, the mature plants live long enough to drop seeds that will wait through the long sleep until the next growing season. A similar way of life holds true for plants such as the desert Easter and mariposa lilies, whose bulbs are safely underground throughout the dry months. The seasonal herbaceous cover is by no means beneficial to surrounding shrubs. It uses much of the surface moisture which would otherwise be available to perennial species.

Finally, we come to the plants that survive the long, parched, wind-harried days between rains, not relying on permanent water nor restricted to the extreme dormancy of seed form. There are many ways to resist dehydration, nevertheless, and most drought-enduring plants combine several features and do not depend on just one alone. These include the following:

(1) Succulence. Such species have the ability to store water in fleshy tissue, for example, cacti, agaves, stonecrops, and aloes (old world xerophytes). Their epidermis is often heavily cutinized, drought proofed, as it were, and as a rule they are shallow rooted, taking up surface moisture to enrich their internal reservoirs. They have a remarkable ability to shrink and pucker during the seemingly endless months of drought, only to swell in corpulence when the rains finally return.

(2) Deep rootedness. Many shrubs of desert hillsides and washes are like chaparral species in that their long roots go deep to the water table or sources of moisture in fractured bedrock.

(3) Leaf structure and seasonal growth patterns. As we have already noted, metabolism, the processes involved in the maintenance of life, uses and spends water.

Water balance—moisture loss equivalent to moisture intake —is essential for all plants if they are to continue growth. In the case of annuals, once seed has been dropped and water balance is no longer important, the plants wilt and die. Perennial species, shrubs, trees, and so forth, are out-of-step with such simple rhythms. Tenacious of life, they have modified to cope with the desert's most stern control, the limiting factor of water deficiency.

Conditions vary, but each organism has sets of tolerance ranges within which it must function, or it will die. Such ranges have limits at both ends. When these are approached, the life of the organism is threatened. We tend to first think in terms of a lack of a requirement—too little water; too small an amount of oxygen—but the other end of the scale is also operative. There can be too much of any one thing, either a necessity or a nonessential. Extremes of any nature are potentially lethal; for life as we know it here on the planet Earth is restricted to a rather narrow spectra of conditions. Unprotected living tissue has very little tolerance to fire, intense and prolonged heat, cold, drought, and radical changes in the chemistry of individual environments.

For most desert perennials, water deficit is countered by a number of resistive measures, many having necessarily to do with foliage, where most water loss takes place. Some plants have discarded leaf tissue or reduced it to spines, and manufacture food with chlorophyll bodies in stems or in bark. Cacti are excellent examples of such modification, though species of this large group of plants do have leaves, some of which occur only in infancy and are shed by the plant as it matures. The function of the spines has been debated. There is evidence that the interlacing network provides enough shade so that the tough, leathery epidermis will not heat to damaging temperatures. Such speculation raises the whole interesting point of the reason for the abundance of thorny or spiny plants in desert regions. It has been suggested that, because of its scarcity, the edible vegetation growing here is the target of all the plant-eating animals, which are surprisingly numerous in arid regions. Thorniness may be a protective adaptation, discouraging intensive browsing.

Palo verde trees conduct limited photosynthesis in green bark on their trunks and branches throughout the year. However, it goes into high-gear food production for a short time each spring when it puts forth slim-leaved foliage which it drops at the start of the hot season. Smoke trees and crucifixion thorns behave in like manner, and many saltbushes are summer deciduous. Ocotillo confines its food making to the leafy periods following sufficient rain, regardless of season. When bare of foliage it is dormant, reducing metabolic activity and living off the food stored in stick-like branches protected by resinous bark. Even the plucky creosote bush loses many leaves during times of stress. The evergreen plants that maintain year-round foliage have many features for water conservation and reduction of heat: hairyness, waxiness, the presence of resin, light color, thickened cuticle, small size, and stomata either sunken or protected in other ways. Most have the capacity to endure prolonged wilting. The osmotic pressure within their cells continues to remain high for some time even in adverse circumstances. Some shrubs, such as goatnut, turn only the edges of their leaves, not the full blades, to solar radiation. Sun strength hitting broadside is far more drying than that striking parallel to the surface.

By far one of the most valuable resources of arid region plants is the ability to enter some type of dormancy when conditions are at their worst. Not only are they slow growers in general, they may reduce metabolic rates even further. In some instances, whole portions of the plant die, and the water-using tissue remains roughly proportionate to the amount of moisture available. Creosote bush exemplifies such behavior. When drought is prolonged—and it can extend for several years in the desert—these shrubs decrease the amount of water-losing leaf surface by dying back. One after another of the numerous stems comprising the adult bush drop their shriveled leaves and become lifeless twigs that in time will break off and collect as dead litter. Finally, only a few viable stems and leafy wisps remain, carrying on limited photosynthesis and barely maintaining life. But a good season or two brings remarkable changes. Though the really dead woody tissue cannot be revived, the living branches sprout fresh green leaf crops, and the plant begins rapidly growing new shoots. The ability to recover quickly, making the most of good fortune, is characteristic of most desert plants. Activity and then dormancy, of one degree or another, is the typical rhythmic pattern of nearly all perennials during the desert year.

For many desert shrubs, infancy is the time of greatest danger. They may sprout but fail to live through the following dry period. There are a number of plants, mostly wash dwellers, in which germination can be accomplished only if the seed coat is scarified by abrasion. Scratching of this sort usually happens when the seeds are tumbled along during the floods that periodically rage through the washes. Presumably it allows the entry of water into the seed which dissolves germi-

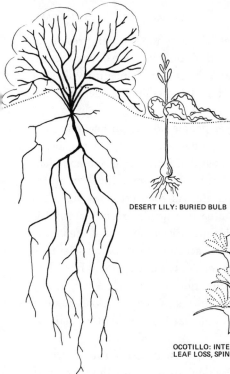

DESERT LILY: BURIED BULB

MORMON TEA: REDUCTION IN LEAF SIZE

SMOKE TREE: SPINES

OCOTILLO: INTERMITTENT TOTAL LEAF LOSS, SPINES

CHOLLA CACTUS: SUCCULENCE, SPINES, AND NO LEAVES

MESQUITE: DEEP ROOTS

GHOST FLOWER: EPHEMERAL

DESERT VELVET: HAIRINESS, LIGHT COLOR

CREOSOTE BUSH: WAXY LEAVES

NAMA: DWARF SIZE

GOAT NUT: VERTICAL LEAVES

PALO VERDE: SEASONAL LEAF LOSS

DESERT HOLLY: WHITE COLOR REFLECTS SOLAR RADIATION

Figure 22. Adaptations to drought in desert plants

nation inhibiting substances. At any rate, water present in quantities sufficient to carry the seeds swiftly down a wash floor is a kind of guarantee that enough moisture will sink beneath the surface to foster the seedlings once they are started.

One of the first things that people notice, on becoming acquainted with desert flora, is the spacing between shrubs. It is so uniform as to seem almost deliberate, as if someone had planted them so many feet apart. Root competition for water effectively keeps plants separate. As each creosote bush has very widespread roots, the area it controls extends around it for a number of feet. There is much discussion about the mechanisms whereby this spacing is accomplished. Some scientists have proved the existence of certain toxic substances from leaf or root which discourage competition from too close neighbors. Whether this is true for such shrubs as creosote bush has not yet been generally accepted, but that it is for brittle bush appears little doubted.

On the other side of the coin, most desert shrubs serve as nursemaids for the annuals taking advantage of the shade and protection afforded by their taller associates. In a region as rigorous as a desert, microclimates become particularly important. An overhanging rock, a sheltering bush or tree, a shaded cranny—these are fortuitous and fortunate circumstances providing habitats a little less xeric, where moisture remains somewhat longer than in more open environments. Any place that collects runoff favors vegetation. Highway pavement edges are classic examples. Concentrations of plants flourish here because of the additional moisture draining off the highway. It is also true of bases of "dry" waterfalls, edges of rock slabs, and other places where water, flowing off the nonporous surface, sinks into the waiting soil.

Life has not found deserts to be impossible places; however, there are secrets to survival here. A shrub can spend water when it is available, but it does so at its peril when moisture is in short supply. It is a way of life based on frugality, stamina, adaptability, and the premise that good fortune will come once in a while if life remains to take advantage of it.

Sand dunes near Kelso, Mojave Desert

# 18. Sand Dune

When we first began our slow journey across California, we paused briefly in the coastal dunes. Their smooth flanks revealed an unsuspected traffic. Beachcombers other than human make their way over the sandy hummocks and leave behind telltale patterns that remain until wind or tide erases them. Then the clean page records a new set of encounters, travels, or adventures.

Desert sand dunes have even more story-telling potential. The number of possible plots and characters is almost endless, particularly in spring when the resident animals are joined by migrants, and the winter's pale green fuzz has suddenly sprouted into fields of wildflowers. Then the smaller sand hillocks, especially those with some vegetative cover, tell stories of remarkable complexity and detail. Their language may be difficult to understand, and only trained eyes can discover all they have to say. With a little curiosity, however, and reference books on California deserts—and there are several very helpful ones available—you should be able to spend a most entertaining morning reading a history that has its own surprises and excitement. Notice the word "morning." Though many desert animals are diurnal, equally many, if not more, are nocturnal. The best time to read a dune is right after dawn, before the wind has had a chance to rearrange the sandy surfaces.

Where can one find such a series of hummocks? Wherever there are sand and wind whose direction is fairly constant. In past years, a fine collection was just at the outskirts of La Quinta, now a high-priced piece of real estate southeast of Palm Springs. Much of the country around the upper end of the Salton Sea is sandy, and dunes may be found where urbanization and agriculture have not yet claimed them. These hummocks are the offspring of mountain and air current. Particles weathered from the surrounding ranges and brought down by the Whitewater River are buffeted by westerly winds channeled through the lower passes. Some dunes are large, such as those near Garnet, at one time an important station stop, but now only an offramp of a freeway that ignores the once omnipotent authority of the railroad. Most dunes are small, a dozen or so feet high, and from the air they look like arrested white caps in a sea of gravel.

All dunes result from local interruptions in the general wind flow patterns. When the wind is obstructed by rocks, plants, and even fence posts, it is forced to drop its load of sand grains, and a dune or series of dunes build up. There are many variations in dune appearance and behavior. Where the wind remains relatively constant in direction, eddies just below the crest on the leeside compel abrupt deposition of material. The windward flank has a gentle gradient, and the lee is steep. Sand like other erosional debris can accumulate on a slope pitch only until the angle of repose is reached. At that point, additional deposited material must roll down to the base. Thus dunes migrate with the prevailing wind as sand is transported from windward to leeward where it gathers at the foot, constantly encroaching on new territory. There are many instances of dunes invading forests and, after a few years, moving on to leave behind hundreds of destroyed trees. Crescent-shaped dunes usually occur in regions where the sand supply is small and prevailing winds are moderate in strength. The milder air currents sweep around rather than over the summit ridge and carry their burdens out to the tapering tips. Serpentine and even star-shaped dunes have been described, all subject to the vagaries of the wind. Larger sand seas occur in many arid places of the world. There is an excellent example in the great dunes area near Yuma, east of the Imperial Valley. Such expanses often bunch into elongate mounds roughly parallel to each other. At times, the sand surface is crinkled by ripple marks, thousands of tiny ridges that in early morning or late afternoon catch shadows in the troughlets separating them.

Not all dunes travel. Where winds seasonally reverse or are multidirectional, they tend to stay put. Vegetation often stabilizes the smaller ones, particularly those that have developed around an embedded plant. Many desert hummocks feature mesquite, a tree peculiarly adapted to remaining alive while sand accumulates around it. Both honey and screw-bean mesquite have extremely long roots. They tap the water table where it comes within fifty feet or so of the ground surface. In addition, these plants cope with clay soils periodically low in oxygen as well as mineralized. Hence they are strong contenders for riparian space. Before the lower Colorado River was channelized, unfortunately so, some contend, by the Corps of Army Engineers and the Bureau of Reclamation, thickets of willow, cottonwood, catclaw, tamarix, and mesquite massed on either side of the stream, sheltering much wildlife.

To those accustomed to this type of riverine growth, the clumps of mesquite decorating many local sand dunes seem to be venturing into unfriendly territory. Nothing is as dry as a sand dune—or so it would appear. There is more than meets the eye. The seedling began its career, perhaps, when wind had exposed moist soil or when rains were plentiful and the surface water sources at no great depth. As drifting sand piled up through the years, the mesquite grew with it, and its leafy top is all that is exposed. We see only a very small part of the entire tree. Below the sand surface, its bare and gnarled branches reach down to the trunk buried deep in the heart of the dune. This is why sand hill mesquite looks shrubbier than the tree forms we find in riparian sites. That it taps the water table is indicated by its behavior. It is winter deciduous, a sure sign that moisture sources are available during the summer months.

Nowhere in California are there the large savannas of mesquite so typical of the relatively well-watered, semidesert plains of southern Arizona, New Mexico, and Texas, with their summer rains. Perhaps it is just as well for the tree is proving quite a problem. Useful as it is for wood, fodder, browse, and shade, it is keenly competitive. When overgrazing weakens the perennial grass cover, mesquite moves in easily. Dunes forming around it also destroy valuable range. In common with many trees of desert wash and oasis, it is frequently host to a very fragrant plant, desert mistletoe. Unlike the leafier species such as that infesting cottonwoods or oak trees, it forms snarls of reddish-brown twinelike stems whose leaves are very little more than scales. Its points of attractiveness are limited to the translucent rosy berries and the odor of its inconspicuous little flowers, a combination of perfume and spice.

Other plants are not strange to dune environments, even those whose roots are unable to extend down to the water table. Almost all the rain received by sand sinks in; very little runs off. Though the surface dries quickly, giving the impression that the interior is moistureless, water is often present in the lower levels of the dunes long after the surrounding plains are sear. Four-winged saltbush frequently accompanies mesquite in the sand hills near the Salton Sea, but both yield to the halophytes, the only species able to contend with the saline soils edging the great playa.

Ricegrass takes to sandy soils as does big galleta, a gramineous species often found on dunes. Creosote bush, desert buckwheat, goldenbush, and Mormon tea find their way up on the unstable slopes. A number of annuals flood the hummocks with color when rains have been abundant—sand verbena (notice its rich, sweet smell), the large white evening primrose, desert sunflower, and the little golden gilia, which though uncommon is not a real rarity. Sand food is another of the desert's oddities. Unlike other members of its family, the water leaf group, it is parasitic and looks like nothing more than a piece of fluffy wool that has escaped from an old comforter and has come to rest on the desert sand. If examined closely, the hairs are seen to cover a mass of purple flowers which are perched on top of a buried but edible fleshy stem, hence the peculiar name. Like another fuzzy plant, Spanish needles, it has made itself a home on the Yuma dunes.

Where sand grains constitute a large part of the substrate, almost any bush or shrub encourages little drifts that pile up around it. For that matter, aeolian sand tends to gather in patches over most of the desert plains and washes. Dune, drift, patch, or even soft shoulder, if their particles are fine enough, traces of animal traffic will be imprinted on the surface, if only for a short while.

If one were to be suddenly dropped within the La Quinta dunes on some spring morning, with a bit of examination one could even backcast the weather. Very recent rain will have moistened the sand so that it feels damp to the touch. As sand is very absorbent, precipitation that occurred several days before the visit is no longer detectable at the surface; but by digging down a foot or so, evidence of a recent soaking rain can be found. Another story is told by circular sweep marks in the sand under bushes whose twig tips angle or arch so that they are in contact with the ground. The graceful curves drawn in the sand are indicative of strong winds that whipped the ends of the shrubs back and forth. Where the streaks intersect, charming patterns are traced in the drifts much like the elaborate penmanship exercises of Victorian times. Smaller plants, particularly annuals, are often dehydrated, damaged, or partially buried by high wind. Tiny drifts banked around belly plants or the presence of grains blown into tufts of dense foliage hints that windstorms have scourged the area in the not-so-distant past. If lizards become active just at sunrise and thriving ephemerals show signs of recent wilting or drying, the weather is warming rapidly to high temperatures, and the nights are failing to cool to midspring norms. On the other hand, if these small reptiles deliberately bask in the open sun, and the wildflowers maintain their jauntiness, chances are that the night before has been cool, though probably not cold. Any visitor then will have a day of pleasant breeze and warmth, without the extremes so typical of this part of the world.

After a mild spring night, when the nocturnal animals have been active, the surface of a dune records much coming and going on the part of its residents and visitors. If you are fortunate enough to find one that has been tunneled by kangaroo rats (look for such a colony near creosote or other bushes where the root network provides support for the runways and prevents cave-ins), the entrances to their burrows will sprout trails leading to numerous intersections where their tracks cross each other. As these agile creatures hop about, they leave lines of double prints where their hairy hind feet land simultaneously, with elongate depressions where their tails hit the ground in rhythm with their progress. Two converging trails that have been disrupted by scattered sand and other marks of scuffle are unmistakable evidence that two rats were disputing territory or possessions, or engaging in strenuous play, all characteristic behavior traits in these attractive but often agressive animals. Smaller dune-dwelling rodents such as grasshopper and silky-haired pocket mice have such diminutive feet that they barely dimple the surface of the sand.

More ominous are the doglike tracks of hunting coyotes. Each of the four claw marks is commonly quite visible if the sand is firm enough to keep the imprint. Owls, on the other hand, like most avian predators, seldom leave terrestrial evidence of their skill in attack unless a struggle ensues before the victim is borne off. Sidewinders, small horned rattlers well-adapted to travel on unstable ground, leave unmistakable traces. As the snake advances, he does so sideways with a peculiar looped motion resulting in a series of diagonal depressions, parallel to each other. This method of travel provides more traction with less drag on sandy surfaces. Long wiggling traces in the sand are characteristic of other snakes. It is rather difficult for an untrained person to distinguish between the various types of snakes by marks alone. The heavy-bodied species such as the larger rattlers leave broader and deeper marks, while the smaller types make shallower impressions whose undulations are closer together; this generalization is only true, however, of adults. An encounter between a constricting snake, such as a desert gopher snake, and a rodent is commonly marked by some signs of disturbance. Both predator and prey are equally determined to survive, one by eating and the other by escaping.

Most desert snakes are nocturnal, even those species whose habits are diurnal in less rigorous environments. When they emerge from hibernation hideouts, they are lean from the long fast. On mild spring nights, one can often see a goodly aggregation of these reptiles on the pavement of the less traveled roads. Cold-blooded animals, they have interrupted their hunting to warm their bellies, as the road surface retains heat long after the sun has set. One can soon learn to identify some of the more common desert snakes. The rattlers are unmistakable with their horny tail ends. Long-nosed and shovel-nosed snakes are attractively banded, some quite spectacularly in black and red. The glossy snake has dusky spots on a light-gray background. Rosy boas have blunt tails; yellow-bellied and red racers are the color their names suggest. Desert gopher snakes generally have a paler ground color than their brush or woodland cousins but are similarly marked. Patch-nose snakes have yellow or tan stripes down their backs, often with dark edging. Very few lizards are nocturnal, but one of the most delightful, the banded gecko, is night active, fortunately, as his velvety pink skin is covered with tiny, granular scales that are not as protective as those covering most other lizards.

As the morning progresses, it becomes noticeably warmer. The now limbered lizards are wary of the harsher sun and scud over the hillocks from bush to bush. Zebra-tailed and leopard lizards are miniature dinosaurs as they charge along on their hind feet, front legs held near their bellies. Where the grains are fine and loosely compacted, the scurrying feet of the larger lizards push aside little heaps of sand like strings of diminutive crater rims. Dragging tails make streaks when lizards are moving slowly. During bursts of speed, they are held off the ground. A series of miniscule dunes with parallel troughs reveals the temporary hiding places of several sand-burrowing lizards—horned lizard and fringe-toed sand lizard. The last is as adjusted to its dune environment as its far-distant cousin, the sidewinder. It not only has fringes or special scales on its toes which help it "swim" through the sand, but the ear, eye, nose, and mouth openings are protected by flaps, valves, and other structural devices. The long-tailed brush lizard, though a sand-burrowing form on occasion, is one of the very few southwestern lizards that are largely arboreal. When stretched out along twigs, it closely resembles the perch to which it clings, a good example of protective disguise.

Bird tracks multiply during the morning activity peak. One is obvious. Freshly made crosses, two inches long, hint that a roadrunner, or paisano, is bent on breakfast. It is no surprise then to see this large bird striding along, usually away from the observer, with a limp leopard, whiptail, or other small lizard dangling from its bill. His large feet help him negotiate the soft dune sand. Snakes are not neglected by this ungainly looking ground cuckoo. Red racers, one of the few day-active snakes, range over the sand hills long after night-hunting species have taken to seclusion during the warmer part of the day.

Other creatures now wander over the hummocks. Here is a strip of needlework stitched by the feet of a large beetle, one of the acrobat beetles perhaps. He is known by several names —tumblebug, stinkbug, and pinacate—but the reference to his headstanding ability is most apt. Not all the mammals have retreated to burrow or shelter, though most take care to avoid prolonged exposure to the powerful noonday sun even on a day not overly hot. They remain in the shade when they can. A quiet observer of dune life can sometimes catch a glimpse of round-tailed ground squirrels out foraging or a jackrabbit nibbling on moisture-rich vegetation. Crested iguanas, relatively large, vegetation-eating lizards, endure surprisingly high air temperatures. They are often observed scampering over sandy hillocks in the full heat of a summer day.

The desert's harsh demands on life have forced its animals to adapt as well as its plants. Both types of living organisms need and use water. Because all living cells are largely fluid, several processes are common to the two kingdoms. Food, wastes, and other dissolved substances are transported in a liquid medium, blood in the case of the higher animals, sap in the more advanced plants. Both plants and animals respire, converting food to energy through oxidation. One of the by-products of this chemical reaction is water, a factor of extreme importance. Leaf structures of most desert perennials are considerably modified to prevent water waste. Such modifications are relatively simple. Some are permanent adaptations typical of desert plants—resinous coatings and the like. The leaf pores, where most gas exchange occurs and water vapor is lost, are smaller in size and recessed within the epidermis. In addition— and this is true for most plants, not just those in desert regions —each stomate is enclosed between two guard cells. During drought, when the plant is in danger of wilting by losing too much water through its stomata, the cells become flabby, the pore closes, and transpiration stops.

Water conservation for the higher animals involves a whole complex of anatomical features, physiological processes, and behavioral procedures. Respiration occurs externally (in contrast to internal gas exchange which involves oxidation within the individual cell) in but one set of organs, gills in tadpoles and fish, lungs and connected respiratory passages in reptiles and warm-blooded animals. Therefore, loss of water vapor from a centralized area such as a lung should be subject to easy regulation. No such adaptations, however, have evolved within the higher animals which, on the face of it, seems somewhat inefficient. There are no automatic or self-regulatory devices to decrease respiration rates within the lungs themselves.

If water is to be conserved, other systems must be employed, and many have developed that help maintain water balance— some specific to a limited group of organisms and some common to a large number of desert dwellers. Regardless of degree of restriction, such adaptive machinery works, or it would have been tossed onto the biological scrapheap long ago by the ruthless hand of evolution.

Animals also lose water in ways other than through respiration. All terrestrial animals facilitate the passing of solid wastes with liquid, the amounts of which vary from species to species. With the exception of those that hibernate or experience normal diurnal fluctuations in body warmth, warm-blooded animals maintain a constant temperature when healthy. Not only must they produce and conserve heat during exposure to cold, they must have ways by which they can lower body temperatures when those of the environment at large are higher. These are of real significance in arid regions where the mechanisms for this decrease involve potentially harmful water loss.

One device is to use the natural cooling resulting from evaporation. One of the first lessons taught in high school science classes is that when water changes its state from liquid to vapor there is an accompanying loss of heat. Man has made use of this handy little physical principle ever since the first tribesman thought to hang an oozing skin bag of water in a tree to catch the breeze. He could very well have been inspired by his own body. Countless sweat glands are scattered in much of the human skin. When perspiring animals are warm, water is shunted out into the sweat glands from the blood. The glands open, water is flushed out over the skin, it evaporates, and the body is cooled; a breeze is enjoyed on a hot day because it speeds evaporation. However, the human species is unusual, for most other terrestrial vertebrates have fewer sweat glands. Evaporative cooling can only occur where there is moist skin, or tissue such as the mucus secreting membranes of nose, mouth, throat, and the lung itself. Many desert animals open their mouths and some even pant while under heat duress, exposing as much moist surface as possible to the open air. The long, dripping tongues of overheated canine friends point up the usefulness of saliva as a moisture source for evaporative cooling. Some ground squirrels, the cactus mouse, and Merriam's kangaroo rat have been seen to actually spread saliva around on their heads and chests as a last-ditch method of keeping body temperatures below lethal levels.

Though water is very scarce over much of the desert, the animals living here must maintain a liquid level in their body cells. At the same time, its loss is unavoidable through several vital processes: respiration, voiding wastes, and keeping cool. In addition, a great drain is placed on the internal water resources of females in the production of young. Amphibians have an even harder time. They are prone to desiccation and must keep their skin surfaces moist at all times.

Needless to say, the story of the maintenance of water balance by animals in the desert is one of ultimate trimph, though the delicate equilibrium is sometimes upset by climatic or other conditions that place great stress on some or all desert populations. In general, animals rely on a number of features that enable them to avoid water deficit, not just one alone. None of the vertebrates is without some protective skin cover, and many have additional epidermal features. Reptilian scales, for instance, are very effective in retarding water vapor loss. Feathers and fur insulate the body from heat as well as cold.

The wastes of vertebrate animals are usually discharged while suspended in fluid or in a moist state. Many desert species absorb most of the liquid passing through the lower intestines, and the discharged feces are relatively dry. In birds and reptiles, the urine is concentrated to the point where its solid particles precipitate out as crystals of uric acid. They are voided with the feces with little loss of water. In some of the desert rodents, urinary wastes are almost pasty in consistency, in contrast with the liquid discharge of more water-spending species. The desert tortoise has a water-storing bladder, an internal resource upon which it can draw when drought has killed or prevented the growth of the moist vegetation on which it feeds.

By following certain patterns of behavior, organisms can regulate the need for water. The simplest ways are to decrease

activity and to seek cooler environments. Though low metabolic rates generally are typical of many desert animals, minimal exertion during the warmer hours reduces the amount of
water used in temperature regulation and respiration. Such
curtailment ranges all the way from resting under a shady
bush during the summer afternoon to complete withdrawal
from the hot, dry environment and cessation of most activity.
The length to which each species goes depends partly on its
structural water-conserving modifications and partly on what
moisture sources are available.

A number of desert animals are restricted to a damp or
aquatic environment, if they are to survive. They rarely, if
ever, expose themselves to desiccating air and heat. Toads and
frogs are among those unable to live far from moisture. Both
the red-spotted and spadefoot toads retreat to damp burrows
and crannies when their pools contract after the swelling of
winter. There is some evidence that they estivate, or enter summer dormancy, akin to hibernation or winter sleep. Neither
food nor water is needed in what amounts to a state of suspended animation. The California treefrog also spends part
of the time holed up in moist, underground pockets. For all
three species, rainy spells are times of busy activity which are
usually coincidental with an increased insect supply. They feast
on juicy grubs and the emerged adults alike. Breeding usually
takes place during the same period of optimum conditions; the
tadpoles hatch in rain pools and renewed streams.

Though some aquatic forms such as the little desert pupfish
are confined to permanent water, brine shrimp can exist for
years as viable eggs encased in the dried mud of a playa bed.
When rains and runoff create temporary lakes or puddles in
these basins, almost miraculously they hatch into lively little
crustaceans, swarming in the salty water. Fairy shrimp, near
relatives, behave in the same way, but they cannot survive
highly saline solutions.

All but a few desert species must somehow take in liquid.
For many, diet alone is sufficient—succulent leaves and fruit,
juicy insects, and other animal tissue. Several lizards—chuck-
wallas and desert iguanas—utilize fresh, moisture-rich vegeta-

tion such as flowers, leaves, and stems. Others supplement it
with water when it is available. Snakes have been observed to
drink from temporary rain pools; on the other hand, quite a
large group of animals must drink regularly. Bighorn sheep
have their waterholes which they visit on their rounds. Coyotes
dig for water in washes when pools are scarce.

Most birds habitually seek water. Limited as such resources
are in most deserts, one would suppose that few birds would
live and be active here the year around. The resident population
of birds is surprisingly large and includes a number of carnivores and carrion feeders, species which, because their kidneys
work harder, need more liquid for excretion. Vultures circle in
the hot updrafts. Prairie falcons, red-tailed and sparrow hawks
quarter the washes and slopes below. Screech and horned owls
move in on the night shift. Occasionally, the diminutive elf
owl moves over from Arizona where he usually keeps to the
giant saguaros serving as his home. Shrikes and roadrunners
harvest the lizards that dart about under the sparse cover.

A host of insectivorous and seed-eating birds are rarely encountered away from desert haunts. In common with all species living here, they must defend themselves against desert
hostility. Fortunately for birds, they are what has been called
preadapted to arid environments. It has already been noted
that their disposal of fecal and urinary wastes is very water
conservative in nature. In addition, they are insulated by feathers which they hold close to their bodies when temperatures
are high. Few birds, however, spend much time in the open sun
of a summer day. Though they may sing or bask on unprotected perches for short periods of time, most seek the shade
of foliage, buildings, and other sheltering places while the
sun is at its worst and may pant in effort to reduce body heat.
The power of flight allows them to be more mobile than most
other desert animals. They can cover wide distances, ranging
over arid heights and plains, looking for water, spotting oases
and streams, seeking cover.

Say's phoebe is one of the more colorful of the resident flycatchers, a drab group in general. Its orange tinted belly contrasts with a body mostly brown. Though it has a wide

distribution, extending from Mexico to Alaska, it is permanently settled in the desert of the Southwest where it seemingly fares well. Another desert flycatcher is not only one of the most gayly clad of its group, but one of California's brilliantly plumaged birds. The vermillion flycatcher is unmistakable. The male is a puff of flame as he waits on a twig or pursues his food with the agile forays so typical of his family. He keeps to the Colorado Desert, but is occasionally seen in the southern Mojave. Two tiny birds are restricted to the southwestern deserts, verdin and black-tailed gnatcatcher. The former has a bright yellow face and cap. Look for him in mesquite patches where he builds a baseball-round nest that opens at the side. The other mite is almost wrenlike, with a long flexible tail he often holds straight up. Though the bird is named for this sooty appendage, the cap of the male is just as black.

One of the desert's most moving experiences is hearing the silvery waterfall of notes poured out by the canyon wren. Though not as exquisite as the fluting of the hermit thrush, his song is one of the most beautiful to be heard anywhere. He is a bird of dry, rocky hillsides. The other characteristic wren of the desert is the cactus wren, one of many birds making use of the natural protection afforded by this spiny vegetation. It builds its nest among the stems of cholla, a formidable type of cactus, and stutters its *chur-r-r* from the needled tips. Several other cactus dwellers are very closely related. They are all large birds with the long curving bills that place them in the thrasher group—Le Conte's, the rare Bendire's, and an occasional crissal.

White-winged, mourning, and Mexican ground doves and Gambel's quail are often seen as they come to tanks and pools for a drink. The California Fish and Game Department has constructed "guzzlers," primarily for the use of such avian visitors, in many desolate areas of the desert, where natural water is hard to find. The most characteristic bird of the open desert is the phainopepla. The male is jet black, and the female gray-brown. Both have sprightly crests peaked over red eyes and startlingly white wing patches. Fond of mesquite clumps, it feeds on berries of infesting mistletoe. Several sparrows compete with the rodents for the seeds of ephemerals and shrubs—black-throated and Bell's among them.

A number of nonresident birds winter over on the desert: western and mountain bluebirds, water pipits, Townsend's solitaires, and Audubon's warblers among others. Some of these same species are found throughout large areas of lowland California during the cool season, and the desert perhaps is peripheral to the center of the range. A few seem to prefer the desert in the summer—Costa's hummer and hooded oriole—while one, Lucy's warbler, occurs in California only in the extreme southeastern corner of the state, where it nests in the hotter part of the year. By far, the avian activity peak is in the spring when both residents and migrants make the most of the desert's awakening. Warblers, tanagers, lazuli buntings, orioles, and a whole host of colorful feathered creatures pause on their migratory wanderings.

With springtime sprouting seeds, rejuvenated shrubs, and restored water supplies, the smaller worlds of legs and wings stir to life. The larvae of sphynx, owlet, and measuring-worm moths work over the flourishing vegetation, crawling about on pudgy pads. Longhorn beetles find their solitary way along tree limbs, venturing down to the blossoms of the ephemerals, but seldom further. They leave the ground surfaces to the scarab and acrobat beetles. Blister beetles, some strikingly marked, often cling in clusters to perennial shrubs. A number of butterflies—swallowtails, painted ladies, monarchs, and queens—along with several kinds of bees visit the wild gardens. Cicadas begin their shrill rattle in tamarisks and cottonwoods to be continued through most of the summer. Grasshoppers and crickets move out through the cultivated fields. Life in abundance bursts forth from pupa cases, both the original species and those that have parasitized them. At dusk the ground seems to quiver as solpugids, centipedes, flightless sand dune cockroaches, Jerusalem crickets, and scorpions take the place of velvet "ants," roving cadres of harvester and honey ants, and spiders.

Tarantula and tarantula hawk, fly and flycatcher, larva and

lizard—take their places in ever-expanding food webs. Seed-eating birds, insects, and rodents begin round-the-clock assaults on the mature annuals and fruiting shrubs, while jackrabbits, gophers, ground squirrels, and wood rats compete for tender shoots and other moist vegetation. The carnivores feast on the burgeoning numbers of plant and insect feeders. The whole desert has become a picnic ground.

The migrants leave when the portions become skimpy; when the annuals have dried to straw, the seeds are picked over, and much of the insect world rests in eggs and pupa cases underground or in hidden crannies. Now the days bake in the pitiless summer sun. Waterholes constrict, and the runoff streams in the desert ranges shrivel and disappear. The year-round inhabitants adjust in many ways. One of the most common is to either cease or abate daytime activity. Some just relax under cover, jackrabbits in forms hollowed out of compact vegetation, speckled rattlesnakes in the shade of rocks. Coyotes rest deep under leafy shade hardly caring about the birds that may share shrub or tree. The lizards continuing to forage throughout the summer day minimize contact with the hot ground surface. They never linger long out in the open sun, but quickly scamper from one shade patch to another, usually holding their bellies and tails up from the scorching earth. The antelope ground squirrel is one of the few mammals that continue to be day active throughout the summer, though it may retreat into its burrow during the warmest part of the day. Though essentially a seed eater, juicy plant material—such as juniper berries, cactus, and Joshua tree fruits—contributes liquid to its diet, and the ability to concentrate urine helps maintain favorable water balance. In addition, the attractive little rodent can tolerate high body temperatures.

It has often been pointed out that animals living in warm climates have larger appendages than those living in colder areas. The desert kit fox is an excellent example of this general rule. Though he is smaller in size than his cousins, the gray fox of the brushlands and the forest dwelling red fox, his ears are much larger. Presumably, this allows him more body surface from which heat can radiate. In addition, a covering of coarse hair prevents sand from entering the ear orifices, and his feet are thickly tufted with hair to form natural "snow-shoes" for traveling over sand.

The most industrious hours of a number of animals are those of dawn and dusk. They are crepuscular rather than strictly diurnal or nocturnal species. Some of the latter, however, extend their foraging times into early morning and evening, such as bats and the desert-dwelling cottontail rabbit. Two crepuscular birds are of particular interest, poorwill and nighthawk. Both are desert residents and closely related. Though much of their insect hunting is at dusk, they continue pursuit throughout the night, though not so intently. The soft *poor-will, poor-will* of the former is one of the desert's most attractive calls. While diving, the nighthawk rips apart the air, creating a little sound shiver quite audible to human ears below.

The desert has many strictly nocturnal animals. These include the several kangaroo rats, pocket mice, wood rats, grasshopper mice and many of their predators—snakes, kit foxes, and owls. Though some merely tuck into shaded nooks or holes, most of the rodents have underground runways in which they seek refuge when morning comes. Unless you have very tough-soled feet, don't try to walk barefoot over a sand dune, at noon, on a sunny July day in the desert. Surface soil temperatures of 180°F. and even higher have been recorded. Yet, only a few inches of vertical depth can make a tremendous difference as soil is excellent insulation. Soil temperatures can fall a hundred degrees from burrow entrance to nest level. Air temperatures drop accordingly, so what better place to wait out the broiling heat of a summer day than in your own micro-environment, a burrow where it is but 80°F. and the humidity is far higher than in the open air. Because of the animal's inactivity and cool surroundings, respiration and evaporation rates drop considerably, and its water balance can restabilize after the busy night. The burrow serves as hiding place for food caches, as well. Much food gathering involves the transport of seeds and other plant material to underground storage places or nests.

Several mammalian species avoid the problem of summer existence by estivating. Sometime in August, the Mojave ground squirrel disappears into underground hideaways and becomes torpid, automatically reducing its metabolic and water-spending rates. The ground squirrel's sleep is not broken after the onset of autumn. It continues in dormant state through the chill months. Though technically it is now hibernating, rather than estivating, there is no real physiological difference between the two states. Thus it is active only during spring and early summer, when conditions are at their best.

Hibernation is not a rare phenomenon in the desert. Though this region, particularly in lower altitudes, rarely becomes very cold, high desert winter nights regularly drop below freezing. Reptiles, being cold-blooded, can little tolerate temperature extremes. Most of them and several rodents avoid this trying time by remaining underground, quiescently dormant. Until just recently, it was thought that birds did not hibernate. A few years ago, however, Dr. Edmund Jaeger, famed desert naturalist, found a torpid poorwill, much to his amazement, in a rocky crypt near the Chuckawalla Mountains. Many other such individuals have been observed since, and it appears that other bird species may reduce body temperatures to alleviate heat loss on cold nights.

The deserts of California have their animal residents, more of them than is often suspected, bound as we are by our own diurnal activity patterns. They get their water when and where they can, from crunchy grubs and cactus pads, waterholes and dripping faucets. Through various types of adjustment, they husband their intake and spend it as frugally as possible. One animal, however, is the "desert rat" supreme, the kangaroo rat, whose defense of territory is part of the nightly drama of the dunes. He is one of the few animals in the world that need no external liquid source. He never drinks, and he eats only seeds. When carbohydrates (starch or sugar based food) are converted to energy in the body, the by-products are water and carbon dioxide. But most animals cannot live on the small amount of fluid obtained in this way. Not so the kangaroo rat. Being strictly nocturnal, having highly efficient kidneys and

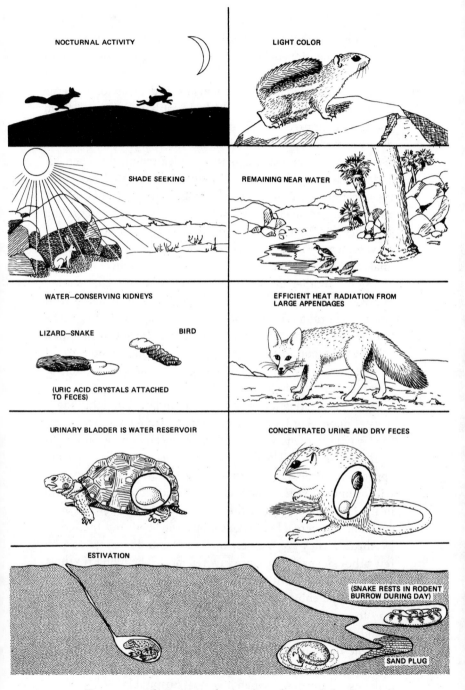

NOCTURNAL ACTIVITY

LIGHT COLOR

SHADE SEEKING

REMAINING NEAR WATER

WATER—CONSERVING KIDNEYS

LIZARD—SNAKE          BIRD

(URIC ACID CRYSTALS ATTACHED TO FECES)

EFFICIENT HEAT RADIATION FROM LARGE APPENDAGES

URINARY BLADDER IS WATER RESERVOIR

CONCENTRATED URINE AND DRY FECES

ESTIVATION

(SNAKE RESTS IN RODENT BURROW DURING DAY)

SAND PLUG

Figure 23. Adaptations of animals to desert conditions

many of the other water-hording devices and behavior characteristics mentioned in this chapter, he thrives on his seed diet.

Many of the adaptive mechanisms and behavior patterns that enable animals to cope with a desert habitat protect them also from their predators. The sparse plant cover of much of the desert provides some protection, but the refuge-seeking habits of much of its animal population foil attempts by enemies. Species ranging from harvester ants to kangaroo rats plug their entrance holes to retain humid air and keep out both heat and foraging invaders. Speed not only takes lizards and ground squirrels into coverts away from the punishing sun, but removes them from predatory interest. Most small desert animals are very light in color. This may serve to reflect both heat and light, another mechanism for the control of temperature and water balance. There is no doubt, too, that blending with one's background is a good way to escape detection. The horned lizards are capable of very subtle shifts in population color. One group may be light gray, matching the dull gravel of its territory, while a neighboring assemblage is the tan or pale rust of its sandy home.

Desert vegetation looks no different under moonlight than it does at noon. April seems little changed from October, except for its wild gardens which are by no means universal or annually dependable. The desert plains, unless disturbed by man, appear much the same as they did a hundred years ago, and will a hundred years hence. The successional patterns we note in the hills and valleys of the coastal ranges are, for the most part, missing here. No foliage canopy will shade out the scrubby shrubs. They are the best the desert can do, except for the few arboreal species in more favored sites. The living rhythms here pulse in time with its animals. Each dawn and dusk, triggered by the ebb and flow of light, one host retires and gives way to another that takes up in turn its struggle to survive in a land that is only occasionally generous. So with the seasons. Like the tide, spring rises and falls, releasing the hibernating creatures, stimulating reproduction, inviting the migrants to make use of the desert when it is most hospitable.

Joshua tree in Joshua Tree National Monument

# 19. The Small World of a Joshua Tree

Deserts have a way of turning out peculiar looking trees, almost as if someone sat at a drawing board and deliberately thought up parodies, grotesque foolery of these familiar features of the natural world. The deserts of Africa have their dragon trees whose branches are tipped with masses of foliage that give the appearance of iris leaves, cut, tied together and glued into place. Baja California's Viscaino Desert has, among other oddities, boojum trees (*Idria columnaris*)—giant hairy asparagus stalks that twist and bend until the tip of the stem may be but six inches from the ground. The Mojave Desert has Joshua trees which are actually more treelike in form than many of the exotic species from other desert areas. They have trunks from which spring branches and leaves of a sort. Webster's *College Standard Dictionary* defines trees as "a perennial woody plant having a single self-supporting trunk, the whole ranging from about ten feet to a considerable height." *Yucca brevifolia* is a lily, yet it has a woody trunk, lives for many years, and is often taller than ten feet. With its precise tufting of spiky leaves that becomes a shaggy thatch when dead, it may not look like the elm in Aunt Cora's back yard in Schenectady, but it is one of the most fascinating trees of the California deserts.

Yucca is a common genus in southern California. *Yucca whipplei*, Our Lord's Candle, is a tall white flame of creamy blossoms erupting from a spike-guarded base. It is thick on chaparral and coastal sage scrub hillsides of the southern counties in late spring. Spanish bayonet and Spanish dagger are two other types of yucca extending east from desert California to Arizona, Nevada, and south down into northern Mexico. The word "yucca" is derived from a native name for cassava or manihot, a food plant of South America from which tapioca is produced. The plants actually have nothing in common, and it is one of the flukes of natural history, no doubt from the time of energetic but sometimes misguided plant explorers, that the two genera became confused. The name "Joshua" was supposedly given to it by early Mormon pioneers who might have been inspired by its aged, bearded appearance and uplifted arms.

Joshua trees are not confined to California, but occur also in Nevada, Utah, and Arizona. However, they are restricted to the higher desert, between 2,500 and 5,000 feet. Their occurrence marks the southern boundary of the Mojave Desert on the slopes of the Little San Bernardino Mountains, where Joshua Tree National Monument is located. Though there are fine groves in the monument, by no means are they the most extensive nor are the individual trees particularly large. There are excellent stands of these tree lilies in many places in the Mojave: Cima Dome not far from the Colorado River, on the northern slopes of the Transverse Ranges back of Mount Baldy and San Gorgonio, and out in the western section of Antelope Valley near Gorman. Until recently vast numbers of them were scattered on the buttes of the valley east of Lancaster and Palmdale, but ruthless bulldozing has severely depleted their ranks. For the most part they are confined to gravelly slopes of alluvium skirting the mountains of the region. They extend roots that make use of surface water and underground moisture draining off higher elevations.

Unlike plants of the lower deserts, Joshuas are able to withstand a fair amount of frost. A favorite shot of photographers is a Joshua swansdowned with snow, and it is a real bonanza if the tree happens to be in bloom with bursts of musty-smelling, six-petaled white blossoms at the ends of its angled boughs. The blue-white of snow on the eggshell tint of its flowers is unforgettable.

The differences between the Mojave and the Sonoran deserts are those which allow Joshuas to live in the former, but not in the latter. The western and northern Mojave is higher by two to three thousand feet on the average. Its higher elevation and more northerly latitude encourage increased rainfall, particularly on the mountain slopes so common to this broken country. Being higher it is also cooler, and the hot season is neither as long nor as severe as in the lower desert.

Like all desert plants, Joshuas have features which enable them to withstand prolonged drought, heat, and drying winds, three characteristics of the world's hot deserts. The dark green spearpoint leaves are fearsomely dagger sharp, stiff, and leathery. The tree is considered an evergreen, though each year some of the foliage shrivels and dies, much of it eventually falling off; during the spring growing period, a ring of new spikes encircles the tip of each living branch. These rings accompany the flowers which appear during the same season. Though most Joshuas have one inflorescence or two every year after maturity, heavy blooming, with clusters of white on almost every branch end, is irregular. Several years may pass between times of massive flowering.

A sequential change in foliage appearance is an outstanding feature of Joshua trees. New leaves, either on the upright poles of youth or sprouting from the branches of older trees, resemble numerous green bayonets thrust into the woody tissue, points outward. It is this stage when the seasonal leaf growth rings are most observable. Leaves more than a year old tend to lose their stiffness and droop, finally dying and becoming part of a bristling thatch that covers a good portion of the plant. After an interval some of this shaggy matting drops off the trunk and larger branches, exposing the bark beneath. Only a relatively small part of the plant has green leaves; it is uneconomical to support more food-making foliage than necessary. In common with most woody desert plants, a balance is needed between water-absorbing devices—roots—and water spending organs—leaves. The specific name, *brevifolia*, refers to the fact that its leaves are shorter than those of most other yucca species; relatively small leaf size helps control evaporation. Its gaunt, awkward posture is intensified by the pattern of branching. Unlike ordinary trees whose boughs move gracefully from the supporting trunk, Joshuas branch into arms twisting and gesturing in upsettingly human fashion. Young trees are unbranched until they are old enough to flower when about 8 to 10 feet tall. Then shoots fork out at oblique angles to the parent stem just below the dead flower stalk. As the same thing happens to the young branch when it blossoms, the stiff-jointed pattern repeats itself again and again as the tree adds to its size and years. A few observers are of the opinion that branching will not occur unless injury such as insect infestation triggers the production of an offshoot.

Joshua trees do not live alone though there are few other plants of the desert that compare with them in size. California junipers and pinyon pine accompany them on some of the higher slopes and hills. Together they form a woodland with shade and shelter reminiscent of moister areas. Desert shrubs and ephemeral herbs are joint residents with tree yuccas, oc-

cupying the spaces between the larger plants. A scrubby undercover of creosote bush, buckwheat, Morman tea, brittle bush,
bladder sage, cotton thorn, cliffrose, and bitterbrush commonly shares their gravel slopes, sandy stretches, and rock
outcrops. Joshuas seldom can afford to live too close to one
another, though underground runners produce shoots around
the bases of vigorous trees, and occasionally one will see several adults entwined together in a clumsy embrace.

Camera enthusiasts would do well to visit a stand of Joshua
trees in April of a wet year. When the rain gods have been
kind, there is an emblazonment of yellow, white, lavender,
orange, and pink displayed by desert dandelions, several kinds
of evening primrose, sand verbena, thistle sage, bird's-eye gilia,
nama, poppies and mallow, and other flowers typical of the
Mojave Desert. Then Scott's orioles sing from gray-green
knife-blade leaves and the wind is sweet with fresh stem and
petal, sun and bird chorus.

A number of organisms spend much or all of their lives in
or close to a single Joshua tree, some of them so dependent on
it for a variety of reasons that they would not exist except for
its presence. In fact, there is such a close relationship among
several species living in or with Joshua trees that it seems unbelievable considering the chance directions taken by the flow
of the tides of life during evolutionary history. Here, for instance, are a moth, a lizard, and one-celled animals called protozoa. The first two are so intimately associated with Joshua
trees that there would be no tree but for the moth and no lizard
but for the tree.

The story of the *Tegeticula* moths and yuccas is a classic example of mutualism, the interactive or symbiotic pattern of
mutual benefit to both organisms involved. Lilies, like all flowers, must be pollinated for seed propagation. Insects rather
than wind carry out the task because of the nature of the
pollen. Instead of being dust dry like the pollen of pines and
other cone-bearing trees, that of the lily family is sticky and
needs the instinctive efforts of an insect rather than the chance
attentions of a wayward wind to ensure the transportation of

these vital cells to their seed-producing counterparts. *Tegeticula* moths are crepuscular, flying at dusk, when they are attracted to the white blossoms of yuccas. Collecting pollen from one flower and working it into a tiny ball, the female moth flies to others for additional material until her burden is of proper size. Now she prepares to lay her eggs which she does by inserting her ovipositor, a needlelike egg-laying organ, into the ovary, the portion of the yucca flower containing the tiny cells which are potential seeds. She makes sure of the development of seed by depositing enough pollen grains on the stigma of the flower so that all the ovules are fertilized, and the seeds will grow. Later the newly hatched larvae of the moth feed on these seeds. Only a few are consumed, the small price the Joshua tree pays for the privilege of pollination. Somewhere and at some time in the long history of the southwestern deserts, yuccas and moths joined in a mutual task of producing more yuccas and moths, and the partnership still continues.

More creatures than moths depend on these huge lilies. Living parts such as branch ends and shoots are homesteaded by several insects having special requirements for food and shelter. The giant yucca skipper lays eggs in young Joshuas clustering around the parent trunk, and the larvae feed on food supplied by underground stems. Yucca boring weevil larvae prefer working over the woody material out at limb tip. Dead branches frequently accumulate. Joshuas are self-pruning and often rid themselves of old limbs. Without a long, stabilizing taproot, they blow over in the high winds of the desert; a forest of yuccas is cluttered with careless piles of slowly decaying trunks and boughs. These are the homes of colonies of termites, beetles, and other insects. Often the interior of an older branch or trunk is hollow as the central pith dries and disintegrates. Though it has been thought that Joshuas have no real annual rings, being more like a palm stem than true wood, rings have been noted in cross sections of Joshuas. Unlike their more herbaceous cousins, these lilies have woody portions under the bark, particularly in older parts of the plant. The periodic increment of fiber between bark and the central pith results in ring-type growth. The true interior pith is not woody and often rots away. Joshua trunks, whether downed or upright, are easily penetrated and become the homes of many animals such as flickers and ladder-backed woodpeckers. Other birds take over their abandoned nesting holes. Ash-throated flycatchers, house wrens, sparrow hawks—a long list of feathered desert dwellers makes use of these conveniently placed apartments as well as the concealing clumps of spiky foliage.

Termites prefer dead wood and, by staying deep in the tissues beneath the bark, avoid the desiccation inherent in this climate. They digest the fibrous material by means of the protozoa and bacteria in their intestines, chemically breaking it down and initiating a vital step in the return of minerals to the soil. In this way, termites perform a most useful task, one of great benefit to Joshua tree, shrub, and annual alike. The food web begun by plant, protozoa, and termite is not at end, for a number of animals eat termites. *Xantusia*, the yucca night lizard, makes his home in the masses of overlapping dried leaf spears covering much of the deadfall. One of the smallest of the American lizards, it is a dainty thing, almost fragile in appearance with its soft, easily desiccated skin. Living in the Joshua's discarded limbs or toppled body, sheltered by its foliage, feeding on its insects, *Xantusia* is another dependent, another dweller in this complex microhabitat. This is not to say that these little lizards do not occur elsewhere. They can be found in many places in the high desert, occasionally where yuccas do not even occur. However, they are typical of Joshua forest, and one can see them by overturning a dead branch or two, uncovering their hiding places where they often avoid exposure to the most trying times of the day. The common name implies night activity or nocturnalism but diurnal and crepuscular behavior is more typical. If *Xantusia* is active during the darker hours he runs the risk of meeting a number of formidable enemies, screech owls, rattlesnakes, and leaf-nosed and spotted night snakes. The food web widens out in patterns of interrelationships involving many inhabitants of the high-desert woodland.

Individual Joshuas offer shelter to various other species. Wood rats, often called pack or trade rats, build huge nests of desert debris at the bases of the larger yuccas and on accumulations of fallen material. These rodents are common to most of California, wherever there is green vegetation. Unlike their kangaroo rat relatives, they cannot metabolize all their water needs from a dry grain diet and must depend on juicy food for necessary liquid. Succulent cactus pads and fruits are harvested for this purpose. Wood rats show amazing agility in maneuvering themselves over the obstacle course of a cholla cactus. They also eat the new green Joshua leaves and use them for nest building. Several other features of physiology and behavior make it possible for the wood rat to live comfortably in the desert. His nest under the shade of a tree yucca or other cover shelters him from the intense heat of the direct desert sun. He is able to eat cacti and plants toxic to most animals because of high concentration of oxalic acid.

Throughout the coastal parts of southern California, the wood rat's nest and his food supply are occasionally shared by a free-loader, the so-called parasitic California white-footed mouse.

Both of these rodents and many more related species of the higher desert are potential meals to a red-tailed hawk perching on the outflung arm of a Joshua, keeping a close lookout for just such a dinner. Other common predators are horned owls, whose great yellow eyes move on silent wings through the ghostly skyline of a Joshua forest at night. One bird in particular prefers to nest in the spiky foliage. Black and yellow, the Scott's oriole is a warm flash of color as it slips swiftly and gracefully under the overlapping leaves. Not only does the tree give it protection, but the nest is woven from yucca fibers, and much feeding is done on the plant itself as the birds consume both nectar and flower parts as well as the insects attracted to this source of food.

A small world it is, a world nourishing and giving shelter to insects, birds, rats, and lizards; a world that has accepted the harsh conditions of the upland heart of the desert; a world of leaves and wood and flowers, dead and living, hospitable in its way to all who seek it.

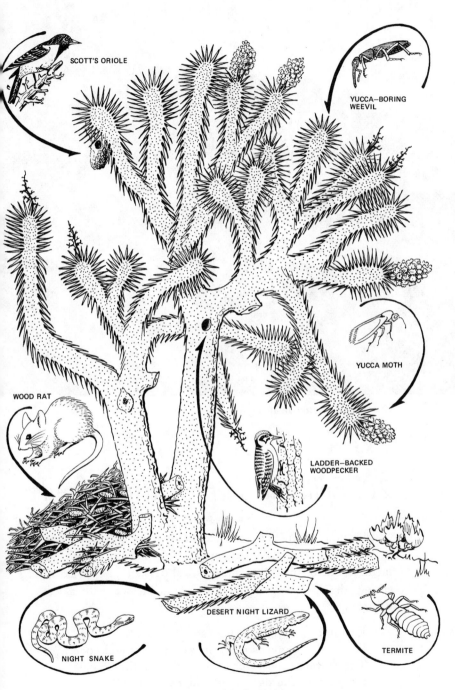

SCOTT'S ORIOLE

YUCCA–BORING WEEVIL

YUCCA MOTH

WOOD RAT

LADDER–BACKED WOODPECKER

NIGHT SNAKE

DESERT NIGHT LIZARD

TERMITE

Figure 24. The small world of a Joshua tree

Outer Coast Range near Big Sur

# 20. Epilogue: Return to an Island

The singer of the Songs of Solomon was not only a consummate lover, but an articulate observer of his natural environment. In one of the Bible's most lyrical passages, he speaks of spring, the special spring of a dry land blessed with a wet winter:

> Rise up, my love, and come away.
> For lo, the winter is past, the rain is over and gone.
> The flowers appear upon the earth, and the time of
> the singing of birds is come, and the voice of the
> turtledove is heard in our land.

Such a plea would have particular meaning to someone who, as a child, perhaps, herded the family's sheep over the hot and barren slopes of summer. In spite of all the references to a "land of milk and honey," stony wilderness and drought were common enough in ancient Palestine to serve as threatened destinies for backsliders and idol worshippers. But a warm, thyme-scented hillside, sung to by larks and carpeted with anemones and crocuses is wonderfully appealing. Who could resist such a tempting rendezvous?

Many early visitors to California were as enchanted. Charles F. Saunders, whose *With the Flowers and Trees in California* (New York, 1914) is a delightful if slightly self-conscious introduction to natural California, quotes from the diaries of Father Crespi: "Both sides of our way were lined with rose bushes of Castile, from which I broke one bunch with six roses opened and about twelve in bud." David Douglas, Scottish gardener whose name appears in much California botanical nomenclature, wrote enthusiastically in 1832 of "the beautiful wild gooseberry not surpassed in beauty by the finest fuchsia," and, "a humble but lovely plant, the harbinger of spring," which we know by the rather sentimental name of baby-blue-eyes.

Though many of the flower fields of the valleys and foothills have been inundated by the Human Wave, they remain symbolic of the Golden State. Few postcard stands lack pictures of poppy fields or of a sea cliff, startlingly magenta from the massed flowers of mesembryanthemum, a South African genus that has donated a number of colorful species now so common to coastal bluffs that they are usually thought to be native.

Impressive floral displays are characteristic of all subtropical wet-winter, dry-summer climatic systems. The plains of southwestern Australia are bright with Sturt pea, everlasting, clumps of kangaroo paw, and multicolored shrubs. Some of the most glorious displays are concentrated in the Cape region of South Africa. For mile after mile, the brilliant whorls of mesembryanthemum and related succulents, flame and sun-tinted gerberas and gazanias, ixias, gladioli, and other Cape bulbs are spread in an unending carpet. Scattered through the scrub of central Chile are open patches of wood sorrel, yellow gum plant, and the blue trumpets of nolana.

Lavish wildflowers, of course, are not confined to Mediterrania and climatically sister lands. Alpine and Arctic tundra, mountain meadows, prairies, and heaths offer bright collections of blossoms when at their best. But none of these communities comes close to the arid or summer-dry subtropics in terms of numbers of species. The standard guide to California's seed plants, *A California Flora* (P. A. Munz and D. Keck, Berkeley and Los Angeles, 1963), is 1681 pages long. In contrast, *Gray's Manual of Botany*, which covers the entire northeastern portion of the continent, is 926 pages in length. Nine-tenths or 14,400 of the 16,000 South African flowering plants are confined to the Cape coastal strip.

Though species count alone is sufficiently impressive to underscore the uniqueness of Mediterranean climate type floral kingdoms and those of their desert edges, a large number of endemics is another outstanding feature. Santa Lucia fir, a conifer restricted to the coastal mountains of central California, has its Mediterranean counterpart, *Abies hebrodensis*, native to the northern coast of Sicily. The Cape's silverleaf and western Australia's honey-myrtles are endemic types that, as attractive ornamentals, have traveled far from their original and limited homegrounds.

Known as "bush" in South Africa and *macchia* or *maquis* in the Mediterranean lands, drought-resistant chaparrel-type scrub is an additional shared characteristic of the summer-dry subtropics. Photographs of brush-covered hills from all five regions are so similar in appearance that only experts can readily distinguish between them. The firm hand of physical environment nowhere exercises more control than here in the olive tree latitudes. Bear this in mind when you next visit a botanical garden featuring specimens from many areas of the world. Any shrub with small, thick, light-colored, evergreen leaves is likely to be from these climatic regions.

One can become so fascinated by differences between California and the rest of the United States that one forgets that the state is part of a larger whole. It is attached to a land mass, and its ecological, physiographic, and climatological isolation can be overemphasized. Political boundaries are seldom coincidental with ecotones. Extending far south of the misted inlets of the Alaska panhandle, a slender ribbon of spruce and cedar follows the California coast until it finally unravels in the increasing summer drought. A mantle of Utah juniper, sagebrush, and pinyon pine, triumvirate species of the intermountain West, folds a ragged edge over the highlands of eastern California. Palo verde, trees of the Southwest arboreal desert, winds along wash floors as far west as San Diego County; and Mexican palo verde is reported to have become naturalized in parts of the Mojave Desert, far from its center of distribution in Sonora, Mexico. Moreover, a number of far-ranging species such as yellow and limber pine, Great Basin sagebrush, and Douglas-fir serve to knit California firmly into the vegetation complex of the West. Mariposa lilies may be called sego lilies in Utah, but they are basically the same flower. California poppies are as richly orange in the Arizona desert as they are in Antelope Valley.

Nevertheless, an area roughly the shape of an ovoid spearhead, whose point is placed on Mount Shasta and whose rounded base covers coast and mountain southern California, is truly an "island called California," a singular piece of country with extremes unknown in more temperate or less diverse regions. Frozen peaks reach up over scorched valleys. Lichen-shrouded seamist forest is but an hour's drive from a mineral encrusted dry lake. Prairie and the world's tallest forest are only a few feet apart. Not many landscapes are as dull and unattractive as the littered, weed-patch fields of the southern San Joaquin Valley. On the other hand, the cypress-crowned coves of Point Lobos and carved ivory of the Sierran scarp west of Independence are among the world's most magnificent scenes.

Isolated by sea, mountain range, and desert, this area has developed in its own way and at its own pace; evolutionary history here has woven numerous distinctive patterns of interaction between life form and the land. Like the fire pines and cypresses, many such patterns are tag ends, remnants of much larger biological designs. Others, like chaparral and coniferous forest, run repeatedly through the warp and woof of natural California.

Such are the patterns of survival through a rainless summer, on a serpentine slope, in a Sierran canyon; patterns that have similarities but no exact duplicates elsewhere in the world; patterns that are incredibly intricate, multiple, and unfortunately irreplaceable if obliterated by man's heedlessness or apathy.

# Selected Bibliography

GENERAL ECOLOGY

Buchsbaum, R., and Buchsbaum, M. *Basic Ecology*. Pittsburgh: Boxwood Press, 1957.

Dice, L. R. *Natural Communities*. Ann Arbor: University of Michigan Press, 1952.

Farb, P., and the editors of Life. *Ecology*. New York: Time, Inc., 1963.

Hanson, H. C. *Dictionary of Ecology*. New York: Philosophical Library, 1962.

Knight, C. B. *Basic Concepts of Ecology*. New York: Macmillan, 1965.

Kormondy, E. J. *Concepts of Ecology*. Englewood Cliffs, New Jersey: Prentice-Hall, 1969.

Martin, A. C.; Zim, H. S.; and Nelson, A. L., *American Wildlife and Plants*. New York: McGraw-Hill, 1951.

Odum, E. P. *Ecology*. New York: Holt, Rinehart, and Winston, 1963.

Odum, E. P., and Odum, H. T. *Fundamentals of Ecology*. Philadelphia: Saunders, 1959.

Shelford, V. E. *The Ecology of North America*. Urbana: University of Illinois Press, 1963.

Whitaker, R. H. *Communities and Ecosystems*. New York: Macmillan, 1970.


PLANT ECOLOGY

Billings, W. D. *Plants and the Ecosystem*. Belmont, California: Wadsworth, 1964.

Dansereau, P. *Biogeography*. New York: Ronald, 1957.

Daubenmire, R. F. *Plants and Environment*. New York: Wiley, 1959.

Gleason, H. E., and Cronquist, A. *The Natural Geography of Plants*. New York: Columbia University Press, 1964.

Humphrey, R. R. *Range Ecology*. New York: Ronald, 1962.

Oosting, H. J. *The Study of Plant Communities*. San Francisco: Freeman, 1958.

Spurr, S. *Forest Ecology*. New York: Ronald, 1964.

Weaver, J. E., and Clements, F. E. *Plant Ecology*. New York: McGraw-Hill, 1938.


ANIMAL ECOLOGY

Kendeigh, S. C. *Animal Ecology*. New York: Prentice-Hall, 1961.

SOILS

Farb, P. *Living Earth*. New York: Harper, 1959.

Kellogg, C. E. *The Soils that Support Us*. New York: Macmillan, 1961.


MARINE ENVIRONMENT

Amos, W. H. *The Life of the Seashore*. New York: McGraw-Hill, 1966.

Baxter, J. L. *Inshore Fishes of California*. Sacramento: California Department of Fish and Game, 1960.

Chapman, V. J. *Salt Marshes and Salt Deserts of the World*. New York: Interscience Publishers, 1960.

Conradson, D. R. *Exploring Our Baylands*. Palo Alto: Palo Alto Chamber of Commerce, 1966.

Daughtery, A. E. *Marine Mammals of California*. Sacramento: California Department of Fish and Game, 1965.

Dawson, E. Y. *Seashore Plants of Northern California*. Berkeley and Los Angeles: University of California Press, 1966.

Engel, L., and the editors of *Life*. *The Sea*. New York: Time, Inc., 1961.

Fitch, J. E. *Offshore Fishes of California*. Sacramento: California Department of Fish and Game, 1958.

Hedgpeth, J. *Introduction to Seashore Life of the San Francisco Bay Region and the Coast of Northern California*. Berkeley and Los Angeles: University of California Press, 1964.

Keep, J., and Baily, J. L. *West Coast Shells*. Stanford: Stanford University Press, 1935.

Light, S. F., et al. *Intertidal Invertebrates of the Central California Coast*. Berkeley and Los Angeles: University of California Press, 1957.

Moore, H. B. *Marine Ecology*. New York: Wiley, 1958.

Munz, P. A. *Shore Wildflowers of California, Oregon, and Washington*. Berkeley and Los Angeles: University of California Press, 1964.

Reid, G. K. *Ecology of Inland Waters and Estuaries*. New York: Reinhold, 1961.

Ricketts, E. F., and Calvin, J. *Between Pacific Tides*. Stanford: Stanford University Press, 1962.

Sverdrup, H. U.; Johnson, M. W.; and Fleming, R. H. *The Oceans*. New York: Prentice-Hall, 1942.

Tierney, R. J., et al. *Exploring Tidepool Life*. Berkeley-Tidepool Associates, 1966.

FRESHWATER ENVIRONMENT

Amos, W. H. *The Life of the Pond*. New York: McGraw-Hill, 1967.

Macan, T. T. *Freshwater Ecology*. New York: Wiley, 1963.

Mason, H. L. *A Flora of the Marshes of California*. Berkeley and Los Angeles: University of California Press, 1957.

Needham, J. G., and Needham, P. R. *A Guide to the Study of Freshwater Biology*. San Francisco: Holden-Day, 1962.

Niering, W. A. *The Life of the Marsh*. New York: McGraw-Hill, 1966.

Pennack, R. W. *Fresh-water Invertebrates of the United States*. New York: Ronald, 1953.

Usinger, R. L. *Aquatic Insects of California*. Berkeley and Los Angeles: University of California Press, 1956.

———. *The Life of Rivers and Streams*. New York: McGraw-Hill, 1967.


BIRDS

Bent, A. C. "Life Histories of the Birds of North America." Smithsonian Institution United States National Museum, *Bulletins* 107, 113, 121, 126, 130, 135, 142, 146, 162, 167, 170, 176, 191, 195, 196, 197, 203, 211.

Dawson, W. L. *The Birds of California*, Vols. 1–4. San Diego, Los Angeles, San Francisco: South Moulton Co., 1923.

Grinnell, J., and Miller, A. H. *The Distribution of the Birds of California*. Pacific Coast Avifauna, no. 27. Berkeley: Cooper Ornithological Club, 1944.

Grinnell, J., and Wythe, M. W. *Directory to the Bird Life of the San Francisco Bay Region*. Pacific Coast Avifauna, no. 18. Berkeley: Cooper Ornithological Club, 1927.

Hoffmann, R. *Birds of the Pacific States*. Boston: Houghton-Mifflin, 1927.

Peterson, R. T. *A Field Guide to Western Birds*. Boston: Houghton-Mifflin, 1961.

Robbins, C. S.; Bruun, B.; and Zim, H. S. *Birds of North America*. New York: Golden Press, 1966.

Welty, J. C. *The Life of Birds*. Philadelphia: Saunders, 1962.


REPTILES AND AMPHIBIANS

Stebbins, R. C. *Amphibians and Reptiles of Western North America*. New York: McGraw-Hill, 1954.

———. *Field Guide to Western Reptiles and Amphibians*. Boston: Houghton-Mifflin, 1966.

———. *Reptiles and Amphibians of the San Francisco Bay Region*. Berkeley and Los Angeles: University of California Press, 1959.

MAMMALS OF CALIFORNIA

Berry, W. D., and Berry, E. *Mammals of the San Francisco Bay Region*. Berkeley and Los Angeles: University of California Press, 1959.

Ingles, L. G. *Mammals of the Pacific States*. Stanford: Stanford University Press, 1965.

INSECTS

Essig, E. O. *Insects and Mites of Western North America*. New York: Macmillan, 1926.

Smith, A. C. *Western Butterflies*. Menlo Park, California: Lane, 1961.

Tilden, J. W. *Butterflies of the San Francisco Bay Region*. Berkeley and Los Angeles: University of California Press, 1965.

CALIFORNIA FLORA

Bowerman, M. L. *The Flowering Plants and Ferns of Mount Diablo, California*. Berkeley: Gillick Press, 1944.

Brockman, C. F. *Trees of North America*. New York: Golden Press, 1968.

Burchman, L. T. *California Range Lands*. Sacramento: California Department of Natural Resources, Division of Forestry, 1957.

Critchfield, W. B., and Little, E. L. *Geographic Distribution of the Pines of the World*. Forest Service, United States Department of Agriculture, Miscellaneous Publication 991, 1966.

Ferris, R. S. *Native Shrubs of the San Francisco Bay Region*. Berkeley and Los Angeles: University of California Press, 1968.

Fowells, H. A. *Sylvics of the Forest Trees of the United States*. Agriculture Handbook 271, Forest Service, United States Department of Agriculture, 1965.

Grillos, S. J. *Ferns and Fern Allies of the San Francisco Bay Region*. Berkeley and Los Angeles: University of California Press, 1966.

Howell, J. T. *Marin Flora*. Berkeley and Los Angeles: University of California Press, 1949.

McMinn, H. E. *An Illustrated Manual of California Shrubs*. Berkeley and Los Angeles: University of California Press, 1964.

Metcalf, W. *Native Trees of the San Francisco Bay Region*. Berkeley and Los Angeles: University of California Press, 1960.

Mirov, N. T. *The Genus Pinus*. New York: Ronald, 1967.

Munz, P. A. *California Desert Wildflowers*. Berkeley and Los Angeles: University of California Press, 1962.

———. *California Mountain Wildflowers*. Berkeley and Los Angeles: University of California Press, 1963.

———. *California Spring Wildflowers*. Berkeley and Los Angeles: University of California Press, 1961.

Munz, P. A., and Keck, D. D. *A California Flora*. Berkeley and Los Angeles: University of California Press, 1963.

Orr, R. T., and Orr, D. B. *Mushrooms and Other Common Fungi of the San Francisco Bay Region*. Berkeley and Los Angeles: University of California Press, 1968.

Peattie, D. C. *A Natural History of Western Trees*. Boston: Houghton Mifflin, 1953.

Sampson, A. W., and Jesperson, B. S. *California Range Brushlands and Browse Plants*. Division of Agricultural Sciences, Manual 33. Berkeley: University of California, 1963.

Sampson, A. W.; Chase, A.; and Hedrick, D. W. *California Grasslands and Range Forage Grasses*. The College of Agriculture Bulletin 724. Berkeley: University of California, 1951.

Sharsmith, H. S. "The Flora of The Mount Hamilton Range of California," *American Midland Naturalist*. Vol. 34, no. 2 (September 1945).

————. *Spring Wildflowers of the San Francisco Bay Region*. Berkeley and Los Angeles: University of California Press, 1965.

Sudworth, G. B. *Forest Trees of the Pacific Slope*. United States Department of Agriculture, Forest Service, 1908 (a Dover reprint was published in 1968).

Thomas, J. T. *Flora of the Santa Cruz Mountains of California*. Stanford: Stanford University Press, 1961.

Twisselmann, E. *A Flora of Kern County*. San Francisco: University of San Francisco, 1967.


GEOLOGY

Bascom, W. *Waves and Currents*. New York: Doubleday, 1964.

Fenniman, N. M. *Physiography of the Western United States*. New York: McGraw-Hill, 1931.

*Geologic Guidebook: Along Highway 49–Sierran Gold Belt*, Bulletin 141. California Department of Natural Resources, Division of Mines, 1948.

*Geologic Guidebook of the San Francisco Bay Counties*. Bulletin 154, California Department of Natural Resources, Division of Mines, 1951.

Howard, A. *Evolution of the Landscape of the San Francisco Bay Region*. Berkeley and Los Angeles: University of California Press, 1962.

Iacopi, R. *Earthquake Country*. Menlo Park: Lane, 1964.


CLIMATE AND WEATHER

Felton, E. L. *California's Many Climates*. Palo Alto: Pacific Books, 1965.

Gilliam, H. *Weather of San Francisco Bay Region.* Berkeley and Los Angeles: University of California Press, 1966.

DESERT ENVIRONMENT

Bailey, H. P. *The Climate of Southern California.* Berkeley and Los Angeles: University of California Press, 1966.

Benson, L., and Darrow, R. A. *A Manual of Southwestern Desert Trees and Shrubs.* University of Arizona Biological Science Bulletin no. 6, 1944.

Dawson, E. Y. *Cacti of California.* Berkeley and Los Angeles: University of California Press, 1966.

Jaeger, E. *Desert Wildflowers.* Stanford: Stanford University Press, 1941.

———. *Desert Wildlife.* Stanford: Stanford University Press, 1961.

———. *The California Deserts.* Stanford: Stanford University Press, 1933.

Kearney, T. H., and Peebles, R. H. *Arizona Flora.* Berkeley and Los Angeles: University of California Press, 1960.

Leopold, A. S., and the editors of *Life. The Desert.* New York: Time, Inc., 1961.

Schmidt-Neilson, K. *Desert Animals: Physiological Problems of Heat and Water.* New York: Oxford University Press, 1964.

Sutton, A., and Sutton, M. *The Life of the Desert.* New York: McGraw-Hill, 1966.

REGIONAL GUIDES

Grinnell, J., and Storer, T. I. *Animal Life in the Yosemite.* Berkeley: University of California Press, 1924.

Jaeger, E., and Smith, A. C. *Introduction to the Natural History of Southern California.* Berkeley and Los Angeles: University of California Press, 1966.

Miller, A. H., and Stebbins, R. C. *The Lives of Desert Animals in Joshua Tree National Monument.* Berkeley and Los Angeles: University of California Press, 1964.

Muir, J. *The Yosemite.* New York: The Century Co., 1912.

Schumacher, G. ed. *Deepest Valley: Guide to Owens Valley and Its Mountain Lakes, Roadsides, and Trails.* San Francisco: Sierra Club Books, 1963.

Smith, A. C. *Introduction to the Natural History of the San Francisco Bay Region.* Berkeley and Los Angeles: University of California Press, 1960.

Storer, T. I., and Usinger, R. *Sierra Nevada Natural History.* Berkeley and Los Angeles: University of California Press, 1963.

CONSERVATION

Dasmann, R. *The Destruction of California*. New York: Collier, 1966.

Hardin, G. *Population, Evolution, and Birth Control*. San Francisco: Freeman, 1964.

Leopold, A. *A Sand County Almanac*. New York: Oxford University Press, 1949.

Udall, S. L. *The Quiet Crisis*. New York: Holt, Rinehart and Winston, 1963.

Williams, E. A. *Open Space: The Choices Before California*. Berkeley: Diablo Press, 1969.

# List of Animals

abalone, black, *Haliotis cracherodii*
abalone, red, *Haliotis rufescens*
alder-fly, *Sialis* spp.
amphipod, Amphipoda
ant, carpenter, *Camponotus* spp.
ant, harvester, *Myrmicinae*
ant, honey, *Prenolepis imparis*
ant, velvet, Mutillidae
antelope, pronghon, *Antilocapra americana*
aphid, Aphidae
auklet, Cassin's, *Ptychoramphus aleutica*
avocet, *Recurvirostra americana*
back swimmer, Notonectidae
badger, *Taxus taxaid*
banana slug, *Ariolimax columbianus*
barnacle, acorn, *Balanus glandula*
barnacle, leaf, *Pollicipes polymerus*
barracuda, *Sphyraena argentea*
bass, Centrachidae
bat, Chiroptera
beach hopper, *Orchestoidea californiana; O. corniculata*
bear, black, *Euarctos americanus*
bear, grizzly, *Ursus horribilis*
beaver, golden, *Castor canadensis*
beaver, mountain, *Aplodontia rufa*
bee, carpenter, Xylocopidae
beetle,
  acrobat, *Eleodes* spp.
  bark, Scolytidae
  blister, Meloidae
  cone, *Conophthorus* spp.
  diving, Dytiscidae
  longhorn, Cerambycidae
  Oregon pine engraver, *Ips oregoni*
  riffle, Elmidae
  scarab, desert, *Ochrosidia villosa*
  wood-boring, Buprestidae
bittern, *Botaurus lentiginosus*
blackbird, red-winged, *Agelaius phoeniceus*
blackbird, yellow-headed, *Xanthocephalus xanthocephalus*
blenny, *Anoplarchus* spp.; *Epigeichthys* spp.; etc.
bluebird, mountain, *Sialia curracoides*
bluebird, western, *Sialia mexicana*
bluegill, *Lepomis macrochirus*
bobcat, *Lynx rufus*
bryozoa, Bryozoa
buffalo, *Bison bison*
bug, box elder, *Leptocoris rubrolineatus*
bug, creeping water, Naucoridae
bug, flat, Aradidae
bullhead, *Ictalurus* spp.
bunting, lazuli, *Passerina amoena*
bushtit, *Psaltriparus minimus*
butterfly,
  California sister, *Limenitis bredowii*
  hairstreak, California, *Strymon californica*
  hairstreak, canyon oak, *Habrodais grunus*
  monarch, *Danaus plexippus*
  painted lady, *Vanessa cardui*
  queen, *Danaus gilippus*
  silver blue, *Glaucopsyche lygdamus*
  swallowtail, *Papilio* spp.
  tailed copper, *Lycaena arota*
caddis-fly, Trichoptera
carp, *Cyprinus carpio*
centipede, *Scolopendra* spp.
chat, *Icteria virens*
chickadee, mountain, *Parus gambeli*
chickadee, chestnut-backed, *parus rufescens*
chickaree, *Tamiasciurus douglasii*
chipmunk, alpine, *Eutamias alpinus*
chipmunk, Merriam, *Eutamias merriami*
chipmunk, Sonoma, *Eutamias sonomae*

chipmunk, Townsend, *Eutamias townsendii*
chiton, Amphineura
cicada, Cicadidae
clam,
    bean, *Donax gouldii*
    bent-nosed, *Macoma nasuta*
    boring, *Pholadidea* spp.; *Teredo* spp.; *Zirfaea* spp.; etc.
    gaper, *Tresus nuttalli*
    Manila, *Corbicula manilensis*
    Pismo, *Tivela stultorum*
    razor, *Siliqua patula*
    sand, *Mecoma secta*
cockle, basket, *Clinocardium nuttalli*
cockroach, flightless sand dune, *Arenivaga* spp.
coot, *Fulica americana*
copepod, Copepoda
coral, red, *Balanophyllia elegans*
cormorant, Brandt's, *Phalacrocorax penicillatus*
cormorant, Farallon, *Phalacrocorax auritus*
cormorant, pelagic, *Phalacrocorax pelagicus*
coyote, *Canis latrans*
crab,
    hermit, *Pagurus* spp.
    hermit, hairy, *Pagurus hirsutiusculus*
    kelp, *Pugettia producta*
    lined shore, *Pachygrapsus crassipes*
    masking, *Loxorhynchus crispatus*; *Scyra acutifrons*; etc.
    mud-flat, *Hemigrapsus oregonensis*
    pea, *Scleroplax granulata*, among several other crab species commensal with *Urechis*
    sand, *Emerita analoga*
    shore, *Hemigrapsus nudus*
crayfish, *Astacus* spp.
creeper, brown, *Certhia familiaris*
cricket, Gryllidae
cricket, Jerusalem, *Stenopelmatus longispina*
crossbill, *Loxia curvirostra*
crow, *Corvus brachyrhynchos*
cuckoo, yellow-billed, *Coccyzus americanus*
curlew, Hudsonian, *Numenius phaeopus*

curlew, long-billed, *Numenius americanus*
damsel-fly, Zygoptera
daphnia, *Daphnia* spp.
deer, black-tailed, *Odocoileus hemionius columbianus*
deer, mule, *Odocoileus hemionius*
deer, red, *Cervus elaphus*
dobson-fly, *Corydalus* spp.; *Chauliodes* spp.
dove, Mexican ground, *Columbigallina passerina*
dove, mourning, *Zenaidura macroura*
dove, white-winged, *Zenaida asiatica*
dowitcher, *Limnodromus* spp.
dragon-fly, Anisoptera
duck,
    baldpate, *Mareca americana*
    canvasback, *Aythya valisineria*
    gadwall, *Anas strepera*
    goldeneye, *Bucephala clangula*
    mallard, *Anas platyrhyncos*
    merganser, *Mergus merganser*
    pintail, *Anas acuta*
    redhead, *Aythya americana*
    ruddy, *Oxyura jamaicensis*
    scaup, greater, *Aythya marila*
    scaup, lesser, *Aythya affinis*
    teal, blue-winged, *Anas discors*
    teal, cinnamon, *Anas cyanoptera*
    teal, green-winged, *Anas carolinensis*
dunlin, *Erolia alpina*
egret, *Casmerodius albus*
elk, Rocky Mountain, *Cervus canadensis nelsoni*
elk, Roosevelt, *Cervus canadensis roosevelti*
elk, tule, *Cervus canadensis nannodes*
empidonax, *Empidonax* spp.
*Ensatina*, *Ensatina eschscholtzi*
falcon, prairie, *Falco mexicanus*
finch,
    Cassin's *Carpodacus cassinii*
    Darwin's, *Geospiza* spp.
    purple, *Carpodacus purpureus*
    rosy, brown, *Leucosticte australis*
    rosy, gray-crowned, *Leucosticte tephrocotis*
flea, Siphonaptera
flicker, red-shafted, *Colaptes cafer*

desert spiny, *Sceloporus magis-
ter*
fence, *Sceloporus occidentalis*
fringe-toed sand, *Uma* spp.
gecko, *Coleonyx variegatus*
granite spiny, *Sceloporus orcutti*
horned, *Phrynosoma* spp.
iguana, crested, *Dipsosaurus
dorsalis*
leopard, *Crotaphytus wislizenii*
skink, *Eumeces gilberti; E. skil-
tonianus*
whiptail, *Cnemidophorus tigris*
yucca night, *Xantusia vigilis*
zebra-tailed, *Callisaurus dracon-
oides*
lobster, spiny, Palinura
loon, *Gavia* spp.
louse, beach, *Leptochelia* spp.
louse, rock, *Ligia occidentalis*
louse, sea, *Idothea* spp.
magpie, black-billed, *Pica pica*
magpie, yellow-billed, *Pica nuttalli*
marmot, *Marmota flaviventris*
marten, pine, *Martes americana*
mayfly, Ephemeroptera
meadowlark, *Sturnella neglecta*
midge, Nemocera
millipede, Diplopoda
mockingbird, *Mimus polyglottos*
mole, *Scapanus latimanus*
mosquito, Culicidae
moth,
    cutworm, Noctuidae
    measuring-worm, Geometridae
    needleminer, Gelechiidae
    oak, *Phryganidia californica*
    owlet, Noctuidae
    pinecone, *Eucosma bobana*
    sphynx, Sphingidae
    tent caterpillar, *Malacosoma*
    spp.
    yucca, *Tegeticula* spp.
mountain lion, *Felis concolor*
mouse,
    brush, *Peromyscus boylii*
    cactus, *Peromyscus eremicus*
    California, *Peromyscus califor-
nicus*
    deer, *Peromycus maniculatus*
    grasshopper, *Onychomys* spp.
    harvest, *Reithrodontomys meg-
alotis*
    harvest, salt marsh, *Reithrodon-
tomys raviventris*

jumping, *Zapus princeps*
meadow, *Clethrionomys* spp.;
*Lagurus* spp.; *Microtus* spp.;
*Phenacomys* spp.
pinyon, *Peromyscus truei*
pocket, *Perognathus* spp.
pocket, California, *Perognathus
californicus*
pocket, San Joaquin, *Perognathus inornatus*
pocket, silky-haired (little),
*Perognathus longimembris*
red tree, *Phenacomys longicau-
dus*
sagebrush vole, *Lagurus curtatus*
white-footed, *Peromyscus* spp.
murre, California, *Uria aalge californica*
mussel, bay, *Mytilus edulis*
mussel, California, *Mytilus californianus*
mussel, horse, *Modiolus demissus*
mysid, opossum, Mysidacea
newt, California, *Taricha torosa*
nighthawk, *Chordeiles minor*
nudibranch, Nudibranchia
nutcracker, Clark's, *Nucifraga co-
lumbiana*
nuthatch, pygmy, *Sitta pygmaea*
nuthatch, red-breasted, *Sitta canadensis*
nuthatch, white-breasted, *Sitta
carolinensis*
octopus, *Octopus* spp.
olivella, *Olivella* spp.
oriole, Bullock's, *Icterus bullockii*
oriole, hooded, *Icterus cucullatus*
oriole, Scott's, *Icterus parisorum*
ostracod, Ostracoda
owl,
    burrowing, *Speotyto cunicularia*
    elf, *Micrathene whitneyi*
    horned, *Bubo virginianus*
    long-eared, *Asio otus*
    pygmy, *Glaucidium gnoma*
    screech, *Otus asio*
    spotted, *Strix occidentalis*
oyster, Ostreidae
oyster borer, *Ocenebra japonica*
oystercatcher, *Haematopus bach-
mani*
oyster drill, *Urosalpinx cinereus*
pecten, *Pecten* spp.
pelican, brown, *Pelecanus occidentalis*

petrel ashy, *Oceanodroma homochroa*

phainopepla, *Phainopepla nitens*

phalarope, Wilson's, *Steganopus tricolor*

phoebe, Say's, *Sayornis saya*

piddock, Pholadidae

pigeon, band-tailed, *Columba fasciata*

pika, *Ochotona princeps*

pill bug, Oniscidae

plover, black-bellied, *Squatarola squatarola*

plover, snowy, *Charadrius alexandrinus*

poorwill, *Phalaenoptilus nuttallii*

porcupine, *Erethizon dorsatum*

puffin, *Lunda cirrhata*

pupfish, *Cyprinodon* spp.

quail, California, *Lophortyx californicus*

quail, Gambel's, *Lophortyx gambelii*

quail, mountain, *Oreortyx pictus*

rabbit, cottontail, *Sylvilagus auduboni*

rabbit, jack-, *Lepus californicus*

raccoon, *Procyon lotor*

rail, black, *Laterallus jamaicensis coturniculus*

rail, clapper, *Rallus longirostris*

rail, Virginia, *Rallus limicola*

rat, kangaroo, Great Basin, *Dipodomys microps*

rat, kangaroo, Heermann, *Dipodomys heermanni*

rat, kangaroo, Merriam, *Dipodomys merriami*

rat, kangaroo, San Joaquin, *Dipodomys nitratoides*

rat, wood, desert, *Neotoma lepida*

rat, wood, dusky-footed, *Neotoma fuscipes*

raven, *Corvus corax*

ray, Elasmobranchii

ringtail, *Bassariscus astutus*

roadrunner, *Geococcyx californianus*

robin, western, *Turdus migratorius propinquus*

rotifer, Rotifera

salamander, California slender, *Batrachoseps attenuatus*

salamander, giant, *Dicamptodon ensatus*

salamander, tiger, *Ambystoma tigrinum*

salmon, *Oncorhynchus* spp.

sand dollar, *Dendraster excentricus*

sanderling, *Crocethia alba*

sand flea, *Orchestia* spp.

sandfly, Psychodidae

sandpiper, least, *Erolia minutilla*

sandpiper, pectoral, *Erolia melanotos*

sapsucker, Williamson's, *Sphyrapicus thyroideus*

sapsucker, yellow-bellied, *Sphyrapicus varius*

scorpion, Scorpionida

sculpin, tide pool, *Oligocottus maculosis*

sea anemone, aggregated, *Anthopleura elegantissima*

sea anemone, burrowing, *Anthopleura artemesia*, etc.

sea anemone, green, *Anthopleura xanthogrammica*

sea cucumber, Holothuroidea

seal, elephant, *Mirounga angustirostris*

seal, northern fur, *Callorhinus ursinus*

sea lion, California, *Zalophus californianus*

sea lion, Steller, *Eumetopias jubata*

sea otter, *Enhydra lutris*

sea pen, Pennatulacea

sea spider, Pycnogonida

sea squirt, Ascidiacea

sea star,

    blue, *Pisaster giganteus*

    brittle star, Ophiuroidea

    common starfish, *Pisaster ochraceous*

    red, *Evasterias troschelii*

    sand star, *Pisaster brevispinus*

    serpent star, *Amphiodia* spp.

    sun star, *Solaster dawsoni*

sea urchin, purple, *Strongylocentrotus purpuratus*

sea urchin, red, *Strongylocentrotus franciscanus*

shark, Elasmobranchii

sheep, bighorn, *Ovis canadensis*

shrew, Trowbridge, *Sorex trowbridgei*

shrike, *Lanius ludovicianus*

shrimp,

    brine, *Artemia salina*

broken back, *Spirontocaris* spp.
fairy, Phyllopoda
ghost, *Callianassa californiensis*
gray, *Crago* spp.
mud, *Upogebia pugettensis*
pistol, *Crangon dentipes*
skeleton, *Caprella* spp.
transparent, *Spirontocaris* spp.
silverfish, Thysanura
skate, Elasmobranchii
skipper, giant yucca, *Megathymus yuccae*
skunk, spotted, *Spilogale putorius*
skunk, striped, *Mephitis mephitis*
snail,
  barrel, *Acteon* spp.
  bubble, *Haminoea* spp.
  horn, *Cerithidea californica*
  moon, *Polinices lewisi*
  purple, *Thais* spp.
  rock, *Thais* spp.
  turban, *Tegula* spp.
  turban, black, *Tegula funebralis*
snake,
  boa, rosy, *Lichanura trivirgata*
  boa, rubber, *Charina bottae*
  coachwhip, *Masticophis flagellum*
  coral, *Micrurus fulvius*
  garter, *Thamnophis* spp.
  glossy, *Arizona elegans*
  gopher, *Pituophis melanoleucus*
  king, *Lampropeltis getulus*
  king, mountain, *Lampropeltis zonata*
  leaf-nosed, *Phyllorhynchus* spp.
  long-nosed, *Rhinocheilus lecontei*
  patch-nosed, *Salvadora* spp.
  racer, red, *Masticophus flagellum piceus*
  racer, yellow-bellied, *Coluber constrictor*
  rattle-, Pacific, *Crotalus viridis oreganus*
  rattle-, speckled, *Crotalus mitchelli*
  rattle-, western, *Crotalus viridis*
  sidewinder, *Crotalus cerastes*
  shovel-nosed, *Chionactis occipitalis*
  spotted night, *Hypsiglena torquata ochrorhyncha*
snipe, Wilson's, *Capella gallinago*
solpugid, Solpugida

sparrow,
  Bell's, *Amphispiza belli*
  black-chinned, *Spizella atrogularis*
  black-throated, *Amphispiza bilineata*
  Brewer's, *Spizella breweri*
  chipping, *Spizella passerina*
  fox, *Passerella iliaca*
  Lincoln's, *Melospiza lincolnii*
  rufous-crowned, *Aimophila ruficeps*
  savanna, *Passerculus sandwichensis*
  song, *Melospiza melodia*
  song, desert, *Melospiza melodia saltonis*
  vesper, *Pooecetes gramineus*
  white-crowned, *Zonotrichia leucophrys*
spider, Araneida
sponge, Porifera
springtail, Collembola
squawfish, *Ptychocheilus grandis*
squirrel, flying, *Glaucomys sabrinus*
squirrel, gray, *Sciurus griseus*
stilt, black-necked, *Himantopus mexicanus*
stone-fly, Plecoptera
swan, whistling, *Olor columbianus*
swift, black, *Cypseloides niger*
tanager, summer, *Piranga rubra*
tanager, western, *Piranga ludoviciana*
tarantula, *Aphonopelma* spp.
tarantula hawk, *Pepsis* spp.
termite, Isoptera
tern, Sterninae
thrasher, Bendire's, *Toxostoma bendirei*
thrasher, California, *Toxostoma redivivum*
thrasher, crissal, *Toxostoma dorsale*
thrasher, LeConte's, *Toxostoma lecontei*
thrasher, sage, *Oreoscoptes montanus*
thrush, hermit, *Hylocichla guttata*
thrush, russet-backed, *Hylocichla ustulata*
thrush, varied, *Ixoreus naevius*
titmouse, *Parus inornatus*
toad, red-spotted, *Bufo punctatus*

toad, spadefoot, *Scaphiopus hammondi*
toad, western, *Bufo boreas*
toebiter, Belostomatidae
top shell, *Calliostoma ligatum*
tortoise, desert, *Gopherus agassizi*
towhee, brown, *Pipilo fuscus*
towhee, green-tailed, *Chlorura chlorura*
towhee, rufous-sided, *Pipilo erythrophthalmus*
Townsend's solitaire, *Myadestes townsendi*
trout, cutthroat, *Salmo clarkii clarkii*
trout, steelhead, *Salmo gairdnerii gairdnerii*
tunicate, Urochordata (Tunicata)
turtle, western pond, *Clemmys marmorata*
unicorn, *Acanthina spirata*
verdin, *Auriparus flaviceps*
vireo, solitary, *Vireo solitarius*
vireo, warbling, *Vireo gilvus*
vulture, *Cathartes aura*
wandering tattler, *Heteroscelus incanum*
warbler,
   Audubon's, *Dendroica auduboni*
   black-throated gray, *Dendroica nigrescens*
   hermit, *Dendroica occidentalis*
   Lucy's, *Vermivora luciae*
   MacGillivray's, *Oporornis tolmiei*
   Nashville, *Vermivora ruficapilla*
   Wilson's, *Wilsonia pusilla*
   yellow, *Dendroica petechia*
   yellowthroat, *Geothlypis trichas*
wasp, braconid, Braconidae
wasp, cynipid, Cynipidae
water boatman, Corixidae

water ouzel, *Cinclus mexicanus*
water pennies, Psephenidae
water pipit, *Anthus spinoletta*
water strider, Gerridae
weasel, *Mustela* spp.
weevil, yucca-boring, *Scyphophorus yuccae*
whale, killer, *Orcinus orca*
whelk, basket, *Nassarius fossatus*
whelk, dog, *Ilyanassa obsoleta*
whimbrel, *Numenius phaeopus*
wildebeest, *Connochaetes taurinus*
willet, western, *Catoptrophorus semipalmatus*
woodpecker,
   acorn, *Melanerpes formicivorus*
   downy, *Dendrocopos pubescens*
   hairy, *Dendrocopos villosus*
   ladder-backed, *Dendrocopos scalaris*
   Lewis', *Asyndesmus lewis*
   pileated, *Dryocopus pileatus*
   three-toed, *Picoides arcticus*
   white-headed, *Dendrocopos albolarvatus*
wood pewee, *Contopus sordidulus*
worm, bristle, Polychaeta
worm, earth, Oligochaeta
worm, tube, a number of species in Polychaeta
wren,
   Bewick's, *Thryomanes bewickii*
   cactus, *Campylorhynchus brunneicapillus*
   canyon, *Catherpes mexicanus*
   house, *Troglodytes aedon*
   marsh, *Telmatodytes palustris*
   winter, *Troglodytes troglodytes*
wrentit, *Chamaea fasciata*
yellowlegs, greater, *Totanus melanoleucus*
zebra, *Equus burchelli*

# List of Plants

agave, *Agave* spp.
Alaska fringe cup, *Tellima grandiflora*
alder, red, *Alnus rubra*
alder, white, *Alnus rhombifolia*
alkali sacaton, *Sporobolus airoides*
alkali blite, *Suaeda fruticosa*
allscale, *Atriplex polycarpa*
almond, tropical, *Terminalia* spp.
aloe, *Aloe* spp.
alpine gold, *Hulsea algida*
alumroot, *Heuchera* spp.
anemone, *Anemone* spp.
Apache plume, *Fallugia paradoxa*
arrow-grass, *Triglochin* spp.
arrowhead, *Sagittaria* spp.
arrowscale, *Atriplex phyllostegia*
arrowweed, *Pluchea sericea*
ash, Oregon, *Fraxinus latifolia*
aspen, *Populus tremuloides*
aster, alpine, *Aster peirsonii*
aster, Mojave, *Aster mohavensis*
avocado, *Persea* spp.
azalea, western, *Rhododendron occidentale*
baby-blue-eyes, *Nemophila menziesii*
baldcypress, *Taxodium distichum*
basswood, *Tilia* spp.
bay, California, *Umbellularia californica*
bee plant, *Cleome serrulata*
beech, *Fagus* spp.
big-cone spruce, *Psuedotsuga macrocarpa*
big tree, *Sequoiadendron giganteum*
birch, paper, *Betula papyrifera*
birch, water, *Betula occidentalis*
bird's-foot trefoil, *Lotus* spp.
bitterbrush, *Purshia tridentata*
bitterroot, pygmy, *Lewisia pygmaea*
blackberry, *Rubus ursinus*
blackbush, *Coleogyne ramosissima*
bladderpod, *Isomeris arborea*
bladderwort, *Utricularia* spp.

blazing star, *Mentzelia* spp.
bleeding heart, *Dicentra formosa*
blueberry, mountain, *Vaccinium occidentale*
blue dicks, *Brodiaea pulchella*
blue-eyed grass, *Sisyrinchium bellum*
bluegrass, *Poa* spp.
bluejoint grass, *Calamagrostis canadensis*
boojum tree, *Idria columnaris*
box elder, *Acer negundo*
bracken, *Pteridium aquilinum*
brittle bush, *Encelia farinosa*
brodiaea, harvest, *Brodiaea elegans*
brome, red, *Bromus rubens*
brome, ripgut, *Bromus rigidus*
buckeye, California, *Aesculus californica*
buckwheat, California, *Eriogonum fasciculatum*
bud-sage, *Artemisia spinescens*
buffaloberry, *Shepherdia argentea*
bulrush, *Scirpus* spp.
burning bush, western, *Euonymus occidentalis*
bur-sage, *Franseria dumosa*
buttercup, alpine, *Ranunculus eschscholtzii*
buttonbush, *Cephalanthus occidentalis*
cactus,
  barrel, *Echinocactus acanthodes*
  cholla, *Opuntia* spp.
  fishhook, *Mammillaria tetrancistra*
  Mojave prickly pear, *Opuntia mojavensis*
  saguaro, *Cereus giganteus*
calico plant, *Langloisia matthewsii*
camas, *Camassia leichtlinii*
cassava, *Manihot esculenta*
cassiope, *Cassiope mertensiana*
catclaw, *Acacia greggii*
cattail, *Typha* spp.

ceanothus, blue blossom, *Ceanothus thyrsiflorus*
ceanothus, jim brush, *Ceanothus sorediatus*
ceanothus, squaw mat, *Ceanothus prostratus*
ceanothus, tobacco brush, *Ceanothus velutinus*
cedar, Alaska, *Chamaecyparis nootkatensis*
cedar, canoe, *Thuja plicata*
cedar, incense, *Calocedrus decurrens*
cedar, Port Orford, *Chamaecyparis lawsoniana*
century plant, *Agave* spp.
chamise, *Adenostoma fasciculatum*
chara, *Chara* spp.
cheese bush, *Hymenoclea salsola*
cheeseweed, *Malva parviflora*
cherry, bitter, *Prunus emarginata*
cherry, choke-, *Prunus virginiana*
cherry, hollyleaf, *Prunus ilicifolia*
chess, downy, *Bromus tectorum*
chess, soft, *Bromus mollis*
chia, *Salvia columbariae*
chiming bells, *Mertensia ciliata*
Chinese houses, *Collinsia heterophylla*
chinquapin, *Castanopsis chrysophylla*
chuparosa, *Beloperone californica*
cinnamon, *Cinnamonum* spp.
cinquefoil, shrubby, *Potentilla fruticosa*
clarkia, *Clarkia* spp.
clematis, *Clematis* spp.
clintonia, red, *Clintonia andrewsiana*
coffeeberry, *Rhamnus californica*
columbine, alpine, *Aquilegia pubescens*
columbine, blue, *Aquilegia coerulea*
columbine, red, *Aquilegia formosa*
cone flower, *Rudbeckia californica*
cordgrass, *Spartina foliosa*
coreopsis, *Coreopsis* spp.
cotton thorn, *Tetradymia spinosa*
cottonwood, black, *Populus trichocarpa*
cottonwood, Fremont, *Populus fremontii*
cow clover, *Trifolium wormskjoldii*
cow parsnip, *Heracleum lanatum*

coyote brush, *Baccharis pilularis* var. *consanguinea*
cranesbill, *Geranium richardsonii*
creambush, *Holodiscus discolor*
cream cup, *Platystemon californicus*
creosote bush, *Larrea divaricata*
cress, cushion-, *Draba lemmonii*
cress, rock, *Arabis* spp.
cress, water-, *Rorippa nasturtiumaquaticum*
crocus, *Crocus* spp.
crucifixion thorn, *Holacantha emoryi*
cucumber, wild, *Marah fabaceus*
cypress,
  Abrams, *Cupressus abramsiana*
  Arizona, *Cupressus arizonica*
  Arizona smooth, *Cupressus glabra*
  Cuyamaca, *Cupressus stephensonii*
  Gowen, *Cupressus goveniana*
  Macnab, *Cupressus macnabiana*
  Modoc, *Cupressus bakeri*
  Monterey, *Cupressus macrocarpa*
  Piute, *Cupressus nevadensis*
  pygmy, *Cupressus pygmaea*
  Sargent, *Cupressus sargentii*
  Tecate, *Cupressus forbesii*
daisy, seaside, *Erigeron glaucus*
Dalea, Mojave, *Dalea arborescens*
dandelion, *Taraxacum officinale*
deergrass, *Muhlenbergia rigens*
desert almond, *Prunus fasciculata*
desert apricot, *Prunus fremontii*
desert candle, *Caulanthus inflatus*
desert dandelion, *Malacothrix glabrata*
desert holly, *Atriplex hymenelytra*
desert marigold, *Baileya multiradiata*
desert peach, *Prunus andersonii*
desert star, *Monoptilon bellioides*
desert sweet, *Chamaebatiaria millefolium*
desert thorn, *Lycium* spp.
desert trumpet, *Eriogonum inflatum*
desert velvet, *Psathyrotes ramosissima*
desert willow, *Chilopsis linearis*
dock, *Rumex crassus*
dodder, *Cuscuta* spp.

dogwood, *Cornus nuttallii*
dogwood, creek, *Cornus stolonif-era*
Douglas-fir, *Psuedotsuga menziesii*
draba, glacial, *Draba densifolia*
dragon tree, *Dracaena draco*
duckweed, *Lemna* spp.
eel-grass, *Zostera marina*
elderberry, blue, *Sambucus coe-rulea*
elderberry, red, *Sambucus racemo-sa*
elephant tree, *Bursera microphylla*
elephant's head, *Pedicularis attol-ens; P. groenlandica*
elm, *Ulmus* spp.
*Eriophylum, Eriophylum pringlei*
fairwell-to-spring, *Clarkia* spp.
fairy duster, *Calliandra eriophylla*
fairy lantern, *Calochortus albus*
Farallon weed, *Baeria minor*
fern,
    chain, *Woodwardia fimbriata*
    five-finger, *Adiantum pedatum* var. *aleuticum*
    goldenback, *Pityrogramma tri-angularis*
    lady, *Athyrium filix-femina* var. *californicum*
    maidenhair, *Adiantum* spp.
    polypody, California, *Poly-podium californicum*
    sword, *Polystichum munitum*
    wood, *Dryopteris* spp.
fescue, European, *Festuca derton-ensis*
fescue, foxtail, *Festuca megalura*
fescue, six-weeks, *Festuca octo-flora*
fiddleneck, *Amsinckia* spp.
fig, wild, *Ficus* spp.
filaree, *Erodium cicutarium*
fir,
    lowland, *Abies grandis*
    noble, *Abies procera*
    red, *Abies magnifica*
    Santa Lucia, *Abies bracteata*
    silver, *Abies amabilis*
    subalpine, *Abies lasiocarpa*
    white, *Abies concolor*
fivespot, *Malvastrum rotundifol-ium*
flannel bush, *Fremontia californica*
flax, *Linum* spp.
fleabane, *Erigeron* spp.

forget-me-not, *Cryptantha* spp.
four-o'clock, *Mirabilis bigelovii*
*Frankenia, Frankenia grandifolia*
fuchsia, *Fuchsia* spp.
furse, *Ulex europaeus*
gaillardia, *Gaillardia* spp.
galleta, big, *Hilaria rigida*
gazania, *Gazania* spp.
gentian, blue, *Gentiana* spp.
gentian, green, *Frasera speciosa*
gerbera, *Gerbera* spp.
ghost flower, *Mohavea* spp.
gilia,
    bird's eye (several species in *Gilia* are commonly called bird's eye, including *G. davyi; G. latiflora;* and *G. tricolor*)
    globe, *Ipomopsis congesta* ssp. *montana*
    golden, *Linanthus aureus*
    granite, *Leptodactylon pungens*
    scarlet, *Ipomopsis aggregata*
    yellow-throated, *Linanthus montanus*
ginger, wild, *Asarum caudatum*
gladiola, *Gladiolus* spp.
goatgrass, *Aegilops* spp.
goatnut, *Simmondsia chinensis*
goldenbush, *Haplopappus* spp.
goldenrod, *Solidago* spp.
goldenstar, *Bloomeria crocea*
goldfields, *Baeria chrysostoma*
grape, Oregon, *Berberis aquifolium*
grape, wild, *Vitis californica*
grass nut, *Brodiaea laxa*
grass-of-Parnassus, *Parnassia pal-ustris* var. *californica*
gray thorn, *Condalia lyciodes*
greasewood, *Sarcobatus vermicu-latus*
groundsel, *Senecio* spp.
gum plant, *Grindelia* spp.
hairgrass, *Deschampsia* spp.
harebell, *Campanula rotundifolia*
hazelnut, *Corylus cornuta* var. *cal-ifornica*
heather, red mountain, *Phyllodoce breweri*
hemlock, mountain, *Tsuga mer-tensiana*
hemlock, western, *Tsuga hetero-phylla*
hickory, *Carya* spp.
hollyhock, wild, *Sidalcea reptans*
honey-myrtle, *Callistemon* spp.

honeysuckle, *Lonicera* spp.
hopsage, spiny, *Grayia spinosa*
horehound, *Marrabium vulgare*
horsebrush, *Tetradymia* spp.
horsetail, *Equisetum* spp.
huckleberry (bilberry), *Vaccinium* spp.
ice plant, *Mesembryanthemum crystallinum*
indigo bush, *Dalea fremontii*
inkweed, *Suaeda torreyana* var. *ramosissima*
iris, Douglas, *Iris douglasiana*
iris, Sierra, *Iris hartwegii*
ironwood, desert, *Olneya tesota*
*Ivesia*, pygmy, *Ivesia pygmaea*
ixia, *Ixia* spp.
Jacob's ladder, *Polemonium caeruleum*
Jaumea, *Jaumea carnosa*
Joshua tree, *Yucca brevifolia*
juniper,
    alligator, *Juniperus deppeana*
    ashe, *Juniperus ashei*
    California, *Juniperus californica*
    common, *Juniperus communis*
    creeping, *Juniperus horizontalis*
    drooping, *Juniperus flaccida*
    one-seed, *Juniperus monosperma*
    red-berry, *Juniperus pinchotii*
    Rocky Mountain, *Juniperus scopulorum*
    Utah, *Juniperus osteosperma*
    western, *Juniperus occidentalis*
kangaroo paw, *Anigozanthos manglesii*
Labrador tea, *Ledum glandulosum*
larch, alpine, *Larix lyallii*
larch, western, *Larix occidentalis*
*Lasthenia*, *Lasthenia glabrata*
laurel, alpine, *Kalmia polifolia* var. *microphylla*
laurel sumac, *Rhus laurina*
lemonade berry, *Rhus integrifolia*
lenscale, *Atriplex lentiformis*
lily,
    alp, *Lloydia serotina*
    corn, *Veratrum californicum*
    desert, *Hesperocallis undulata*
    mariposa, *Calochortus* spp.
    Sierra, *Lilium kelleyanum*
    star, *Zigadenus fremontii*
    water, *Nuphar polysepalum*
live-forever, *Dudleya* spp.

lobelia, *Lobelia* spp.
locoweed, *Astragalus* spp.
locust, *Robinia* spp.
loosestrife, *Lythrum californicum*
lovegrass, *Eragrostis* spp.
lupine, dune, *Lupinus chamissonis*
lupine, harlequin, *Lupinus stiversii*
lupine, tree, *Lupinus arboreus*
madrone, *Arbutus menziesii*
mallow, apricot, *Sphaeralcea ambigua*
manzanita, pinemat, *Arctostaphylos nevadensis*
manzanita, white-leaf, *Arctostaphylos viscida*
maple, big-leaf, *Acer macrophyllum*
maple, vine, *Acer circinatum*
marsh pennywort, *Hydrocotyle verticillata*
marsh rosemary, *Limonium commune*
melicgrass, *Melica* spp.
menodora, smooth, *Menodora scabra*
mesquite, honey, *Prosopis juliflora*
mesquite, screwbean, *Prosopis pubescens*
miner's lettuce, *Montia perfoliata*
mistletoe, desert, *Phoradendron californicum*
mistletoe, oak and other broadleaf trees, *Phoradendron villosum*
mitrewort, *Mitella breweri*
mock heather, *Haplopappus ericoides*
mock orange, *Philadelphus lewisii*
molly, green, *Kochia americana*
molly, rusty, *Kochia californica*
monkeyflower,
    Bigelow, *Mimulus bigelovii*
    bush, *Mimulus aurantiacus; M. longiflorus*
    Mojave, *Mimulus mohavensis*
    scarlet, *Mimulus cardinalis*
    yellow, *Mimulus guttatus*
monkshood, *Aconitum columbianum*
Mormon tea, *Ephedra* spp.
morning glory, beach, *Convolvulus soldanella*
morning glory, western, *Convolvulus occidentalis*
moss, club, *Lycopodium* spp.
moss, sphagnum, *Sphagnum* spp.

moss campion, *Silene acaulis*
mountain mahogany, birch-leaf, *Cercocarpus betuloides*
mountain mahogany, curl-leaf, *Cercocarpus ledifolius*
mountain misery, *Chamaebatia foliolosa*
mountain sorrel, *Oxyria digyna*
mouse barley, *Hordeum leporinum*
mugwort, *Artemisia douglasiana*
mule fat, *Baccharis viminea*
mullein, common, *Verbascum thapsus*
mullein, turkey, *Eremocarpus setigerus*
mustard, *Brassica* spp.
nama, *Nama demissum*
needlegrass, *Stipa* spp.
nettle, *Urtica gracilis*
nightshade, *Solanum* spp.
ninebark, *Physocarpus capitatus*
nolina, *Nolina bigelovii; N. parryi*
nutmeg, California, *Torreya californica*
oak,
  black, *Quercus kelloggii*
  blue, *Quercus douglasii*
  canyon, *Quercus chrysolepis*
  deer, *Quercus sadleriana*
  desert scrub, *Quercus turbinella*
  Engelmann, *Quercus engelmannii*
  Garry, *Quercus garryana*
  huckleberry, *Quercus vaccinifolia*
  island, *Quercus tomentella*
  leather, *Quercus durata*
  live, coast, *Quercus agrifolia*
  live, interior, *Quercus wislizenii*
  MacDonald, *Quercus macdonaldii*
  Palmer, *Quercus palmeri*
  scrub, *Quercus dumosa*
  valley, *Quercus lobata*
  white, *Quercus alba*
oat, slender, *Avena barbata*
oat, wild, *Avena fatua*
oatgrass, *Danthonia* spp.
ocotillo, *Fouquieria splendens*
onion, wild, *Allium* spp.
orchid, coralroot, *Corallorhiza maculata*
orchid, rein, *Habenaria leucostachys*
orchid, stream, *Epipactis gigantea*

osoberry, *Osmaronia cerasiformis*
owl's clover, *Orthocarpus purpurascens*
oxalis, *Oxalis* spp.
paintbrush, alpine, *Castilleja nana*
palm, blue, *Erythea armata*
palm, native fan, *Washingtonia filifera*
palo verde, *Cercidium floridum*
palo verde, littleleaf, *Cercidium microphyllum*
palo verde, Mexican, *Parkinsonia aculeata*
pea, beach, *Lathyrus japonicus* var. *glaber*
pea, chaparral, *Pickeringia montana*
pea, Sturt, *Clianthus formosus*
pearlwort, Arctic, *Sagina saginoides*
pennyroyal, *Monardella* spp.
pentstemon, *Pentstemon*, spp.
peppergrass, *Lepidium oxycarpum*
phacelia, wild-Canterbury-bell, *Phacelia campanularia*
phlox, alpine, *Phlox douglasii* ssp.
phlox, spiny, *Phlox stansburyi*
pickleweed, *Allenrolfea occidentalis; Salicornia* spp.
pine,
  Alleppo, *Pinus halepensis*
  Apache, *Pinus engelmannii*
  beach, *Pinus contorta*
  bishop, *Pinus muricata*
  bristlecone, *Pinus aristata*
  Chihuahua, *Pinus leiophylla*
  Coulter, *Pinus coulteri*
  digger, *Pinus sabiniana*
  foxtail, *Pinus balforiana*
  island, *Pinus remorata*
  Japanese, *Pinus densiflora*
  Jeffrey, *Pinus jeffreyi*
  knobcone, *Pinus attenuata*
  limber, *Pinus flexilis*
  lodgepole, *Pinus murrayana*
  Monterey, *Pinus radiata*
  pinyon, four-needled, *Pinus quadrifolia*
  pinyon, Mexican, *Pinus cembroides*
  pinyon, one-needled, *Pinus monophylla*
  pinyon, two-needled, *Pinus edulis*

silver, *Pinus monticola*
Southwestern white, *Pinus stro-biformis*
stone, *Pinus pinea*
sugar, *Pinus lambertiana*
Torrey, *Pinus torreyana*
whitebark, *Pinus albicaulis*
yellow, *Pinus ponderosa*
pipevine, *Aristolochia californica*
pitcher plant, *Darlingtonia californica*
plantain, *Plantago maritima*
podistera, *Podistera nevadensis*
poison oak, *Rhus diversiloba*
pond scum, *Spirogyra* spp.; *Zygnema* spp.
pond weed, *Potamogeton* spp.
popcorn flower, *Plagiobothrys nothofulvus*
poplar, Lombardy, *Populus nigra*
poppy,
  California, *Eschscholzia californica*
  flame, *Papaver californicum*
  prickly, *Argemone munita*
  tree, *Dendromecon rigida*
  wind, *Stylomecon heterophylla*
potentilla, *Potentilla* spp.
primrose, dune, *Oenothera cheiranthifolia*
primrose, evening, desert, *Oenothera deltoides*
primrose, fairy, *Primula augustifolia*
primrose, Sierra, *Primula suffrutescens*
prince's plume, *Stanleya pinnata*
pussy paws, *Calyptridium umbellatum*
pygmy cedar, *Peucephyllum schottii*
rabbitbrush, *Chrysothamnus nauseosus*
rabbitbrush, Mojave, *Chrysothamnus nauseosus* var. *mohavensis*
radish, wild, *Raphanus sativus*
ranunculus, aquatic, *Ranunculus aquatilis*
ratany, *Krameria parvifolia*
rattlesnake weed, *Euphorbia albomarginata*
redberry, *Rhamnus crocea*
redbud, *Cercis occidentalis*
redwood, *Sequoia sempervirens*

redwood, dawn, *Metasequoia glyptostroboides*
reed, *Phragmites communis*
reedgrass, *Calamagrostis* spp.
rhododendron, *Rhododendron macrophyllum*
ricegrass, Indian, *Oryzopsis hymenoides*
rock fringe, *Epilobium obcordatum*
rose, cliff, *Cowenia mexicana* var. *stansburiana*
rose, wild, *Rosa californica*
roseroot, *Sedum rosae* ssp. *integrifolium*
rush, *Juncus* spp.
sage,
  black, *Salvia mellifera*
  bladder, *Salazaria mexicana*
  blue, *Salvia dorrii*
  Mojave, *Salvia mohavensis*
  purple, *Salvia leucophylla*
  thistle, *Salvia carduacea*
  white, *Salvia apiana*
sagebrush,
  alpine, *Artemisia rothrockii*
  beach, *Artemisia pycnocephala*
  black, *Artemisia nova*
  California, *Artemisia californica*
  flat, *Artemisia bigelovii*
  Great Basin, *Artemisia tridentata*
  hoary, *Artemisia cana*
  low, *Artemisia arbuscula*
salal, *Gaultheria shallon*
salmonberry, *Rubus spectabilis*
saltbush, four-winged, *Atriplex canescens*
salt grass, *Distichlis spicata*
salt grass, desert, *Distichlis stricta*
saltwort, *Batis maritima*
sand food, *Ammobroma sonorae*
sand verbena, *Abronia* spp.
sandwort, *Arenaria macradenia*
saxifrage, goldenbloom, *Saxifraga serpyllifolia*
scale bush, *Atriplex* spp.
scarlet bugler, *Pentstemon centranthifolius* (two other species are commonly called by that name: *P. bridgesii*; *P. labrosus*)
scarlet pimpernel, *Anagallis arvensis*
sea blite, *Suaeda californica*

sea fig, *Mesembryanthemum chilense*

sea rocket, *Cakile maritima*

sea strawberry, *Fragaria chiloensis*

seaweed,
    coralline algae, *Bossiella* spp.; *Calliarthron* spp.; *Corallina* spp.; *Lithophyllum* spp.; *Lithothamnium* spp.

    delicate sycophant, *Microcladia* spp.

    green rope, *Spongomorpha coalita*

    kelp, bladder, *Macrocystis pyrifera*

    kelp, bull, *Nereocystis leutkeana*

    kelp, feather boa, *Egregia menziesii*

    lissom red sea fire, *Farlowia* spp.

    mermaid's hair, *Gracilaria verrucosa*

    nailbrush, *Endocladia muricata*

    oar blade, *Laminaria* spp.

    ocean pincushion, *Cladophora* spp.

    red fan, *Hymenena* spp.; *Cryptopleura* spp.

    red laver, *Porphyra* spp.

    red point, *Prionitis* spp.

    red sea feather, *Erythrophyllum delesserioides*

    rockweed, *Fucus distichus*; *Pelvetia fastigiata*

    ruffled sword, *Dictyoneurum californicum*

    sea lettuce, *Ulva* spp.

    sea palm, *Postelsia palmaeformis*

    seersucker, *Costaria costata*

    tassel wing, *Pterochondria woodii*

sedge, *Carex* spp.

seep willow, *Baccharis glutinosa*

service berry, *Amelanchier alnifolia*

shadscale, *Atriplex confertifolia*

shooting star, *Dodecatheon* spp.

Sierra pride, *Pentstemon newberryi*

silene, California, *Silene californica*

silk tassel, *Garrya* spp.

silverleaf, *Leucadendron argenteum*

silver mat, *Raillardella argentea*

sky pilot, *Polemonium eximium*

smoke tree, *Dalea spinosa*

snakeweed, broom, *Gutierrezia sarothrae*

snakewood, *Colubrina californica*

sneezeweed, *Helenium* spp.

snowberry, *Symphoricarpos* spp.

snow plant, *Sarcodes sanguinea*

Solomon's seal, *Smilacina* spp.

Spanish needles, *Palafoxia linearis*

speedwell, *Veronica alpina* var. *alterniflora*

spice bush, *Calycanthus occidentalis*

spikenard, *Aralia californica*

spirea, *Spiraea densiflora*

spirea, rock, *Petrophytum caespitosum*

spruce,
    blue, *Picea pungens*
    Engelmann, *Picea engelmannii*
    Sitka, *Picea sitchensis*
    weeping, *Picea breweriana*
    white, *Picea glauca*

squaw bush, *Rhus trilobata*

squirreltail, *Sitanion hystrix*

stonecrop, *Sedum* spp.

sugar scoop, *Tiarella unifoliata*

sulfur flower, *Eriogonum umbellatum*

suncups, *Oenothera primiveris*

sunflower, *Helianthus* spp.

surf grass, *Phyllospadix scouleri*; *P. torreyi*

swamp whitehead, *sphenosciadium capitellatum*

sweetbush, *Bebbia juncea*

sycamore, *Platanus racemosa*

tamarix, *Tamarix gallica*

tanoak, *Lithocarpus densiflora*

tar weed, *Madia* spp.

thimbleberry, *Rubus parviflorus*

thistle, *Cirsium* spp.

three awns, *Aristida* spp.

ticklegrass, *Agrostis scabra*

tidytips, *Layia platyglossa*

toyon, *Heteromeles arbutifolia*

trillium, *Trillium ovatum*

trisetum, *Trisetum* spp.

tule, *Scripus acutus*

turpentine broom, *Thamnosma montana*

twinberry, *Lonicera involucrata*

valley tassel, *Orthocarpus attenuatus*
velvetgrass, *Holcus lanatus*
vetch, *Vicia* spp.
violet, white, *Viola macloskeyi*
violet, yellow, *Viola pedunculata*
wallflower, *Erysimum asperum*
walnut, California, *Juglans californica*
walnut, wild black, *Juglans hindsii*
water starwort, *Callitriche* spp.
wax myrtle, *Myrica californica*
wedgescale, *Atriplex truncata*
wheatgrass, *Agropyron* spp.
whispering bells, *Emmenanthe
penduliflora*
whitlow-grass, *Draba* spp.

wild rye, blue, *Elymus glaucus*
willow, *Salix* spp.
willow herb, *Epilobium* spp.
winter fat, *Eurotia lanata*
wintergreen, *Pyrola* spp.
woodland star, *Lithophragma af-
finis*
wormwood, *Artemisia* spp.
yarrow, *Achillea borealis*
yellow-eyed grass, *Sisyrinchium
californicum*
yerba santa, *Eriodictyon californicum*
yew, western, *Taxus brevifolia*
yucca, banana, *Yucca baccata*
yucca, Mojave, *Yucca schidigera*

# Index

Map. 3. From the Golden Gate to the High Sierra

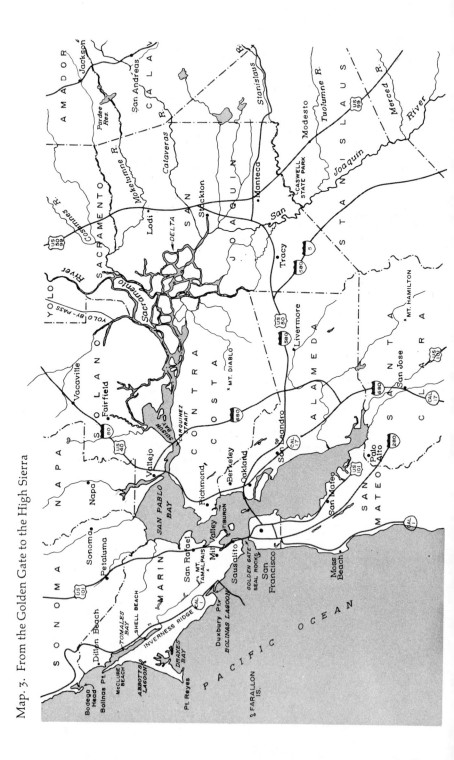

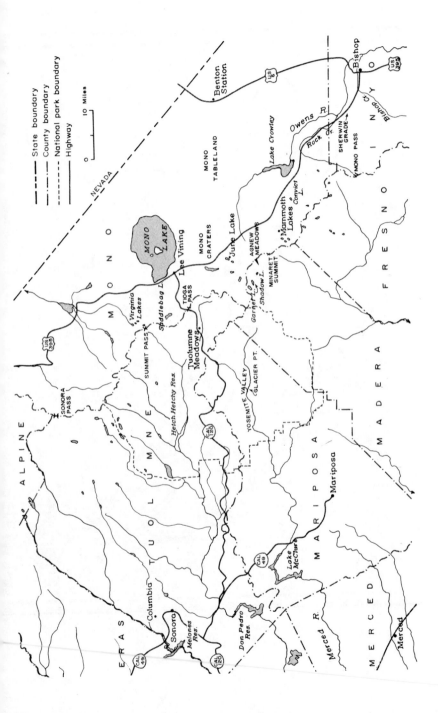

LE NOUVEAU MEXIQUE,
et LA FLORIDE :
Tirées de diverses Cartes, et Relations.
Par N. Sanson d'Abbeville Geogr ord.re du Roy.
A PARIS
Chez Pierre Mariette. Rue S.t Iacque. a l'Esperance.
Avec Privilege du Roy, pour vingt Ans.
1656.